Prime Time Crime

Prime Time Crime
Balkan Media in War and Peace

Kemal Kurspahic

UNITED STATES INSTITUTE OF PEACE PRESS
Washington, D.C.

Cover photographs copyright Reuters NewMedia Inc./Corbis, *Oslobodjenje*, Kontos Yannis/Corbis Sygma, and AFP/Corbis. Used by permission.

The views expressed in this book are those of the author alone. They do not necessarily reflect views of the United States Institute of Peace.

UNITED STATES INSTITUTE OF PEACE
1200 17th Street NW, Suite 200
Washington, DC 20036-3011

First published 2003

Printed in the United States of America

The paper used in this publication meets the minimum requirements of American National Standard for Information Sciences—Permanence of Paper for Printed Library Materials, ANSI Z39.48-1984.

Library of Congress Cataloging-in-Publication Data

Kurspahic, Kemal, 1946–
   Prime time crime : Balkan media in war and peace / Kemal Kurspahic
   p. cm.
   Includes bibliographical references and index.
   ISBN 1-929223-39-0 (alk. paper) – ISBN 1-929223-38-2 (paper : alk. paper)
   1. Mass media–Former Yugoslav republics. 2. Yugoslav War, 1991–1995–Mass media and the war. 3. Mass media–Moral and ethical aspects. 4. Mass media and propaganda–Former Yugoslav republics. I. Title

P92.Y8 K87 2003
302.23'497–dc21
                                                            2002032922

To Vesna, Tarik, and Mirza, with love

Contents

Acknowledgments

I WANT TO THANK the many colleagues and media analysts who contributed, through interviews and an exchange of messages and materials, to my understanding of developments in Balkan media in the 1990s. That list includes—in regional and alphabetical order—in Serbia, Stojan Cerovic, Gordana Logar, Veran Matic, Branka Mihajlovic, Aleksandar Nenadovic, Dusan Reljic, Dusan Simic, and Manjo Vukotic; in Croatia, Heni Erceg, Mirko Galic, Zivko Gruden, Miljenko Jergovic, Damir Matkovic, Goran Milic, and Bozo Novak; and in Bosnia-Herzegovina, Gojko Beric, Brane Bozic, Zlatko Dizdarevic, Zdravko Grebo, Mehmed Husic, Gordana Knezevic, Slavo Kukic, Rizo Mehinagic, Senad Pecanin, Spasoje Perovic, Zekerijah Smajic, Milos Solaja, Zoran Udovicic, Miljenko Vockic, and Zdravko Zlokapa.

I owe special gratitude to the United States Institute of Peace for granting me a senior fellowship in the Jennings Randolph Program for International Peace in the academic year 1999–2000. The Institute provided a wonderful work environment; stimulating ongoing dialogue among the fellows, staff, and public; and a high bar of intellectual and academic expectations and standards. My personal thanks go to Institute president Richard H. Solomon and executive vice president Harriet Hentges; fellowship director Joseph Klaits; Institute Balkan specialists Daniel Serwer and Bill Stuebner; and—more than anyone else—my program officer, Sally O. Blair, and book editor, Cynthia Roderick, for their valuable contribution in shaping this book from my first chapter outline to the final manuscript. And finally, my special thanks go to my research assistant, Haris Alic, for all the hard work he has done in collecting the books, reports, and transcripts I needed in my work on the book.

Introduction

"Indifference is not a beginning, it is an end. And, therefore, indifference is always the friend of the enemy, for it benefits the aggressor—never his victim, whose pain is magnified when he or she feels forgotten. The political prisoner in his cell, the hungry children, the homeless refugees—not to respond to their plight, not to relieve their solitude by offering them a spark of hope is to exile them from human memory. And in denying their humanity we betray our own.

Indifference, then, is not only a sin, it is a punishment. And this is one of the most important lessons of this outgoing century's wide-ranging experiments in good and evil."

ELIE WIESEL[1]

IN THE FALL OF 2002, seven years after the Dayton Peace Agreement ended three-and-a-half years of war in Bosnia, the media and the public in countries engaged in that war—in Serbia, Croatia, and Bosnia—are still agonizing between the two extremes: denial or acknowledgment of the atrocities of the 1990s. A months-long debate rages in the pages of the Belgrade weekly *Vreme* (*Time*), with even the founders of that magazine finding themselves in the two bitterly opposing camps. One side criticizes the "moral fundamentalism" of those who argue for a full accountability for war crimes: They believe there is no point in debating "the tragedy for which there is no medicine." The other side insists that "tragedy" here is a euphemism for crimes against innocent people. They call for three levels of responsibility: criminal—for those who ordered and executed crimes; moral—for the creators of public opinion who initiated, condoned, and defended the crimes committed; and political-historical—for those who supported the criminals in power. The debate is not only about the past. It is very much about the future of the region as well. It reflects the basic dilemma over the war crimes issue even among the international sponsors of the Balkan peace process. Some of them believe that insisting on accountability for war crimes—in courts, in political life, in the media—might undermine the peace process. The others believe that acknowledging war crimes is the very essence of that process: to honor victims, to give survivors a sense of justice and closure, to create conditions for reconciliation among the innocent on all sides. Acknowledgment of war crimes and reconciliation depend very much on the media, most of which even seven years after the war remain in the trenches of nationalism they helped dig in the first place.

This book is the story of the media's role in the former Yugoslavia—first in Serbia, then in Croatia, and finally in Bosnia—in perpetrating lies about genocidal threats, awakening forgotten fears and hatreds, and preparing once peaceful neighbors to suspect, hate, confront, and finally, kill each other in the last decade of the twentieth century. Media controlled by the party and state—which in the former Communist countries controlled what the public was allowed to know and what the authorities wanted it to believe—played a major role in causing the Balkan bloodbath of the 1990s. In the hands of Slobodan Milosevic, the Serbian media systematically spread fear among Serbs concerning the genocidal threat of Croat "Ustashas" and Bosnian Muslim "mujahedeen," mobilizing the nation for what became a "preemptive" genocide: "If we don't kill them, they will kill us." In the hands of Franjo Tudjman and his ultranationalist Croatian Democratic Union (HDZ), the Croatian state media were no more civilized in depicting Serbs and Muslims as arch-enemies. As a consequence, victimized by forces from both Milosevic's "Greater Serbia" and Tudjman's "Greater Croatia," Bosniaks developed their own brand of ultranationalist media, spreading anti-Serb and anti-Croat feelings. Once the demons of the Balkan myths and history had been unleashed, flooding the newspaper pages and radio and television programs with horrifying stories of once-good neighbors as dangerous enemies, the nationalist-controlled media became instigators—not just witnesses—of terror, killings, and exodus of genocidal proportions. The front pages of newspapers and evening television newscasts churned out a nightmarish years-long prime-time crime.

This book focuses on the role of the media in the three former Yugoslav republics that were engaged in a deadly war triangle in the early 1990s, Serbia–Croatia–Bosnia. It does not analyze the lower-scale conflicts of 1999 in Kosovo and 2001 in Macedonia. In those two cases, the conflict had the same roots: a failure to balance the integrity of the state and minority rights; conflicting ideas about how to preserve that statehood while recognizing and respecting different religious and ethnic identities; and each group's obsession with its own causes while ignoring the other's grievances. And in both cases, except for some notable exceptions, the majority of the media had been reduced to advocating their own groups' "patriotic causes." One such exception was Veton Suroi's *Koha Ditore* in Kosovo, which even in the worst days of terror argued passionately against blind hatred and revenge.

Prime Time Crime: Balkan Media in War and Peace is the story of media degraded by the very people who should have been passionate defenders—self-serving editors and writers, many of whom led the charge in manufacturing enemies, warmongering, and justifying war crimes. But it is also a story of the few media outlets and brave individuals who, at great personal sacrifice and risk, sometimes including even life itself, refused to be manipulated and used in war propaganda but instead maintained and defended ethical values and professional standards above the patriotic call of duty. This book honors those who knew, even in a country that was handed over from communists to ultranationalists and thus missed the great opportunity for change in the late 1980s, that regardless of who was in power, journalism is a profession and journalists are witnesses, not warriors.

There may not be a balance between good and evil in this book, just as there was no such balance in the Balkans during the 1990s. The forces of evil dominated the decade. Nevertheless, I want to begin with a story about those who, despite everything, tried to practice journalism "pure and simple." Many of them waged exhausting battles against their oppressive regimes. Some were silenced only when cronies of nationalist governments took over their newspapers; some lost their jobs in endless, systematic purges; and very few managed to maintain their independence to the end of the wars, only to see their countries and their professional ideals shattered in a decade of nationalist crusades.

Two editors, Stanislav Stasa Marinkovic of the Belgrade daily *Borba (The Struggle)* and Josko Kulusic of *Slobodna Dalmacija (Free Dalmatia)*, a daily in Split, Croatia, occupy a very special place in the story of the struggle for journalistic integrity in the former Yugoslavia in the late 1980s. I met both of them at the beginning of Yugoslavia's slide into chaos, shortly after Slobodan Milosevic seized power in Serbia. In late spring 1988, together with Zlatko Dizdarevic, my colleague from the Sarajevo daily *Oslobodjenje (Liberation)*, I received *Slobodna Dalmacija's* invitation to a weekend cruise on the Adriatic. Kulusic brought together a dozen prominent journalists from all over Yugoslavia—including Jurij Gustincic and Jak Koprivc (Slovenes); Marinkovic, Zoran Jelicic, and Stevan Niksic (Serbs); and Drazen Vukov-Colic and Drago Buvac (Croats)—for a friendly, professional exchange of experiences with increasing political pressure against the media. The contrast couldn't have been more striking. In a setting that one could see only in exotic travel brochures, on the deck of a sailboat quietly navigating through the azure waters of the Kornati Islands off the Croatian Adriatic coast—with an abundance of the best Dalmatian prosciutto and cheese, local grape brandy, fishermen's catch of the day, and wine from local cellars—we shared stories about the challenges we faced in our respective republics.

Marinkovic had been the first to feel the heat of the ultranationalist offensive against the remaining liberal media. By the time we met, all the major Serbian media, from Radio-Television Belgrade to the papers of the Politika publishing house, were already in the hands of Milosevic loyalists and busily promoting the Serbian nationalist agenda: blaming everyone else in the former Yugoslavia for Serbia's real or alleged griev-ances, producing and expanding daily lists of enemies, and projecting an image of a nation facing imminent danger and thus needing to unite around the leader. Marinkovic's *Borba* had resisted the call to serve the nationalist cause. There was some legal ground for its claim to inde-pendence from Serbian politics: *Borba* was a federal newspaper and in that sense all-Yugoslav, open to the whole country. In the decades of a strong central government and Tito's unchallenged rule, this had been the paper's curse. *Borba* was the most strictly controlled paper because its editorial line was supposed to reflect official Yugoslav policy, making it too formal, less interesting to read, even boring for a general audience. It survived only as required reading for the party and army cadre and was most carefully read by foreign diplomats and analysts looking for between-the-lines hints concerning developments in the country. The weakening of federal authority and the inter-republic quarrels in the post-Tito decade of the 1980s opened a window of opportunity for *Borba*. Under Marinkovic's leadership, the paper used its broad terri-torial status to present all sides of the debate. While each republic's press was obliged to present primarily the position of its own political leadership, ignoring or simply dismissing others' views and interests, Marinkovic offered his readers impartial reporting on the increasingly confrontational Yugoslav political scene.

Presenting the plain facts on who said what provided a rare treat for the public. Marinkovic went so far as to acquire and print, as a special supplement to *Borba*, the full transcripts of several meetings of the Serbian and Yugoslav party leadership. For the first time, the paper exposed the inner workings of the Communist hierarchy—with all its (until then) hidden rivalries and quarrels, accusations and denials, limitations and weaknesses. Suddenly, *Borba* became a sought-after commodity. The paper also invited some of the most controversial par-ticipants in those debates to explain, in interviews or through their own articles, their positions on Yugoslavia's hottest issues. *Borba's* new mis-sion represented a reversal of roles in the Belgrade newspaper market because at the same time the once-liberal *Politika* became the propa-gandistic mouthpiece of the Milosevic regime.

The new Serbian regime, however, could not tolerate *Borba's* challenge to its authority. During the Adriatic cruise, Marinkovic told us of the methods Milosevic's propagandists were using to bring him in line with the new patriotic journalism. Just before joining us in Split, he was summoned to a special session of the information section of the Serbian Socialist Alliance (of Working People) for "a democratic debate about some errors and mistakes in *Borba's* editorial policy." *Borba* was accused of "losing a sense of judgment and moreover losing its political and ideological orientation." Marinkovic was blamed for "undermining relations between *Borba* and Serbia"; "putting the Serbian League of Communists' Central Committee on trial"; and "being obsessed with criticizing Serbia"—a verbal artillery usually used in the final stages of the Party's drive to eliminate political opposition. Attempts by the paper's representatives to explain that the presentation of diverse views is not a symptom of loss of judgment but the very essence of professional, unbiased reporting were taken almost as self-incrimination, as just another piece of evidence that there was "not enough self-criticism" in *Borba* in facing its "errors and mistakes"—another curse in Party vocabulary. The Serbian Socialist Alliance publicly threatened to withdraw support for *Borba*. "Thank God they didn't support us!" Marinkovic told us half-jokingly.

Josko Kulusic, our host, was probably the most successful newspaper editor in prewar Yugoslavia. His paper was not federal, like *Borba*, nor republican like *Politika* in Serbia, *Vjesnik* in Croatia, and *Oslobodjenje* in Bosnia, but a regional daily based in the Adriatic coastal city of Split. It was Kulusic's vision and hard work during his ten-year leadership as editor-in-chief (1983–93) that had transformed *Slobodna Dalmacija* into the finest daily in Croatia. He was a born journalist, attracted to journalism in his teens, even before finishing high school. Kulusic was noticed in the paper's city section for bringing his editor more than twenty news items in a single day. In the 1970s he was named the first editor of *Nedjeljna Dalmacija (Sunday Dalmatia)*, the paper's weekend edition, and he turned it into a respectable weekly with a circulation of more than 50,000. In 1983, even though the ruling Communist Party had its own candidate for the position, *Slobodna Dalmacija* journalists chose Kulusic as their editor-in-chief.

Kulusic set high professional standards and goals. He was the first to arrive at the office each morning and the last to leave at the end of the day, editing and laying out most of the pages himself. Most important, he engaged some of the best writers in Croatia and Yugoslavia as columnists. *Slobodna Dalmacija's* reputation and circulation rose higher than *Vjesnik's*—reaching a circulation of well over 100,000—and the paper became a prosperous business: It bought the most modern printing press and newsroom equipment and developed its own network of kiosks throughout Croatia.

Those few days on a small boat sailing around Kornati engaged in endless professional dialogue with Marinkovic, Kulusic, and others influenced the way I managed the Bosnian daily *Oslobodjenje* in Sarajevo after I became the first editor to be elected by the journalists themselves in December 1988. The trip established bonds and the beginning of friendships that each of us would turn to for understanding and support during the battles that followed.

Sadly, both Marinkovic and Kulusic died untimely deaths of natural causes in the midst of their struggle for professional standards and values. Milosevic's "street revolutionaries," who swept moderates from power in Serbia, Vojvodina, Montenegro, and Kosovo, could not tolerate *Borba's* professed independence. Gordana Logar, another brave *Borba* editor, told me that Marinkovic had challenged Serb nationalism from the very beginning. "When Milosevic staged a Party *putsch*, at the infamous Eighth Session of Serbia's Central Committee in the fall of 1987, [Stasa] did something no other media outlet would do," Logar recalled. "He obtained and published a full transcript of the session, giving the public an exclusive opportunity to read what Milosevic's opponents had to say ['A Night of Rough Words']. All the other Serbian media gave only one side of the story—the Milosevic group's."[2] Milosevic loyalists charged with bringing the media into line called Marinkovic in for numerous sessions of ideological brainwashing, trying to intimidate him into obedience. Although they threatened him with a cut in newsprint subsidy and withdrawal of support for the paper, publicly called for his resignation, and cancelled the official subscription to *Borba,* he continued to resist "with occasional tactical retreats," as Manjo Vukotic, his friend and successor as editor, told me.[3] Marinkovic resigned as editor in fall 1989 after bringing Vukotic from Rome to replace him. Instead, he planned to go to Poland to report on the democratic processes there as *Borba's* correspondent. "That was his greatest professional wish," Logar said.

While undergoing a routine medical checkup required of any Yugoslav leaving the country for a long-term assignment abroad, Marinkovic discovered that he had colon cancer. He died a year later in December 1989. At about that time, *Slobodna Dalmacija* named *Oslobodjenje* the 1989 Newspaper of the Year in the former Yugoslavia in an annual poll among professional journalists—the honor *Borba* had received in 1987. Marinkovic's wife, Dragana, sent me a friendly letter, telling me, "Stasa would have been proud of you if he had lived to know this."

Vukotic and Logar continued Marinkovic's struggle. Under Vukotic's leadership, *Borba* became the voice of the moderate reformist forces in 1990 and reached a circulation of more than 100,000 when it covered the anti-Milosevic protests in Belgrade in 1991. Logar led *Borba's* defiance against the government's takeover in 1994–95 and started a new paper, *Nasa Borba (Our Struggle)*, which provided an alternative voice to the government-imposed official line for a full year before the paper was strangled.

Meanwhile in Croatia, open-mindedness was no longer tolerated after Franjo Tudjman won the presidential election in 1990. The Croatian media were expected to mirror the patriotism of Milosevic's press in Serbia. *Slobodna Dalmacija* and Josko Kulusic became a natural target of Tudjman's nationalist HDZ attacks. The paper's commitment to covering all sides of the debate on the future of Yugoslavia was billed as a lack of Croat patriotism and "Yugo-nostalgia." When the nationalist government mistreated non-Croats—establishing bureaucratic obstacles to Croatian citizenship and requiring a statement condemning the Croatian Serb leadership and a statement of loyalty to Croatia in order to keep jobs—the paper's coverage placed it at the top of the list of media that needed to be silenced. Tudjman used the same method that Milosevic used in silencing *Borba*. He annulled *Slobodna Dalmacija's* privatization and arranged for Miroslav Kutle, the newly promoted HDZ media tycoon, to "buy" the newspaper in early 1993. This led to Kulusic's dismissal. The finest Croatian daily became just another mouthpiece of Croatian nationalism.

Kulusic, arguably the greatest editor in Croatian journalism, found himself on the street, trying to create a new paper, *Dan (The Day,* but also an acronym for "Dalmatian Newspaper"). In the HDZ-controlled media market, however, there were too many obstacles. The ruling Party controlled printing presses and distribution networks, deciding who got printed and at what price, which papers got distributed at kiosks, and which publishers received their money for copies that sold. Businesses owned by Party loyalists were instructed to advertise only in "politically correct" media, and Kulusic's new paper could never be on that list. Starting a new paper despite all those obstacles, first as a weekly and then as daily, took all Kulusic's energy. *Novinar (The Journalist)*, the magazine of the Croatian Association of Journalists, praised publishing under such conditions as his "last act of defiance."[4] Josko Kulusic died of heart failure at his desk as he was editing the last issue of *Dan* during the night of February 20–21, 1998. The next day his paper ceased publication.

Two years later, following the victory of the democratic opposition in Croatia's elections, *Slobodna Dalmacija's* representatives—the same people who had led the HDZ takeover of Kulusic's paper—visited his grave, announcing this event in a note entitled "Pocast sjor Josku" ("In Honor of Mr. Josko").[5] Croatia's Constitutional Court declared the 1993 HDZ takeover of *Slobodna Dalmacija* unconstitutional and had Kutle arrested for his role in the officially sanctioned corruption. Kulusic remains, in the words of those who knew him, an editorial genius who died defending professional dignity in a decade of darkness.

There are other inspiring stories of journalists who maintained their integrity against all odds.

☐ In Serbia these include Nebojsa Popov's monthly, *Republika;* Veran Matic and Radio B92; the group around the *Vreme* weekly in its original form; the independent journalists who maintained solidarity as they lost their jobs in Milosevic's media purges; and courageous individuals, such as media analyst Petar Lukovic, who remained the most outspoken critic of nationalism despite all threats and intimidation. In post-war Serbia a new daily *Danas (Today)*, started by some of those who fought to preserve *Borba* and *Nasa Borba*—Gordana Logar, Grujica Spasovic, Radomir Licina, Nikola Burzan, Bozidar Andrejic, and others—distinguished itself by opening its "Dialogue" pages to a free debate of the hottest issues of the recent past and of the future of the country. In addition, the *Monitor,* a weekly in Montenegro, represented one of the few voices of tolerance in that republic.

☐ In Croatia the most persistent critics of Tudjman's abuse of power were Viktor Ivancic, Predrag Lucic, Boris Dezulovic, and Heni Erceg.

Ivancic, Lucic, and Dezulovic were the founders of the *Feral Tribune*, a political-satirical weekly originally published as a supplement within Kulusic's *Slobodna Dalmacija*. Erceg was a former TV journalist. After the HDZ took over *Slobodna Dalmacija*, the Rijeka regional daily *Novi list (New Paper)* under editor Veljko Vicevic continued as the only independent daily in Croatia to challenge nationalist policies. The Zagreb independent Radio 101 irritated nationalists in power so much that it took mass street protests of citizens to prevent authorities from closing it.

❑ In Bosnia the honor of maintaining the tradition of tolerance in the worst days of the war belongs to my colleagues at *Oslobodjenje*, some of whom, including Kjasif Smajlovic and Salko Hondo, were killed while reporting. In the first five years following the war, Bosnian independent journalism had its best representatives in the Sarajevo weeklies *Dani* and *Slobodna Bosna*, whose editors, Senad Pecanin and Senad Avdic, respectively, regularly challenged the authorities despite intimidation, accusations, lawsuits, and physical threats and attacks. They were joined by the publisher and editor of the Banjaluka daily *Nezavisne novine (Independent Newspaper):* Zeljko Kopanja lost both legs in a car-bomb blast in the fall of 1999 after his paper's courageous and path-breaking reports on Serb war crimes against Muslims.

Prime Time Crime: Balkan Media in War and Peace is the story of a historic episode in the eternal struggle between good and evil. While evil prevailed throughout most of the 1990s, those who fought for the good never gave up. In 2000 the people of the Balkans gained new hope with the fall of Milosevic in Serbia, the victory of the democratic opposition in Croatia, and the first signs of changes in Bosnia. This book is based on my lifelong experience as a journalist in the former Yugoslavia, research that includes dozens of books and reports from the region and abroad, interviews with some of the region's most respected journalists, and hundreds of newspaper articles and radio and TV news transcripts. While several excellent books have been published on the Balkan media during the 1990s, this is the first to cover the full cycle of media manipulation in the Balkans—from Milosevic's rise to power in 1987 to his fall at the end of 2000.

The book is structured into seven chapters. Chapter 1, "The

Yugoslav Media in Tito's Time," examines the developments of the Yugoslav media in what was a unique environment compared to other Communist countries in Eastern Europe: under Communist Party rule but constantly resisting Moscow's control. This special situation made for a more liberal and interesting press than the press behind the Iron Curtain. While in Tito's time there were forbidden subjects, with no room for questioning his or his party's control over society, some pages of the Yugoslav press—including foreign news, culture, and sports—could be compared with the best in the European press. Occasionally, during the "Croatian spring" and the "Serb liberalism" of the 1970s, the press in those two republics reflected new liberal tendencies, opening their pages to reformist ideas. But they were soon silenced in systematic ideological purges of disobedient party functionaries and those who supported them publicly. In this chapter, developments in the Yugoslav media in Tito's time are discussed by the most prominent journalists of that era in the three republics: Bozo Novak, editor-in-chief of Croatia's leading daily, *Vjesnik;* Aleksandar "Sasa" Nenadovic, editor-in-chief of Serbia's leading daily, *Politika;* and Rizo Mehinagic, editor-in-chief of the leading Bosnian daily, *Oslobodjenje.* They talk about the horizons and limits of press freedom in their time. Novak and Nenadovic lost their jobs in Party purges following Tito's crackdown against the Croat and Serb liberal leadership of the 1970s, while Mehinagic was sent— as a punishment—to be a correspondent in New York after his paper printed a cartoon questioning the unity of the country in 1968. The chapter also looks at those aspects of society under Tito that made it possible for his successors, Milosevic in Serbia and Tudjman in Croatia, to assume total control over the press and public life in their countries.

Chapter 2, "Serbia: Manufacturing Enemies," chronicles the rise of Serb nationalism and Milosevic's takeover of the Communist Party machinery, the state, and the media in the late 1980s, leading to the wars against Slovenia and Croatia in 1991. Contrary to common wisdom, which says that Milosevic's first step on the road to unchallenged authority in Serbia was taking control of the Serbian media, the evidence presented in this chapter demonstrates that it was the Serbian media that created Milosevic. Some of the key executives in Serbia's most influential media—such as the Politika publishing house and Radio and TV Belgrade—befriended Milosevic while working with him in Party propaganda headquarters. They participated in behind-the-scenes maneuvers to remove his opponents and all obstacles to his rise to the top. It was Milosevic's televised promise to Kosovo Serbs, "No one is allowed to beat you anymore!" played over and over again on Belgrade TV, that catapulted him into the role of unquestioned leader of the Serb cause. Those media also played instrumental roles in manufacturing an ever-expanding list of Serb enemies from Albanian "Shiptar separatists" to the anti-Orthodox "Catholic alliance" (Slovenes and Croats), from Bosnian "Muslim mujahedeen" and "Jihad warriors" to "Western imperialists" intent on destroying Serbia. Projecting all "others" as enemies, Serbian media helped lay the ground for preemptive wars and even crimes, presenting the siege and bombardment of Croatian cities of Dubrovnik and Vukovar as the "defense of Serbian ancient fireplaces."

Chapter 3, "Serbo-Croatian War: Lying for the Homeland," analyzes the rise of Franjo Tudjman and his party to power in Croatia; their conquest of all relevant media in the country; and their manipulation of radio, TV, and the press as an act of self-defense against Serbia and aggression against Bosnia. An analysis of Serbian and Croatian media during the Serbo-Croatian war in 1991 established "the same frameworks of propaganda on both sides, repeating: 'we' are the victims, 'they' are the culprits; there is no way to save 'ourselves' other than annihilating and vanquishing 'them'; it is 'us' who have been sanctified, while the 'others' have been satanised."[6]

Chapter 4, "Bosnia: Ground Zero," tells the story of the nationalists' three and a half years of systematic destruction in which they targeted, terrorized, and tore apart the most tolerant and open-minded media in prewar Yugoslavia, with its multiethnic editorial staff and tradition of respect for differences. This chapter is the most extensive, primarily because the conflict in Bosnia was the longest and the deadliest of all, involving both Serbia and Croatia. Although Milosevic and Tudjman were in a bloody war over the "Serb areas" of Croatia, they found common ground in their mutual aspiration to expand their countries by conquering and annexing huge parts of Bosnia. This chapter is the most personal because I not only researched but lived the years of the terror against that country. The chapter also offers documentary evidence of the manufacturing of "news" in both the Serbian and Croatian media, aimed at stirring ethnic and religious hatred in Bosnia. The chapter provides an analysis of the gradual destruction of the multi-ethnic alternative in Bosnia, which opened the way for the rise of the extremist Muslim media in the country.

Chapter 5, "Balkan Media Post-Dayton: Missed Opportunities," provides a critical overview of developments in the media in the post-war period, 1995–2000. It includes the few successes and the major failures of international "media intervention" in the Balkans, in which bureaucratic methods and ignorance of local capacities undermined the stated goal of creating a civil society.

Chapter 6, "The Year 2000: The Beginning of Change," describes the dramatic events of the year 2000—the end of the Tudjman era in Croatia and the Milosevic era in Serbia and the rise of antinationalist alternatives in the mostly Bosniak-majority areas of Bosnia, and it looks at the impact of those changes on the regional media. Finally, the closing chapter, "Policy Recommendations," offers some thoughts about what the international community might have done better in its efforts to assist the development of a free media in the Balkans.

It is my hope that the record and recommendations of this book will prove relevant and useful not only to those trying to understand the forces behind the destruction of the former Yugoslavia but also to the people of other countries and regions—and especially to fellow journalists—struggling to make their own transitions to democracy.

Prime Time Crime

The Yugoslav Media in Tito's Time (1945–80)

BOZO NOVAK WAS ONLY 20 when World War II ended in the former Yugoslavia in May 1945. But the young Croat was already a war veteran. He had joined the liberation movement, led by Josip Broz Tito, at the very beginning of the Nazi occupation in 1941. By the war's end, he had been recognized as a talented writer contributing his war reports to partisan publications from the Dalmatian islands of Vis and Hvar. German and Italian forces occupied the country in the spring of 1941, and the Italians controlled a large part of the Adriatic coast, including the Dalmatian islands where Novak lived.[1] Novak, only a teenager at the time, recalls a friend telling him jokingly that he was covering the most dangerous territory in Dalmatia, between the Italian troops' barracks and Croatia's Nazi-installed Ustasha headquarters: "The former would sentence you to ten years in jail and the latter to death."[2]

Novak worked clandestinely from his parents' home in the center of the town of Hvar. The house was located between an office of the Ustasha commander, the Hrvatska Lodja (Croatian Lodge) housing the Italian commander of the town, and a hotel filled with Italian soldiers. The underground People's Liberation Authority, resisting the

occupation, instructed Novak and five or six other young people to collect the news on the antifascist struggle and distribute it throughout the
island. The only technology they had—an old-fashioned typewriter,
primitive copy machine, and short-wave radio—was stationed in
Novak's home, which was surrounded by occupying forces. Novak and
his colleagues would listen to international radio dispatches, mostly
from London, and then compile the news into "battleground reports."
Once they had printed their bulletin, no more than 100–200 copies, a
network of supporters distributed it throughout the island. "Pretending
that we were going night fishing at sea, we would distribute the bulletin
throughout Hvar, with mandatory instructions at the end: 'Read and
distribute further.' Sometimes, when we had a chance to get a copy of
Vjesnik, the Croatian partisans' primary paper, we would reprint it in
four pages and make it available to our 'subscribers.' In our bulletin, we
also reported on the activities of the underground liberation movement's leaders, including their illegal meetings and calls for mobilization, as well as occasional partisan commando actions throughout
Dalmatia," Novak remembered.[3]

In 1942 his work in Hvar became too dangerous. The Italians and
Ustasha knew that "something" was going on right under their noses,
and in July 1942 they raided Novak's home and seized the typewriter.
He escaped through a well-studied route, over the roofs and through
narrow island streets, carrying whatever printing equipment he could.
On a small fishing boat navigating between Italian and Ustasha patrol
boats, he reached Biokovo hill near Makarska on the Adriatic coast.
There, until the end of the war, he reported on the liberation struggle
for *Rijec puka (Voice of the People)*, covering the islands of Hvar, Brac,
and Solta.

The war's end found the 20-year-old war veteran in the streets of
Split, the largest Dalmatian city, looking for a job. An older friend,
prominent in the new regional government, suggested that he go to
work for *Slobodna Dalmacija* to help turn it into a daily newspaper.
"Why not?" Novak answered.

This is how Novak became a full-time journalist. *Slobodna Dalmacija*
was being published three times a week. It was one of the many underground papers published by the partisans during the war to report on
the liberation struggle and prepare the population for a "bright future"

under Communist rule. When Novak went to the paper's office in Split, they gave him copies of several recent issues. "Look at the paper, study its message, and tell us what you would do," an older editor told him. Novak leafed through the papers. They tended to be four pages in length, consisting primarily of unsigned, government-supplied, official notices. He looked at the editor. "Any questions?" asked the editor. "Just one: What is that 'message of the paper' you mentioned?" "Excellent question," the editor told him laughing. "You are the first partisan who comes from the woods admitting that there is something you don't know. Let's have a drink together."

As it turned out, because all the experienced journalists had left Split for either Zagreb or Belgrade, Novak became editor-in-chief in just two years. In this way, he became a firsthand witness, even a major participant, in the history of Yugoslav journalism in Tito's time. And as he tells it, this history was not one of those intriguing yet predictable "behind-the-Iron-Curtain stories" of one-party, one-man, single-minded rule.

Even though Tito himself was a Communist revolutionary, partici-pating in the Russian October Revolution, surviving and rising through the Stalinist purgatory of the twenties and thirties in the Soviet Union, in many ways Tito's Yugoslavia was different from all the other Eastern European countries within the Soviet empire. Yes, at first Tito accepted and imitated the Soviet model of governance—a centralized state under Communist Party dictatorship—but even at that time of Moscow's unchallenged authority over Eastern Europe, the Yugoslav leader distinguished himself from the dictators of other "brotherly countries." First, he enjoyed widespread popular support as liberator and unifier of the country in the aftermath of the bloody, four-year war in 1941–45 that, according to official figures, claimed the lives of 1.7 million people, approximately 11 percent of the prewar population.[4] Second, Yugoslavia entered the socialist countries' orbit at Tito's choice and not by the force of the "liberating" Red Army or political arm-twisting as in most of Eastern Europe. Third, Yugoslav partisans had established a constitutional outline for the postwar state at the mid-point of the war, while fighting both Nazis and "domestic traitors"— the Croatian Nazi-installed Ustasha regime and the Serb royalist Chetniks. At its second session in Jajce, Bosnia, on November 29, 1943, the Anti-Fascist National Liberation Council of Yugoslavia (AVNOJ) declared Yugoslavia a federation of six equal republics. One of the six, Serbia, was to have two autonomous provinces within it—Kosovo, with a huge Albanian majority, and Vojvodina, with sizable Hungarian and other minorities. The federal arrangement was supposed to provide a measure of autonomy and distinct identity for the diverse constituent peoples and to ensure their equal representation at the national level.

In three and a half decades of Tito's rule (1945–80), Yugoslavia went through three different stages of searching for its brand of "socialism with a different face," and in each of those stages, the Yugoslav media shared in the turbulence of the times: (1) playing a strict, Soviet-style propagandistic role (1945–50); (2) searching for a proper role amid society's doomed effort to implement economic and political reform while maintaining firm Party control (1951–74); and (3) adhering to a loyal party line during a period of decentralization when the republics strengthened their control over all spheres of life including the media (1974–80).

In the first period, also known as the period of "Administrative Socialism," the Yugoslav media mirrored the Soviet model. Agitprop, the propaganda arm of the Communist Party, was established and functioned even during the war, so that Tito's right-hand man at the time, Milovan Djilas, built the country's postwar information network based on both the Soviet model and the Yugoslav partisans' own experience. In Belgrade there were two central institutions: the Information Ministry and Agitprop. These were in charge of developing the main lines of Communist propaganda, aimed at spreading the Party's ideology among the population and at mobilizing the masses for a postwar "belt-tightening" and reconstruction. They had a network of information ministries and Agitprop departments in all six republics, not only to transmit directives from the center but also to coordinate, supervise, and control the regional and local media.

In the most comprehensive study of the Yugoslav media in the postwar period, *Tito's Maverick Media: The Politics of Mass Communications in Yugoslavia*, Gertrude Joch Robinson writes that the new Yugoslav press law of 1946 ordered that only political parties, trade unions, and other official groups were allowed to publish. The government subsidized their publications, and, as state enterprises, they were run by a Party-appointed director, who exercised final editorial responsibility.[5]

While freedom of the press was nominally guaranteed, the fact is that only groups showing evidence of loyalty to the authorities received permits to publish and to broadcast. Article 6 of the 1946 press law denied the right of becoming a publisher, editor, or journalist to all those not enjoying political or civil rights and to those who had collaborated with "fascist" or ultranationalist organizations such as Chetniks and Ustasha.[6]

Robinson found that the 1946 Yugoslav press law provided practically the same methods and instruments of Party control over all political, economic, and cultural content as existed in other Communist countries. The "filtering" of the news was guaranteed by the appointment of chief editors and directors by the Central Committee; by checking content before publication and making the top editors personally responsible for what was in their papers; by making distribution and newsprint allocation dependent on good relationships with the Party's economic planning committee; and by making the official news agency, Tanjug (Telegraph Agency of New Yugoslavia), the exclusive source of the "news" for all newspapers and radio stations. The editors did not have their own correspondents but received their information from republican ministry branches that were part of Tanjug's news collection net. Robinson notes that Tanjug's monopoly over news sources and the lack of a trained corps of journalists made political, economic, and cultural reporting "heavy" and official. She says, "The press law prohibited the distribution of publications encouraging revolt, diversionary activities, sabotage, and the violent overthrow of the constitutional order; it also punished the spreading of 'false information' that threatened the national interest."[7]

Such a general description of "threats" to and "enemies" of the state, combined with the unlimited power of the Party *apparatchiks* at all levels—local, regional, republican, and federal—to interpret and implement the "law" in a way that would protect their privileges and authority, imposed on all Yugoslav media a climate of self-censorship and reliance on exclusively official sources. Novak, then editor-in-chief of *Slobodna Dalmacija*, remembers the biggest challenge that Tito's Yugoslavia—and its strictly controlled journalism—faced in that period. It was 1948: Stalin made his final move in punishing Tito for not accepting Moscow's authority and economic exploitation of the country. He orchestrated Yugoslavia's expulsion from the Cominform (Communist Information Bureau), an international organization created in 1947, the aim of which was to consolidate and expand Communist rule throughout Europe. For Yugoslavia, a poor and war-devastated country, expulsion from the Eastern European bloc was a near deadly blow: Yugoslavia had no market or technical support other than the "brotherly assistance" from Communist countries, which now imposed a total blockade. But expulsion was also a deep emotional issue for the majority of Yugoslavs, especially Party members who had been systematically drilled by their leadership that Stalin, Moscow, and the Soviet Union were their guiding lights to a bright future. Now, the question—literally of life or death—was "us or them."

At all levels, from small towns to state institutions, Yugoslavs were asked to choose between Tito and Stalin. All those who remained loyal to Moscow, and even hundreds of those who merely expressed some doubt ("Maybe Comrade Stalin has some reasons for isolating us?"), disappeared overnight, most of them sent to a newly opened "reeducational" prison facility at Goli Otok (Barren Island) in the Adriatic, undergoing long months, even years, of hardship, including torture, confession, self-criticism, and repentance. In the name of legitimate concern for the survival of the country, Tito's party and the secret police embarked on a large-scale hunt for "enemies within" during which, along with hard-line Stalin supporters, thousands of confused and innocent people ended up at Goli Otok, most of them without any due process of law. According to history books, thousands of people were imprisoned at Goli Otok.[8] No one knows how many perished—some executed, others starving to death or dying of exhaustion and epidemics, and some committing suicide.

Under the imminent threat of a Soviet takeover, with the Soviet consul in Split declaring that he "has taken command and will be issuing orders," Novak knew that anything but clear support for Tito's "historical no to Stalin" by any of his staff at *Slobodna Dalmacija* would spell serious trouble, not only for that individual but for him as the editor and for his paper as well. So he instructed his staff, in strict confidentiality, "Just listen to what I have to say, repeat it, support it, and don't say anything else." What Novak was saying—and his staff kept repeating—was the official Party line communicated through "top secret" briefing papers to people in the most sensitive positions such as editors-in-chief. No journalist or staff member of *Slobodna Dalmacija* lost his job in the mass purges following Yugoslavia's breakup with the Soviet Union.

That breakup opened a new chapter in Yugoslav history as the country entered its second stage of searching for a unique brand of socialism. Supported by the West for his brave stand against the Soviet dictatorship, Tito embarked on a search for "socialism with a human face." At home he offered Yugoslavs the promise of workers' self-management, as opposed to strict central control of the economy. Abroad, with presidents Nasser of Egypt, Sukarno of Indonesia, and Nkrumah of Ghana, Tito initiated the creation of a nonaligned movement as an alternative to East–West confrontations and, in the process, managed to gain respect on both sides. The split from Moscow had an immediate positive effect on the Yugoslav media too. In order to counter Soviet propaganda, Tito needed an analytical, critical, and well-documented response. "Foreign Political Propaganda" departments within Party headquarters in Belgrade and the capitals of the five other republics brought together some of the best journalists of the time. Their mission was to counter, on a daily basis, Soviet anti-Yugoslav propaganda and to analyze political and economic developments in the Soviet Union and Eastern bloc in general. Their reporting made Yugoslavia, and especially Belgrade, a strategic observation post for the West as it tried to understand developments behind the Iron Curtain.

Novak was recruited for this counter-propaganda effort, first in Zagreb as head of a department that later included well-known commentators such as Frane Barbieri, Josko Palavrsic, and Zeljko Brihta, and later at the party propaganda headquarters in Belgrade. That's how he met Milovan Djilas, a minister of Agitprop and at that time still Tito's most trusted man in the propaganda field. Djilas named Novak head of the Jugopress news agency, which was supposed to provide some competition to Tanjug.

Djilas argued, both within the Party and also publicly with the support of prominent Yugoslav writers, that there was a need for greater freedom of expression, at least in less politically sensitive fields such as culture, in order to underline the difference from the Soviet model. Djilas himself, in a series of articles in the Party daily *Borba* in 1954, criticized the Party leadership for the slow progress toward political and economic liberalization and even suggested the creation of another party to provide open debate and exchange of ideas. Tito convened a Central Committee meeting during which he sharply criticized Djilas.

Facing the accusation of factionalism within the Party, Djilas turned in his membership card. A propaganda master, he then made the best move to protect himself from further prosecution: He granted an interview with the *New York Times*, becoming the first high-ranking Communist dissident to use international public support in an attempt to fend off prosecution at home.[9]

At that point Belgrade became "too hot" for all those who were close associates of Djilas. The leading Croat politician of that time, Vladimir Bakaric—who, with Serb Aleksandar Rankovic and Slovene Edvard Kardelj, was in Tito's inner circle of confidants—gave Novak some strictly-between-us, friendly advice: "Now that Djilas is down, they will hunt those who worked with him. You'd better flee to Zagreb!" Novak went, joining the leading Croatian daily *Vjesnik* as an editor in the political and economics department. In the meantime, Djilas confronted Tito and the Party with a new challenge; in 1957 he smuggled a manuscript of his book *The New Class* to New York. The book portrayed Communism as a grab for all sorts of privileges by a small group of immoral and corrupt Party bureaucrats.[10] Coming from someone at the top of the Party hierarchy, and Tito's right-hand man, the criticism sealed Djilas's fate as an "internal enemy" on a crusade to "undermine the people's authority" and even "socialism as an idea." Already on suspended sentence for his original sin of 1954, Djilas began to serve a nine-year sentence, ironically in the same prison in Sremska Mitrovica in which he had been jailed for his communist ideas by the prewar Yugoslav royalist regime.[11]

Yugoslavia's break with Moscow in 1948 and the ensuing debate over the need to project the country's image as different from that of its strictly controlled East European neighbors had a positive effect on Yugoslav journalism. Even though all leading republican and federal publishing houses remained under Party-appointed supervisors, the introduction of self-management gave them a limited degree of freedom: Workers' councils took over the responsibility for decisions relating to business, employment, salaries, apartment allocation, and, most important, editorial staff appointments (other then editors-in-chief), which were increasingly based on professional competence. Aleksandar Nenadovic, a prominent journalist and former editor-in-chief of the leading Serbian daily *Politika* (1969–72), said in an interview that the break with Stalinism resulted in "a happier time" for Yugoslav journalism:

> It wasn't, of course, possible to write freely about many things, but it was a time when "the unthinkable became possible": Even Stalin, or Soviet Stalinism, was no longer off-limits. Not only could journalists describe and unmask Stalin-style communism with no hesitation, they were even encouraged and directed to do so. That "freedom of anti-Stalinism" was important for introducing, through comparisons between the Soviet and our own model of socialism, not only a deep criticism of "their ways" but also, step by step, among more courageous editors and writers, the beginnings of questioning the domestic Yugo-version of socialism.[12]

Both Nenadovic and Novak ascribe the awakening of Yugoslav journalism during the 1950s and 1960s to the regime's need to clearly separate the country from the rest of Eastern Europe. Foreign news, once the exclusive domain of official Tanjug reporting, became a prominent feature in all newspapers. The republics' dailies started to develop their own correspondents' network—in New York, London, Moscow, Cairo, Bonn, Beijing, and, in line with Yugoslavia's nonaligned foreign policy, faraway Asian and African countries. At the same time, increased competition for readership led Yugoslav news executives to look to the West for market-oriented strategies and advanced technologies.

In 1956, at the age of 31, Novak became the editor-in-chief of *Vjesnik,* the main Croatian daily in Zagreb, and in 1960 he went on a study trip to London "to learn English and to see for myself how they produce a newspaper." It was in London that this self-made journalist discovered the central role of a news editor—deciding "what's fit to print"—and that there were "at least a hundred books" published on the subject of journalism. Later, after becoming director of *Vjesnik* in 1963, Novak attended school at the American Institute of Journalism in Salzburg, Austria. On his return to Zagreb, with the help of fifty selected journalists from throughout Yugoslavia, he produced an encyclopedia entitled *Contemporary Journalism,* "in which we never mentioned the Party or Communism," Novak recalled. "It was a simple professional guidebook, based on international standards, given to all those who came to work as journalists so that they could learn from it."[13]

While the distancing from Stalinism provided Yugoslav journalism with an unparalleled degree of freedom compared to the rest of the communist world, this freedom was limited to foreign news coverage and, with occasional stiffening of the Party line, to culture and sports. Domestic politics was, of course, "forbidden territory." The continuing political imperative for editors to support and project "Titoism" established clear limits: There was no room for questioning the Party's or Tito's authority. Tito himself set those limits—at least for that stage of Yugoslavia's history—in his speech at the 1958 Congress of the League of Communists:

> During our country's revolutionary period of transition, the press cannot be considered an independent and autonomous factor in society, since all actions of society as a whole must converge towards one aim: the construction of Socialism.[14]

Novak said in an interview that, in his experience, it wasn't so much Tito himself, but mainly the old guard of hard-line communists around Tito, members of his ruling Politburo, who were most concerned with any loosening of the Party's control over the press. As *Vjesnik's* editor and later director, Novak had his worst problems with Party functionaries at the republican and even regional level, officials who wanted to be quoted extensively whenever and wherever they spoke. They liked to visit their hometowns on weekends, sometimes just to hunt or fish, and they would give speeches at various local ceremonies. If their remarks weren't extensively covered, they would call Croatia's Party bosses and the bosses would call Novak, objecting that *Vjesnik's* reports had "missed a key point" in comrade-so-and-so's speech. Novak recalled:

> Once, leaving the country for a couple of days, I instructed a desk editor to print everything they said that weekend. When, as was the custom, the first edition of the paper was delivered to the highest Party officials' homes, there was a shock: There was never so much stupidity in a single issue of the paper as on that occasion. Bakaric himself, in Zagreb for the weekend, rushed to the editorial offices and worked long into the night correcting all those "key points" that the Party bureaucrats had made that weekend. For a long time, I didn't get further complaints of this nature.[15]

Novak remembers the mid-1960s as a time when Yugoslavia had a chance to break further from communism and embrace a market economy. In 1966, in a major affair concerning the alleged bugging of Tito's private quarters, Aleksandar Rankovic, Tito's hard-line associate in charge of the secret police, was removed from power, weakening the

Party's instruments of control over society. Novak was the president of the Association of Journalists of Yugoslavia in 1965–69, a time when, at their congress in Mostar, Bosnia Herzegovina, journalists from throughout the country objected to the proposed law on the control of the press. He explained that "Edvard Kardelj [a Slovene and Tito's close associate at the time] drafted a law that would have amounted to requiring self-censorship. We did not want to be treated either as 'universal incompetents' or 'socio-political workers,' but simply as professionals responsible only to the public. We submitted our own draft law, making a case for the establishment of a journalists' labor union."[16]

This public expression of insubordination on the part of such a "strategic" group as journalists sounded the alarm in Party headquarters and soon a delegation from the Association—led by Novak—was invited to meet Tito at his favorite summer destination, Brioni Island off the Croatian Istrian peninsula. Novak remembers: "Tito wasn't really yelling or anything like that. He listened to what we had to say, and we told him that, with his international reputation and acceptance, he needed a free, not controlled, press. We stayed with him for three hours and, much later, his aide came to my room with a message: 'The Old Man [Tito's nickname] says you can write a press release the way you want it.'"[17]

The regime, of course, had its way; there was never anything like a free union of journalists in Tito's Yugoslavia or Yugoslavia post-Tito, but journalism was occasionally less controlled there than elsewhere in Eastern Europe.

Nenadovic agreed that, depending on global developments—and even more on who was in charge of the media in a given republic at a given time—there were periods of relative freedom of the press that allowed some of the Yugoslav newspapers, *Politika* among them, to compare even with well-regarded European dailies outside of the Soviet bloc. He said:

> In other words, there were some opportunities for professional journalism, as long as some politician at the top didn't, in less dramatic cases, raise a 'yellow card' against journalism 'going astray,' or in the worst cases, raise the accusation of 'enemy propaganda.' Objections were always in defense of the two untouchable guarantors of the political oligarchy's power: Tito and the Party. No one who didn't want to risk his status as a journalist—and even his bare existence outside of journalism—would dare touch those taboos.[18]

Another witness of that time, veteran Bosnian journalist Rizo Mehinagic, had similar experiences through the postwar Yugoslav phases of
development in journalism. In the first phase, during "Administrative
Socialism," all the international "news" came exclusively through TASS,
the Soviet news agency, and the papers, including his—*Oslobodjenje* in
Sarajevo—would carry only endless speeches by the all-important Soviet
comrades. The breakup with Moscow provided the Yugoslav press with
a challenge and opportunity to develop its own international reporting.
Mehinagic himself was named the first foreign correspondent for
Oslobodjenje in Bonn, West Germany, in 1955. After returning to Sarajevo, he served mostly as foreign news editor until 1965 when he was
named editor-in-chief. By that time, *Oslobodjenje* had gained a reputation
for solid international and sports reporting, as well as for one of the finest
cultural news departments in the Yugoslav press. The Party's close watch,
however, limited political reporting. No dissent was allowed in the ethnically sensitive republic of Bosnia.

Mehinagic said in an interview that as editor he didn't need to censor
his journalists: They would censor themselves, avoiding anything that
might anger those "above."[19] Nevertheless, he noted that there were occasional calls from the Party's high offices: Once, the criticism came that
"[Ivica] Bodnaruk's reports on agriculture are contrary to Party policies in
that field." Another time, Dzemal Bijedic, a high-ranking Bosnian politician called (later he became Tito's prime minister and was subsequently
killed in a plane crash on January 18, 1977). Bijedic complained about
"historical inaccuracies" in a series of articles on the Herzegovinian war
hero Miro Popara. "Milan Knezevic, *Oslobodjenje's* Party-appointed director at the time, found an elegant escape route. He countered Bijedic's complaints with a surprising offer: 'You were there, during the war. It would be
great if you would write us a story on how it really was.' Bijedic did not call
us again on that matter," Mehinagic recalled. But he had a more serious
problem with the Party: Just before the 1968 Olympic Games in Mexico,
quarrels arose among the Yugoslav republics. *Oslobodjenje* cartoonist Bozo
Stefanovic was inspired by the Olympic torch to make a cartoon spoofing
the feuds. The Yugoslav national coat-of-arms consisted of six torches representing six constitutive republics. Stefanovic drew a cartoon depicting
two runners, each of them taking his own torch from the Yugoslav coat-
of-arms and then running in different directions. Mehinagic remembered:

As a first reaction, we received a letter from a colonel in the Yugoslav Army, accusing the paper of "attacking the country's unity," and I responded that it was only a cartoonist's benign warning against those who threaten "disunity of the country." But very soon I was invited to the Executive Committee of the League of Communists of Bosnia Herzegovina, and was criticized for the "lack of critical awareness." The paper's director, Knezevic, had to submit a ten-page essay explaining the incident to the Committee's members.[20]

Worst of all, as the editor-in-chief, Mehinagic had to go with Stefanovic to the state prosecutor's office for an "informative talk" in which they both received strong warnings against similar incidents in the future. Remembering the episode, Stefanovic, who remained with *Oslobodjenje* throughout the Bosnian war (1992–95), said in an interview, "As soon as we walked out of the prosecutor's office, Mehinagic reassured me of his support, asking me not to let this incident limit my creativity."[21]

In his years as editor, Mehinagic was especially proud when Belgrade students, during the anti-regime demonstrations in the summer of 1968, posted copies of *Oslobodjenje's* reports on a "Column of Pride" while most reports from the Belgrade press were attached to a "Column of Shame." "[That year,] the students made the most dramatic demand for change in Yugoslavia, and they contributed to the liberalization that followed in both Croatia and Serbia," Mehinagic recalled. "We covered their issues in *Oslobodjenje* pretty well."

As for me, I had my own close encounter with the limits of press freedom during the summer of 1968 as editor of *Student,* a weekly in Belgrade. I had come to the Yugoslav capital three years before, in the summer of 1965, as a freshman at Belgrade University's Law School, but all I really wanted was to be a journalist. Since the first year of high school in Sanski Most, a small town in Bosnia, I had been writing as a stringer-correspondent for a variety of newspapers, including *Oslobodjenje,* and I was so eager to move into professional journalism that I finished the eleventh and twelfth grades in one year. For an aspiring Yugoslav journalist in the mid-1960s, Belgrade was the place of choice: In addition to the traditional, well-established dailies such as *Politika* and *Borba,* there were evening tabloids—*Vecernje novosti (Evening News)* and *Politika ekspres* (sometimes called *Ekspres*)—as well as a dozen or so magazines, including the first Yugoslav news magazine,

Above: Communist authorities accused *Oslobodjenje* of "attacking the country's unity" when the newspaper ran this cartoon by Bozo Stefanovic in 1968. The cartoon spoofs feuds among Yugoslavia's six republics by showing two runners, each taking a torch from the Yugoslav coat of arms and running off in different directions. The torch is a reference to the Olympic Games, which were being held in Mexico at that time.

Above right: The author, then a student at Belgrade University, is knocked to the ground and beaten by a Serbian policeman during a student protest on June 1, 1968. He was covering the demonstration as editor of the university's weekly newspaper, *Student.* (Photo: Tomislav Peternek)

Below right: Belgrade students in 1968 protest the media distortion of their demonstrations. Their sign reads, "Don't Trust the Press." (Photo: Tomislav Peternek)

NIN, and, soon after, the first sports magazine, *Tempo.* Just "being around"—having an early evening beer in the open-air café Sumatovac, located outside the Politika publishing company high-rise, or visiting editors with story ideas—brought a young journalist in touch with star reporters, mostly foreign and sports correspondents, whose reports from around the globe inspired generations of aspiring journalists.

For me, this was the land of opportunity, both a welcoming and a competitive environment. I never sensed that my background posed problems in being accepted into Belgrade's "high society"—my being a small-town newcomer to the city, a Bosnian and a Muslim among Serbs, or a hard-working young man supporting himself. All that mattered was how interesting and well-written my stories were. As a freshman in law school, I was able to write for the sports and city pages of *Borba;* when *Tempo* started up, I had articles—mostly soccer stars' profiles—in almost every issue. It was at the weekly *Student,* however, that I found my full-time occupation. By the summer of 1968, I was a university news editor.

That year, student protests raged in the streets of Paris and other European capitals, and there was a "feeling in the air" that something might happen in Belgrade too. Before closing for summer break in June, we even ran a couple of articles in the last issue of *Student* that challenged traditional teaching at the university and inequalities in Yugoslav society. Nevertheless, the *Student's* editorial staff took their traditional three-month summer break, focusing on the upcoming June exams and—along with the whole country—celebrating Yugoslavia's soccer victory over England and our team's advancement to the final round of the European championship in Italy. So student protests at Belgrade University caught even me, as a *Student* editor, by surprise. On the evening of June 1, 1968, a concert was held in Studentski Grad (Student City on the outskirts of Belgrade), and many more people came than could fit into the hall, so a fight broke out between those inside and those trying to get in. Police intervened, beating "irresponsible hooligans," and word spread through neighboring dormitories, which housed up to 7,000 students, that "police are beating students." Hundreds of students rushed to the scene armed with sticks and stones. While the battle between students and police raged into the night, with one fire engine set afire and lighting up the sky, student protesters formed an Organizing Committee to spell out demands ranging from the investigation of police brutality to changes in the social system that would promote social justice and equality.

The next morning, armed with these demands, the students began their march toward the city's center. A column of some 3,000 protesters, carrying banners and chanting "Murderers, murderers," headed to the federal government building only to be blocked by hundreds of policemen in full riot gear. Coming from the city, I found myself with a group of other journalists and photographers, sandwiched between the mass of students pushing toward the city and the police determined not to let them through. There were some wave-like motions of the crowd—students pushing toward the city, police pushing back—when suddenly an order was issued, "Start beating them!" The police pulled out long rubber sticks, beating mercilessly anyone they could reach—on the head, shoulders, back, and stomach. Being in the worst place, between the protesters and the police, I pulled out my press card and yelled, "I'm a journalist!" but to no avail. They hit me on the head twice, and when I raised my arms to protect my head, they beat me on my back. I fell to the ground, for a moment losing consciousness, while the chase and beating continued all the way back to the dormitories. Later I walked in pain to the *Student* office to work on a special issue of the paper covering the protests with as many of the editorial staff members as could make it.

As I was the editor-on-duty for the issue, I picked up all the edited stories and, following the usual routine, went to the Glas printing company in Vlajkoviceva Street in the center of the city. But the procedure was different this time. With an apologetic gesture, the manager on duty took the manuscripts to his office instead of distributing them to typists. After an hour or so delay, he emerged from his room and, after another couple of hours, a special issue of *Student*—with only four pages of battleground reports—was ready. My front-page story, published with another one written by Milisav Savic (later a prominent Serbian writer), gave a firsthand account of the police brutality. I took some copies and headed toward the exit. But the huge door was locked, and the guard in the entrance boot apologized. "Sorry, police orders." Soon, two trucks with riot police, again in full gear, pulled in front of the building and, holding their sticks ready, ordered us to leave immediately. The paper was banned with the frightening accusation of

"attempting to undermine the constitutional order." The protests lasted
for another week, now with a full list of students' demands for changes
attracting the attention and support of many who until then had been
silent opponents of the regime. Tito, who refrained from commenting
throughout the crisis, suddenly appeared on TV one night, making a
dramatic statement. "The students are right," he said and expressed his
understanding of the impatience among youth concerning the slow
progress of reforms. That night Belgrade students celebrated their "victory," embracing in a traditional folk dance and pledging allegiance to
Tito and the Party.

Tito knew what he was doing. Once he had defused the immediate
tension, he had enough time—the whole summer—to deal individually
with the leaders of the student movement. Relatively small fry in that cat-
egory, I went for a summer vacation to my grandmother's home in Sanski
Most. Some of my local friends, active in the Party or occupying important public positions, shied away from "that rebel from Belgrade." No
longer surrounded by friends who would share a summer afternoon beer
with me, one day I drank a couple by myself and went to take a nap. My
grandma woke me up. "There is someone who wants to talk to you, but
be careful." "Why?" "He said he went to school with you in Mrkonjic-
Grad." I laughed at the incompetence of the infamous Yugoslav secret
police: I was born in Mrkonjic-Grad, Bosnia, but I was only six months
old when my parents moved. Since then I had never even visited
Mrkonjic-Grad. So I was careful, as my old grandma suggested, telling
my "schoolmate" only the things he could find readily available in each
issue of the paper itself. At that time, of course, I didn't even wonder if he
might report our conversation as an act of recruiting another "informer."

The next fall I did not return to *Student*. Instead, I became a full-
time Belgrade sports correspondent for *Oslobodjenje*, reporting—as I
had always wanted—on national and international sports events.
Sports, after all, presented a safe haven from that best of all worlds we
were told we lived in.

Sasa Nenadovic was *Politika's* correspondent in New York at that
time. Along with sports and to a lesser extent culture, international
reporting was another safe haven of free journalism. That's why
Nenadovic wasn't happy when, in the fall of 1969, colleagues from
Politika asked him to return to Belgrade and become the editor-in-

chief. He resisted, telling them that he was only at the half-point of his term as correspondent and that his son had just started school in New York, but some of his best friends—including Frane Barbieri, then foreign news editor, and Vojislav Djukic, political editor—convinced him that his return was crucial in preserving *Politika's* professional standards and reputation. He finally accepted on condition that the journalists themselves decide if they wanted him as the new editor, which they did, and he assumed that position in November 1969.

The events that followed made Novak and Nenadovic both the symbols and the primary victims of the Tito regime's showdown—first with the leaders of the so-called "Croatian spring" in 1971 and then with the "Serbian liberals" in 1972.

What the Party dubbed "Croatian nationalism threatening the constitutional order [of Yugoslavia]," Novak saw as the awakening of public opinion in Croatia and the beginnings of the development of civil society. He explained:

> In the wake of the fall of Rankovic, who lost his position as the head of Yugoslav secret police for allegedly bugging even Tito's private quarters, the regime couldn't control what people thought and said. In Zagreb alone, there were approximately twenty new publications, carrying articles by people who had been silent for twenty or more years. The old guard felt threatened. They couldn't understand this fashionable new approach—that, after they spoke, other people could publicly question or oppose their ideas. Tito was alarmed by this "threat," and he came to Zagreb requesting that Croatia's reformist Party leaders, Savka Dabcevic and Miko Tripalo, "stop it." They said they couldn't. Freedom of expression had reached a level of "anarchy" unacceptable to the old guard, and Tito was compelled to "do something." The rest is history. Tito criticized and removed the Croatian leadership, and in the ensuing purges thousands lost their jobs. Including me.[22]

Novak was asked to submit his resignation so that the Party could conduct its "differentiation" (a Communist name for witch-hunt). He was promised a diplomatic assignment on one condition: He must publicly denounce those "strayed journalists." Novak refused and, in turn, was accused of supporting Croatian nationalism and liberalism, and of using a "techno-managerial" professional style. Novak was also accused of "falling under foreign influence," a serious curse in communist terminology, probably because he went so far with market-oriented strategies at *Vjesnik* that, after a trip to the United States, he decided to develop an investigative journalism team similar to one he had encountered at the *New York Times*. "That was enough to be accused of being, in fact, an agent of the CIA with the intent to undermine Yugoslavia," said Novak, recalling the days of "differentiation," which forced him to retire in 1973 using his veteran's benefits. Croatia's Society of Journalists expelled him from membership for life and forbade him to practice journalism. His mentors at the American Institute of Journalism, which he had attended in Salzburg, Austria, sent him a letter asking whether they could help in any way, but someone in the company he had headed for decades, having risen from obscurity to national prominence, coldly returned it with the stamp "Person Unknown." Blacklisted and banned from public life, Novak spent years documenting and writing a history of Croatian journalism.

Sasa Nenadovic, in the meantime, as the new editor-in-chief of *Politika*, announced his platform, declaring that henceforth the paper would answer only to its readers. It was relatively easy to raise professional standards and encourage freedom of expression in the coverage of foreign policy issues, but it was much more difficult when it came to domestic issues. The new liberal leadership in Serbia, under Marko Nikezic and Latinka Perovic, provided only passive support: They did not interfere. But the Party bureaucracy, Serbian hard-liners, and (even more so) representatives from other republics asked the federal Party leadership to intervene. Nenadovic got a sense of the pressures to come when one of the Serbian federal politicians, Dusan Petrovic Sane, called him to explain nothing less than "subversion" in *Politika*. Petrovic was enraged by the way in which one of his "great speeches" had been presented in the paper: It had been substantially cut, missing "all the key points." The politician wanted to know who was behind *Politika* that it would treat him so disrespectfully. Was the paper under some "foreign influence?"—an obvious allusion to Nenadovic's stint as a New York correspondent. Who should be held "politically responsible" for what had happened? Nenadovic told him the cuts had been made strictly on the professional judgment of the editor on duty, with no political considerations, but Petrovic repeated his key question: "Who is behind *Politika?*" alluding to Serbia's new liberal leadership.

"I don't see any sense in continuing this discussion," Nenadovic told him, hanging up. At the next session of Serbia's political leadership, someone in the old guard, accusing the new leadership of liberal tendencies, commented: "You see how bad things are when someone like that Nenadovic at *Politika* hangs up on comrade Sane." But *Politika* continued the practice of cutting political speeches, trying to present only what was new in them, and it gradually expanded the practice to include the speeches of all Party leaders, with special handling only for Tito's statements. When, for the first time, the paper reported on some of Tito's routine activities in a newly designed column, "From the Office of the President of the Republic," located on page two instead of at the top of page one, Nenadovic received a visit and a polite warning from Tito's protocol office, and Tanjug sent out special instructions to the Yugoslav media that all of Tito's speeches had to be published in full. Nenadovic recalled:

> I insisted within our editorial board that it was professionally unacceptable to follow that order, and, on the occasion of one of Tito's visits to Africa, I cut his courtesy speech, which had no substance, by about one-third. That was the beginning of the end of my tenure as editor. The old guard, already agitated by the first signs of political pluralism in public life—by the opening of the media to alternative thoughts that threatened their monopoly—launched their crusade against liberalism, which was "endangering the country." Pressure was mounting for my resignation and, in the fall of 1972, I resigned with a simple explanation that "conditions were not right for the kind of journalism I wanted to practice."[23]

In this official campaign to clamp down on so-called Serb liberalism, dozens of the finest in Serbian journalism lost their positions and jobs, as did hundreds of reform-minded Party cadres at all levels and thousands of market-oriented business leaders. As for Nenadovic, the old guard hard-liners were not satisfied with his resignation. They wanted to have *Politika's* Party organization condemn him, giving the whole farce a "democratic form," which would then mean that he would not even be able to work as a journalist at *Politika* any longer. Nenadovic's salary was reduced by some 40 percent, to the bare minimum, and he was not allowed to write anything for a full eight years. Some of his friends at the paper resisted the pressure by Party authorities to condemn him, but there were others who, afraid for their status, were careful not to be seen with him and would not exchange a word or shake hands. One of those begged him, "Please go. Otherwise they will break me." "But where can I go?" Nenadovic asked. His name was prohibited in the pages of *Politika* even if only for a rewrite of some international news. After seven years, his initials, A.N., appeared in the cultural section of the paper on an article he wrote on the death of an actor. Vukoje Bulatovic, *Politika's* director at the time, had to explain to the Party bosses "what that meant" until someone higher up decided that this practice was more embarrassing for the Party than if they let Nenadovic write an occasional article. Only in 1983, eleven years after his resignation, was Nenadovic able to write his first article under his full name. It was published in the weekly *NIN*, edited at that time by his long-time *Politika* colleagues Slavoljub Djukic and Dusan Simic.

After the purges in Party leadership in Croatia and Serbia, a new Yugoslav Constitution was adopted in 1974, giving more power to the republics and weakening the federal authorities' grip over the country. For the Yugoslav media, this meant that the command center—which had been first in Moscow, then in Belgrade—was moved to the capitals of the republics, thus opening the third phase of Yugoslavia's search for a distinctive brand of "socialism with a human face." While decentralization could have led to democratization, for the media it was only a changing of the guard and not a change in the methods or instruments of control. The Party was still careful to appoint loyal directors and editors who would make sure that the media reflected their republic's "interests." Each republican radio and television station, as well as the main dailies, promoted exclusively the positions of their political leaderships, ignoring or criticizing what "others" said, which in time led to the first salvos of the "media war" that would characterize the last decade of Yugoslavia.

Tito died on May 4, 1980. It was the irony of his legacy that some of his real achievements, which compared very favorably to the legacy of other Eastern European dictators, also contributed to Yugoslavia's ultimate failure. The better standard of living, the more open borders and communication with the outside world, the greater freedom and diversity of the press (except in the permissible treatment of himself and his Party)—these accomplishments made Yugoslavs less enthusiastic about dramatic changes than other Eastern Europeans. Even the country's reformers spoke more about "improvements" and "changes within the system" than changing the system itself. For Yugoslavs, who had distanced themselves from Stalinism four decades before, the symbolic fall of the Berlin Wall in the fall of 1989, as the final blow to the whole Soviet empire, was a great historic event, but it was only "another people's story." Yugoslavs saw themselves as being on the other side of the Iron Curtain, observers and not participants in the history being made. Having been able to travel, to work in the West, and to invest their savings in their families' prosperity at home, Yugoslavs did not feel the same joy in the new freedom of movement or the promise of acceptance and integration into Europe as did the other Eastern Europeans after decades of life behind the Wall.

While the whole continent was celebrating and embracing a future-oriented Europe that was becoming, finally, "whole and free," the Yugoslav tribes were busy looking for their identity somewhere in the distant past. While the continent was embracing unity and integration, Yugoslavia was heading toward a violent breakup. While Europe was busy dismantling borders and delegating to common institutions such basic elements of sovereignty as armies, currencies, and even passports, Yugoslavs were getting ready to fight and die for new borders and centuries-old ideologies. With Tito gone and with no vision or leadership for a transition to democracy and prosperity, the scene was set for a bloody replay of the past.

What in Tito's time had made it possible for the next generation of Yugoslav leaders—best represented by Serbia's Slobodan Milosevic and Croatia's Franjo Tudjman—to mobilize their peoples for the nationalist crusades of the 1990s? First, the one-man, one-party rule. Used to living under their beloved "father of the nation" for almost four decades, Yugoslav peoples—starting with the Serbs—were primed to embrace new, undisputed leaders. The media led the way. The Serbian media and intellectuals celebrated Milosevic as the "new Tito," while the Croatian media portrayed Tudjman as the "father of the nation," sporting Tito-like uniforms and ceremonial guards. Similarly, most of the media offered new ruling parties the same slavish support they had provided to communists. In Serbia, communists (renamed socialists) maintained steady control over the same instruments of power—the army, police, courts, media—that had kept the party in undisputed control for the previous thirty-five years. In Croatia, not belonging to Tudjman's HDZ—or, worse, publicly questioning its rigid nationalism—was considered an act of national betrayal. All of the regime-controlled media continued to trumpet a single ideological line: While the message had changed, from required brotherhood and unity to required hatred for neighbors, the propagandistic enforcement of that line was practiced with the same degree of well-trained enthusiasm and loyalty in promoting the ideology of the day. Finally, the media manipulation of history under Tito paved the way for nationalists. In Tito's time, some World War II crimes had been buried under the carpet of ideological interpretations, and there had been no critical examination of atrocities. Obfuscation of the past served the new pretenders to Tito's throne who manipulated reality to awaken fears, suspicion, and hatred for "enemies around us." Such a combination of forces set the stage for unspeakable crimes that would be committed "in the service of the nation."

Serbia: Manufacturing Enemies (1980-89)

GORAN MILIC WAS ARGUABLY the most popular journalist in Yugoslavia in the early 1980s. He had all that it takes to be a role model. Born in Zagreb in 1946, the son of Marko Milic, a Dalmatian partisan who became Tito's diplomat serving in France and Uruguay, fluent in three foreign languages (French, Spanish, and English), Milic was tall, good-looking, well-mannered, and outgoing. He held the enviable job of Belgrade TV correspondent in New York for five years, from 1980 to 1985. There was hardly a more attractive job in Yugoslav journalism, and Milic made the most of it: He interviewed U.S. President Jimmy Carter and later Vice President George Bush, U.N. Secretary General Javier Peres de Cuellar, and international celebrities. The regular exchange of programming between central television studios in all six republics and two provinces guaranteed that he was well-known throughout the country. When Milic returned to Belgrade in the summer of 1985, he was troubled to find that the city in which he had grown up and become a celebrity wasn't exactly as he had left it. He noticed early signs of the awakening of Serb nationalism: Chetnik insignia sold in the streets, nationalistic songs, and preoccupation in public life with the Kosovo

27

mythology. Yet his high school friends and colleagues from Belgrade University Law School dismissed his concerns, saying that he had been out of town and working in a foreign culture for a long time. "It was always like this, Goran; you just forgot," friends told him reassuringly.

But in late August to early September 1985, only a month after his return, he realized that indeed something had gone fundamentally wrong in his absence. According to Milic, one of his colleagues was Nenad Ristic, the editor of the late-night newscast, a man known as a solid Orthodox Serb, hailing from a village that observed all the religious holidays, but also a solid Party member and at some point even a member of the Belgrade City Committee of the League of Communists. Ristic went to Kosovo to do a story on Serb monasteries in the province. A woman he interviewed in one of the monasteries told him of her personal tragedy: "Ten years ago, they killed my husband, three months ago, they killed my son," the woman said. "Who killed them?" Ristic asked. "Shiptars, who else!" *Shiptar* is a derogatory term for Kosovar-Albanians. It was not only the first time that such offensive language had been used in a major, Party-controlled media outlet (Serbian television) but also, more significantly, the first time that an entire ethnic group, Kosovar-Albanians, was publicly blamed for a Serb family tragedy in that province. Even though Ristic's report ran late at night on Belgrade TV's Channel 2 in a low-rated cultural magazine with an audience of no more that 3 to 4 percent, in the following days almost every discussion in Belgrade began with "Did you see that woman?"

Milic observed in an interview, "That's the phenomenon of television. Even if only a few people actually saw something shocking, the 'did-you-see-it' network means that, in a couple of weeks it seems as though everyone saw it, too."[1] The "something" that had gone wrong in Milic's five-year absence was Yugoslavia's inability—with no central authority and no transitional democratic institutions to replace Tito or his party—to deal with its first serious challenge to the constitutional order. The eight-member federal presidency, with its representatives from six republics and two provinces rotating as chairmen by established order in mid-May of each year, did not have Tito's authority or his power to silence or confront challenges to national unity, nor were the democratic procedures or mechanisms in place to resolve existing or potential disputes.

In February 1981, less than a year after Tito died, Albanian students at Pristina University staged mass protests, asking for better conditions and better food at the universities, and also demanding something much more serious. "Kosovo-Republic, Kosovo-Republic!" they shouted through Pristina's streets. The students demanded that the province's status be upgraded from an autonomous province within Serbia to a Yugoslav republic equal to the six others. The regime's response was harsh. Kosovo protests were declared a counter-revolution, an attack on Yugoslavia's constitutional order, and organizing for hostile activities. In a matter of months, hundreds of Kosovo Albanians—often just high school teenagers and university students who were "guilty" of carrying "Kosovo-Republic" banners or participating in the street protest, as well as teachers and other intellectuals held responsible for their uprising—were subjected to mass trials and harsh sentences of five to twenty years in prison.

In her book *The Destruction of Yugoslavia: Tracking the Break-Up 1980–92*,[2] Branka Magas illustrates the severity of the regime's response in the three trials held in less than a month during the summer of 1981. On August 3, eleven Albanians charged with organizing demonstrations in local villages and related activities received sentences from one to thirteen years. On August 8, ten college and high school students received sentences from four to eight years for organizing demonstrations and shouting, "We want a republic! Long live the Socialist Republic of Kosovo!" On August 31, three youths were sentenced to two, four, or six years for painting similar slogans on houses. Other trials held that summer across the province ended in stiff sentences, too. "Those identified as having been involved in any way with the events of last spring have in most instances been dismissed from their schools, colleges, and workplaces,"[3] Magas writes.

It was then, in the first year after Tito's death, that the Yugoslav federation faced—and failed—its first test of sustainability. With a weak central authority—all power having shifted to the republics' bureaucracies—the other republics treated the events in Kosovo as "Serbia's affair," accepting Belgrade's official condemnation of the Albanian "counter-revolution" and concurring with the use of federal army and special police units in the ensuing years of repression. After the government's harsh showdown with Albanian "separatism," step-by-step the Serbian media engaged in a campaign of ethnic stereotyping, the first of many to come. The single rape of a Serb woman by an Albanian would be translated into a "they-are-raping-our-mothers-and-sisters" media avalanche (even though official statistics prove that, year-by-year, there were fewer cases of rape in the traditional Kosovo Albanian communities than among Serbs in the province or in Serbia proper).[4] Any land dispute between neighbors, something that is common in predominantly agrarian rural areas, or any sale of a Serb home to an Albanian, was used in the media as evidence of the orchestrated expulsion of Serbs from their "ancient hearths." A single murder of a Serb by an Albanian—and there was only one during the five years preceding the 1981 "counter-revolution"—was enough for a media claim of "Albanian terror." A high birth rate among Albanians was billed as part of a systematic effort at domination amounting even to "ethnic genocide."[5]

These distortions, combined with the special place that Kosovo occupies in Serbian national mythology as the location of the historic battle against the invading Ottoman Empire in 1389 and the "cradle of Serbhood," created the perfect mix to awaken Serb nationalism, which would eventually lead to the breakup of Yugoslavia. The rise of nationalism was also the "something" that Milic had missed by spending five years, 1980–85, in New York: During that time, Tito's ideology of brotherhood and unity, a fragile constitutional federation maintaining a balance between the temptation on the part of the largest ethnic group to dominate and the need of the smaller groups for equality, receded as the Serbian media sniped freely at ethnic Albanians and painted the whole national group as "anti-Serbian" and thus "enemies." Putting on national TV the accusation of a Serb woman in Kosovo that all "Shiptars" were responsible for the deaths of her husband and son was indeed sinking to a new low in the Serb media's satanization of Albanians. The "exodus of Serbs and Montenegrins from Kosovo," as reported in Serbia's media in the mid-1980s, became a rallying point of Serb nationalism, an excuse for reexamining the whole federal arrangement and the "rightful place" of Serbia within Yugoslavia.[6]

The Academy Sets the Tone

In 1986 the media-fed frustration with Kosovo received a new boost when Serbian intellectuals got directly involved. On January 21, 1986, some 200 of them signed a petition to federal and Serbian authorities protesting what they called "genocide" in Kosovo. As summed up in Magas's *Destruction of Yugoslavia*, the petition accused the authorities of national treason in Kosovo:

> "Everyone in this country who is not indifferent has long ago realized that the genocide in Kosovo cannot be combated without deep social . . . changes in the whole country. These changes are unimaginable without changes likewise in the relationship between the Autonomous Provinces and the Republic of Serbia. . . . Genocide cannot be prevented by the . . . gradual surrender of Kosovo and Metohija to Albania: the unsigned capitulation which leads to a politics of national treason."[7]

The themes from that petition were elaborated more completely in a draft Memorandum of the Serbian Academy of Sciences and Arts (SANU), which found its way into *Vecernje novosti (Evening News)*, Serbia's largest-circulation daily. On September 24, a journalist, Aleksandar Djukanovic, published a critical review of the portions of the Memorandum that expanded the nationalists' theory of Serbia's victimization within the Yugoslav federation. Serbia, the Memorandum claimed, was victimized economically by the privileged status of the two more advanced, export-oriented, hard-currency-earning republics, Croatia and Slovenia; it was discriminated against in the Yugoslav constitution because it was the only republic with two autonomous provinces; Serbs were discriminated against because they were the only ethnic group without their own national state (since there were substantial Serb populations in both Bosnia and Croatia); and they were being treated unequally in Yugoslavia's other republics. Additionally, the Memorandum claimed, Serbs were being subjected to genocide in Kosovo.

The Memorandum was the first document to challenge the very foundations of the Yugoslav federation with the unofficial approval of a prominent national institution such as the Serbian Academy of Sciences and Arts. The document disputed the republics' borders as mere "administrative lines"; it insinuated the existence of some kind of "Catholic alliance" (between Slovenia and Croatia) against Orthodox Serbia; and it called for the restoration of Serb dignity in both Croatia and Bosnia Herzegovina. Key assertions of the Memorandum included the following claims:

☐ *A disturbed balance had developed between the principle of unity (of Yugoslavia) and the principle of autonomy (of the republics and provinces), denying the Serbian nation the right to its own state.* This claim amounted to a call for "all Serbs in a single state," a call that could not be realized without the territorial dismemberment of the neighboring republics of Bosnia and Croatia: For example, in Bosnia, Serbs constituted 31 percent of the population, but they lived with Bosnian Muslims and Croats in ethnically mixed, multi-ethnic towns throughout the republic.

☐ *There was consistent discrimination against Serbia's economy "in the context of the political and economic dominance of Slovenia and Croatia."* The Memorandum claimed that the disadvantaged status of Serbia was a consequence of the post-World War II prevailing view elsewhere in Yugoslavia that, before the war, Serbs had been "the oppressors" and others were "oppressed," and that this assessment aimed at inculcating "a feeling of historical guilt" in the Serb population. The document did not take note of Slovenia and Croatia's long-standing complaints concerning their hard currency earning—from exports in Slovenia and from Adriatic tourism in Croatia—being spent on Serb-dominated federal institutions.

☐ *These vindictive policies towards Serbia had grown ever stronger—to the point of genocide.* The watchword of this policy, the Memorandum claimed, was "a weak Serbia ensures a strong Yugoslavia," accomplished through the constitutional division of Serbia into three parts. "A worse historical defeat in peacetime cannot be imagined," the document stated.

☐ *The physical, political, legal, and cultural genocide of the Serbian population in Kosovo and Metohija was a worse defeat than any experienced in the wars waged by Serbia from the First Serbian Uprising against the Ottoman Turks in 1804 to the uprising of 1941.* Again, the SANU academics did not have any interest in trying to look at changes in the Kosovo population through an Albanian prism: Kosovo was the most underdeveloped part of Yugoslavia, with an employment rate and per capita income some 30 percent below the country's average. Much of the Serbs' movement out of the province toward more prosperous Serb majority areas could be explained by the lack of opportunities as well as by the loss of privileges in the governmental sector Serbs had enjoyed in Kosovo prior to the constitutional changes of 1974 (that granted Kosovo autonomy).[8]

The entire document, the very existence of which was initially denied, was a list of Serbian grievances against "the others" from ancient times to present-day Yugoslavia, and a battle cry to rectify those grievances. It reflected the well-known statement of the famous Serbian novelist Dobrica Cosic, who called Serbs "winners in wars and losers in peace."[9] The Memorandum provided Serb nationalism with a coherent platform from which to challenge the Yugoslav federal arrangement. In the decade to come, this would lead to the bloody destruction of the country. The Serbian press, starting with magazines that had no direct Party affiliation, picked up on the themes of Serbian victimization within Yugoslavia. The list of potential enemies was expandable, depending on political developments, as was clearly demonstrated in the Academy's official explanation of why the Memorandum was written. The explanation included the following statement: "The leaders of the artificially created Muslim nation have done everything in their power to turn Bosnia and Herzegovina into a republic under the domination of the Muslim population."[10]

The time was ripe for the birth of a leader. There was the threatened nation. There were enemies all around. There was the ongoing exodus of Serbs and even genocide against them. The nation needed a savior. And the savior appeared in the form of Slobodan Milosevic, who rose to power through a Party *putsch* in the fall of 1987.

It is conventional wisdom among analysts of the Milosevic era that the first thing he did after coming to power was to establish control of the media. The fact is, however, that *the media actually gave birth to Milosevic.* As a low-level Communist Party *apparatchik,* rising through Party ranks from the Belgrade city government propaganda office to become the president of the City Committee and later the president of the Serbian Central Committee, Milosevic befriended a number of influential Belgrade journalists and editors active in different Party propaganda bodies. An instant love affair sprang up between the aspiring politician and the journalist-activists who used their positions in the media to offer their services to the Party in order to advance their careers or to advance to more prosperous positions in the government, the Party, or even the diplomatic service. For Milosevic, developing close relationships with people like Dusan Mitevic, one of the top executives of Belgrade Radio and Television, and Zivorad Minovic, the editor-in-chief of *Politika,* the most prominent Serbian daily, was a way to understand and master the manipulation of the media, which proved to be the most useful art in his own rise through the Party hierarchy. For them, Milosevic was the first politician who, after decades of the old guard communists' contempt for the press, showed an interest in the power of the media, combined with total disrespect for its freedom, and who was willing to give access to behind-the-scenes Party intrigue.

Milosevic belonged to the first generation of post-Tito Yugoslav politicians. Born in 1941 in Pozarevac, a small town in Serbia, he became a Party activist as an above-average student at Belgrade University Law School, earning an 8.9 GPA out of a possible 10. From his earliest days in Party politics, his political mentor was Ivan Stambolic, a nephew of Petar Stambolic, the prominent, old guard Serbian politician. Ivan Stambolic made no secret of his special support for Milosevic: When Stambolic left business for politics, he arranged for Milosevic to succeed him at the huge Naftagas company; when he became Serbia's prime minister, he named Milosevic as head of Beobanka, a Belgrade bank that provided Milosevic with the opportunity for numerous business trips to New York; when Stambolic became Serbian Party president, he promoted Milosevic to City Committee president; and when Stambolic became the president of Serbia, he gave Milosevic his chair as president of the Central Committee of the League of Communists of Serbia. Thus, Milosevic came to be only one step away from the top rung of the Serbian political ladder: the Serbian presidency, occupied by his political godfather, Stambolic.

A Leader Is Born

With pressure rising in Serbia to "do something" to protect Serbs and Montenegrins in Kosovo and to change the Yugoslav constitution in order to "rectify" Serbia's status within the federation, the time for Milosevic to take that final step to become the "threatened nation's" hero had come. In April 1987, a made-for-TV opportunity arose. Serbs and Montenegrins had called for a meeting of political activists in Kosovo Polje (Blackbird Field) to protest their alleged mistreatment at the hands of the Albanian majority. Ironically, it was Stambolic who asked Milosevic to go, to listen to what they had to say, and to calm the situation. It was a mission that would mark the beginning of the end of Stambolic as a political leader—and the beginning of the Milosevic era in Serbia.

As documented by the television series *Yugoslavia: Death of a Nation*, local Serb activists had prepared everything in advance in order to provoke a major incident. Before the staged "spontaneous gathering," they had brought a truck full of stones ready to attack the police. The day before the event, Milosevic's wife, Mirjana Markovic—at that time a Belgrade University professor and later the founder of the Yugoslav United Left party—called a family friend, Belgrade Radio and Television executive Mitevic, to express her concern for "Sloba's safety" in going to a Kosovo hot spot. Mitevic, himself a Serb from Kosovo, offered to accompany him, but Milosevic called him late at night to assure him it wouldn't be necessary. The point had been made. Mitevic saw to it that the event in Kosovo Polje received full TV coverage. When Milosevic went to Kosovo Polje on April 24, this wasn't just a meeting with the province's political leadership. There was a gathering of some 15,000 angry Serbs and Montenegrins who wanted to tell the president their firsthand stories of terror. While Milosevic was at the meeting inside the local Home of Culture, the crowd outside started to throw stones at the police and, when they responded with force at this well-organized provocation, the crowd started to chant "Murderers, murderers!" and "They are beating us!" Local Serb activist Miroslav Solevic said in the television series, "There was not a single policeman who did not get a beating that night."

Responding to the crowd's calls for help, Milosevic came out, struck a memorable pose as the self-confident protector of the oppressed, and made a statement, in front of Mitevic's rolling TV camera, that would elevate him to the status of instant hero of the Serbian national cause. "No one is allowed to beat you!" he said, with the crowd responding instantly, chanting his name, "Slobo, Slobo." Encouraged by the response, he later made a brief speech, strengthening his new role as the champion of the Serbian cause. "The first thing I want to tell you, comrades, is that you need to stay here. This is your land, here are your homes, your meadows and gardens, and your memories. . . . Yugoslavia

and Serbia are not going to give up Kosovo!" The scene from Kosovo
Polje—of a young politician stepping out to protect the terrorized,
frightened, mistreated Serbs and Montenegrins—became the focus of
the evening television news. "We showed Milosevic's promise over and
over again on the TV. And this is what launched him," Mitevic said
later, reflecting on his role in the making of a new Serbian legend.[11]

The event in Kosovo was the beginning of Milosevic's final assault on
the highest office, the presidency of Serbia, occupied by his longtime
political mentor and friend Stambolic. A group of leading Serbian media
bosses, all active in Milosevic's party propaganda commission—Mitevic
first of all, but also Radio and Television director Ratomir Vico, *Politika*
editor Zivorad Minovic, *Politika ekspres* editor Slobodan Jovanovic, and
an expanding list of others willing to serve—played a major, maybe even
decisive, role in his rise to power. They were there not only to provide the
best coverage of the ensuing purge of all the "irresolute" from the state
and party hierarchy. They also participated in behind-the-scenes
intrigues aimed at compromising anyone who posed a threat to Milosevic
on his way to the top. With the help of Milosevic's wife, they drafted articles against his opponents, making sure that these people didn't get a
chance to publicly challenge the promotion of the new leader. The con-
spiratorial nature of this group has been best described by prominent
Belgrade journalist Slavoljub Djukic in his series of four books that actually constitute updated biographies of Milosevic and his wife: *Kako se
dogodio vodja (How the Leader Happened,* 1991), *Izmedju slave i anateme
(Between the Glory and Anathema,* 1994), *On, Ona i mi (He, She and Us,*
1997), and *Kraj srpske bajke (The End of the Serbian Fairy Tale,* 1999).[12] A
longtime political columnist with *Politika* and later the editor-in-chief of
the weekly political magazine *NIN*, Djukic described numerous planning
sessions of the group as they plotted to remove all obstacles to Milosevic's
takeover of Serbia. They were there at every turn in the road.

On May 25, 1987—Tito's birthday—it was Mitevic who provoked
the debate that would lead to the fall of moderates in Serbian politics. At
a session of the Belgrade City Committee to discuss economic issues, he
suddenly introduced an entirely different topic: Mitevic accused the university weekly *Student* of "unquestionably aiming at comrade Tito" with
its cover page entitled "The Ball of the Vampire." "I think that such an
act is unacceptable and non-cultural," Mitevic said.[13] Some of Milosevic's

friends on the Committee supported his view, but the president, Dragisa Pavlovic, cut the debate short. "*Student* is not on the agenda; we have more important things to do," he said. A couple of days later, Serbia's minister of culture, Branislav Milosevic, wrote an article in *NIN* attacking not only Mitevic but also the dogmatic policy attributed to the group obviously represented by Slobodan Milosevic. The next day, Minovic's *Politika* carried a heavy-hitting response, entitled "Why Is the Minister of Culture Defending an Anti-Titoist Line?" The article, signed by "B. Jovanovic," was edited late into the night at Milosevic's house by his wife and Minovic.[14] In a display of coordination that would characterize all stages of Milosevic's rise to power, *Politika's* position was immediately cemented by a press release from Milosevic's party headquarters announcing that "The Presidency [of the League of the Communists of Serbia] has charged the Belgrade City Committee to establish concrete political responsibility for the attacks against Tito."

According to Djukic, Milosevic's inner circle, including Mitevic and Minovic, met for dinner at a private home in Igalo on the Montenegrin coast in August 1987. Milosevic told them: "Eat and drink! Starting next fall, you won't have time for that!"[15] The group, Djukic says, knew well what was to come. They just needed a new motive to reignite the Kosovo debate. It came in a tragic form: On September 3, an Albanian conscript in the Yugoslav Army, Aziz Keljmendi, discharged his automatic rifle in the sleeping quarters of an army barracks in Paracin, a town in southern Serbia, killing four soldiers and wounding six. Djukic has a *Politika* journalist's written statement describing Minovic's excitement at the news: "It is made-to-order: an Albanian soldier killing four Serbs!" Minovic told journalists gathered in his office, ordering full coverage.[16] Minovic was soon informed that not all those who had been killed were Serbs—actually the victims included two Muslims (Hazim Dzananovic and Safet Dudakovic), one Croat (Goran Begic), and one Serb (Srdjan Simic). Of the six wounded, three were Muslims, two were Croats, and one was Slovene. Nevertheless, with some disappointment, he still insisted on "huge publicity." Djukic says, "When *Politika* came out with the first reports on the killings in the barracks, I was frightened by how the paper looked and the intonation of the stories, awakening feelings of revenge. The impression was created that it was a nationalist crime even though, according to the doctors' statements, Keljmendi was a mentally deranged person. He didn't select his victims, he shot at anyone he encountered."[17]

On September 11, Pavlovic called a press conference at the City Committee to warn against the uncontrolled incitement of national passions. "If the struggle against Albanian nationalism is accompanied by intolerance and hatred towards the Albanian nation, which we find in certain media, then that struggle is further and further away from socialist principles, and closer and closer to nationalism."[18] Milosevic's group knew the statement was directed towards them, so they met again, this time on September 13, at the home of Milosevic's wife's grandfather in Pozarevac. Along with Mitevic and Minovic, another of the Party propaganda activists was there—*Ekspres* editor Jovanovic. They decided to attack Pavlovic publicly. Mirjana Markovic dictated the article to Minovic; Jovanovic was to publish it in *Ekspres*, while Minovic would reprint it in *Politika*. The dilemma of who would sign the article was solved in a way that promoted another journalist—a one-time small-town correspondent named Dragoljub Milanovic—to the select group of most-trusted: The comment, entitled "Dragisa Pavlovic's Too Easy Judgment," was published under Milanovic's name in Jovanovic's *Ekspres*,[19] making them both an integral part of the group that would dominate Serbian media throughout the decade to come.

Mitevic would play a decisive role in ensuring Milosevic's showdown with Pavlovic and, soon after, with Stambolic. On September 18, 1987, Milosevic convened a session of the Serbian party leadership with "The Political Consequences of Dragisa Pavlovic's Press Conference" on the agenda. ("In Communist countries, when you are on the Central Committee agenda, there is an 80 percent chance that you're dead," Mitevic commented later.[20]) Pavlovic was accused mostly along the lines of the *Ekspres* commentary. In defending himself, he tried to remind his critics that the key issue should be the danger of Serb nationalism, and he mentioned the inflammatory reporting on the Keljmendi case. But Milosevic's supporters insisted on the City Committee's responsibility for *Student's* "attack on Tito" and for its alleged "weakness in carrying out the Party policy on Kosovo." "I think that, after six and a half years of deepening crisis in Kosovo, we simply don't have the moral right to say that it should be dealt with by 'cool heads.' This phrase, 'cool heads,' has become an excuse for postponing the solution in Kosovo," Milosevic insisted.

Pavlovic alluded to the close connection between Milosevic and two dailies: "When *Ekspres* publishes a comment, as they did, and then *Politika* reprints it, along with other accusations against the City Committee, then one has to wonder whether *Politika* does this on its own," Pavlovic said.[21] But he was besieged, with most speakers arguing that he lacked firmness.

When the meeting was adjourned until the next day—according to Djukic's account—Milosevic's closest circle, including Mitevic, Minovic, and Vico, met at his apartment. "Something is missing here: a final blow," Mitevic said, and he embarked on a mission to produce that missing piece. As a City Committee member, he received a letter from Serbia's President Stambolic, urging them not to include "the Pavlovic case" on their agenda. Mitevic decided to use that letter to alarm the Central Committee concerning Stambolic's use of his authority "to exert pressure" against the Belgrade party leadership.[22] The next morning, Mitevic personally found four other members of the City Committee and asked them to sign a letter to the Serbian Party Presidency. Milosevic then used this as "the final blow" in Pavlovic's execution and as an opening shot against Stambolic. "Comrades, I want to tell you something. Comrades, I agonized about this for the last hour and a half to two hours. We have received a letter. I first asked for a double-check, to make sure it wasn't planted by someone. Then I asked myself whether to close the session for the Presidency members only. But then I decided, since we are working together for two days, to read you this letter," Milosevic said, stating that he was "personally, emotionally hurt" by this event, which was billed as a political conspiracy and usurpation of power.[23]

That night marked the beginning of the political execution of Pavlovic, the end of any moderation in Serbia's approach to Kosovo or, for that matter, to the future of the Yugoslav federation. Just four days later, on September 23, 1987, Milosevic convened the now historic Eighth Session of Serbia's Central Committee with the "case of Dragisa Pavlovic" as the main issue. This was the first Party showdown ever to be broadcast on national TV: Milosevic's "decisive policy" on Kosovo was contrasted with "years of humiliation." The two-day meeting was supposed to be broadcast live but, with some interruptions for news, Belgrade TV was able to delay and cut speeches, which gave

Mitevic maneuvering room to edit material favoring the pro-Milosevic faction.

According to Djukic, Mirjana Markovic called Mitevic to check her own impression that things were going their way. "Victory!" Mitevic told her.[24] He later explained, "Milosevic looked good because he was saying, 'we have had enough of all this empty talk, this blah-blah-blah that has brought us here.'" In a long report on the Eighth Session, entitled "36 Hours of Sleeplessness," the biweekly *Duga* characterized the meeting "as a democratic ritual of political sacrificing: a showdown between courage and hesitation."[25]

The winners did not want to waste any time. They wanted to strengthen their hold on the major media houses. Zekerijah Smajic—a Bosnian television journalist who joined Belgrade TV after being removed by the Croat nationalist editor, Smiljko Sagolj, from the main TV evening journal in Sarajevo as "untrustworthy" to cover political events—remembers the days around the Eighth Session as the time when Belgrade ceased to be a safe haven for decent journalism. A couple of days before the session, he felt the tension in the otherwise "harmonious, and even joyful, newsroom." Since Smajic had been there for only a little more than a year, he tried to understand what was going on, relying on some of the veterans, his close friends, such as Omer Karabeg, Vlado Mares, Branka Mihajlovic, Goran Milic, and Gordana Susa. They told him they were confused too. The day of the Eighth Session, for the first time since coming to Belgrade, Smajic wasn't assigned to cover a major event. Instead, the chief correspondent was Sonja Djuric, who would soon—together with Simo Gajin and Milorad Komrakov—become the most trusted interpreter of the new Serbian policy. While the session was in progress, all employees were asked to attend an emergency staff meeting immediately after the prime-time evening news. Smajic noted in an interview:

> At this staff meeting, a rare guest in those quarters entered the room: Ratomir Vico, the general manager of Belgrade Radio and Television (RTV), obviously euphoric about the expected victory of Milosevic's group. With no delay, we were told that the agenda included a review of the position of the chief editor of the news program, Mihajlo Eric-Era, and his right-hand man in the news department, Karabeg. It was obvious from the very beginning of the meeting that Vico had come to remove Eric from his position. Eric was

accused of being a "Stambolic man," notwithstanding that Stambolic was still the president of Serbia; of running an anti-Serbian program; of unbalanced regional coverage of Serbia. Eric's and Karabeg's counter-arguments fell on deaf ears, while the list of accusations rapidly expanded with, to my amazement, technical personnel—such as cameramen, electricians, drivers—taking the lead in the execution.[26]

Smajic said he openly sided with the attacked colleagues, to no avail. That night-long meeting was followed by a series of Party meetings—held almost nightly after the prime-time news—aimed at systematically purging Belgrade TV of all those who wouldn't follow a new "uncompromising Serbian policy." In that purge, all leading news editors lost their jobs. Eric left journalism for a position in a Belgrade company, and other senior editorial positions went to loyalists ready to serve the cause all the way to the destruction of Yugoslavia. That was the beginning of Milosevic's total control over what had been professional journalism in Serbia.

The purges were immediate and thorough. One by one, other "untrustworthy" politicians and media executives lost their jobs, opening the way to what would become known as Milosevic's "antibureaucratic revolution." Ivan Stojanovic was forced to resign as the director of the *Politika* publishing house, making the way for Minovic to assume both positions—editor and director. In less than three months after the Eighth Session, Ivan Stambolic was forced to resign his post as Serbia's president. Actually, the Serbian Presidency "relieved him of his duty," and Milosevic got a free hand to pursue the confrontations that would lead to the breakup of the country. His victory marked the end of a period in which the Serbian leadership had been trying to change the federal constitution through existing institutions, searching for understanding and consensus on the need to reintegrate the provinces more fully into Serbia and using the "Kosovo card" to speed up that process. Milosevic won on a promise of change, regardless of what anyone else wanted.

The Serbian media played a crucial role in Milosevic's rise to power, not only in promoting him publicly as a protector of all Serbs—as with the repeatedly replayed clip of his "no-one-is-allowed-to-beat-you" speech on television—but also in the direct involvement of key media executives in the conspiracy to bring him to power. To understand Milosevic's success in manipulating the public to give overwhelming support for his drive to "restore Serbia's dignity," one needs to know this simple formula: By controlling just four men who were ready to do whatever it took to propel him to power, including directly participating in the political executions of all opponents (as Vico, Mitevic, Minovic, and Jovanovic participated in the events leading to the Eighth Session), Milosevic was able to control 90 percent of all information available to Serbs. This was the combined outreach of the media outlets controlled by the "gang of four."

Politika Echoes Intolerance

With Milosevic firmly in power, the Serbian Academy's Memorandum themes of Serb victimization, exploitation, and anti-Serbian conspiracy became the dominant lines of argument in most Serbian media. Minovic's *Politika* played a special role in this. Once the finest daily in the Balkans, reflecting the intellectual vitality and cosmopolitan spirit of Belgrade but open to a wider Yugoslav intellectual debate, *Politika* had been for many decades the most trusted newspaper in the region. It had the largest and best foreign correspondents' network of all the Yugoslav dailies; the most extensive sports coverage; the best cultural pages with a special weekend supplement covering arts and literature; and family-oriented content, including pages for children with a daily dose of Donald Duck's adventures. Generations grew up with that paper, and *Politika* managed to maintain a level of self-respect even in the worst years of Communist one-party rule. In some sections— including foreign news, arts and culture, sports, and family-oriented content—the paper pursued and often achieved the high journalistic standards of the European press.

In his essay entitled "*Politika* u nacionalistickoj oluji" ("*Politika* in a Nationalistic Storm"),[27] *Politika's* former editor-in-chief Aleksandar Nenadovic, who lost that job in the Party's purge of "Serbian liberals" in the early seventies, traces the beginnings of his paper's fall from grace to January 18, 1987. That day, a Sunday edition of *Politika* printed a "humorous" piece entitled "Vojko and Savle," which, in Belgrade's intellectual circles, was easily identified as a political-police attack against the free-minded retired general and prominent academic Gojko Nikolis. This personal attack was understood as an attempt to frighten and silence all those who would dare to publicly challenge the Party's monopoly of power. The publication of that "humorous" article caused public outrage, including a protest letter to Minovic signed by 67 of *Politika's* contributing writers asking that the paper publicly apologize to Nikolis's family and a letter signed by 126 citizens stating that the printed article "was a shame not for those you intended to humiliate but for the people whose written and spoken words have been identified with *Politika* for almost a century." The origin of that piece was the best-kept secret in Serbia. On June 4, 1987, almost six months after the article was published, *Politika's* special investigative commission concluded that "it was impossible to find out for sure who was the author of 'Vojko and Savle' or by which means, or, ultimately, by whose order, the text found its way into *Politika's* pages." For Nenadovic and most of the journalists of his generation, one thing was obvious: Thanks to the servile attitude of the top editorial staff, some powerful outside forces without regard for the basic norms of journalism had begun to edit their once proud paper.

With the Eighth Session legitimizing Greater Serbian nationalism as the dominant political option, and with Milosevic as the almost unassailable, charismatic cult figure at the top of the ruling political oligarchy, Minovic made *Politika* the mouthpiece of Serb nationalism. In the summer of 1988, in line with Milosevic's drive to change the federal constitutional arrangement regardless of what others in Yugoslavia might think or want, Minovic introduced a dramatic innovation in *Politika's* editorial policy, "Echoes and Reactions"—up to two pages each day, which he said would be "edited by the people." The pages were in fact an invitation to "the people" to write on the issues of the day, but—by Minovic's design— the space wasn't anything like a free-for-all public forum. The letters were selected and placed in order to give the impression of overwhelming support for the Memorandum's key claims about the victimization of the Serbs, the Slovenian-Croatian "Catholic conspiracy," and the anti-Serb alliance of the rest of Yugoslavia and later of the West.

That summer, Milosevic raised the stakes in his drive to make Serbia "whole, and not a three-part republic, again." In addition to the "Albanian separatists" in Kosovo, the enemies' list was headed by "Vojvodina autonomists." The regime orchestrated, organized, and sponsored mass rallies throughout Vojvodina in support of the "threatened Serbs and Montenegrins from Kosovo," busing tens of thousands of protesters to towns in the province, in many cases at their companies' expense. These "Meetings of Truth," as they were called in the government-controlled media, soon became a tool in the campaign to frighten, denounce, and break any opposition. Among the banners and slogans in the crowd, there were more and more calls for conflict and violence. The banners read, "We Want Arms," "Let's Go to Kosovo," "Hang Vllasi" (an Albanian politician from Kosovo), "Hang Smole" (a Slovenian politician)—all accompanied by the popular song:

> Who is saying, who is lying that Serbia is small.
> It's not small, it's not small!
> It waged three wars, and it will do it again, if God gives us luck . . . .

Politika's "Echoes and Reactions" reflected this new spirit. The pages were flooded with letters demanding the dismissal of all Vojvodina representatives who still pleaded for institutional debate on constitutional changes. Letters against then Yugoslav War Veterans' president Petar Matic occupied a whole page for weeks: "Veterans Don't Want Him as a President," "He Has Lost Our Trust," "He Shames Heroes," "Who Are Matic's Collaborators?" "Ignorance of Veterans' Requests [for resignation] Deserves Condemnation," "They Lost Their Reputations," "Matic Has to Be Replaced." There were dozens of similar letters calling for the ouster of other Vojvodina representatives. In the end, it was a mass street protest on October 5, 1988, that forced the Vojvodina leadership to capitulate. Under the imminent threat of violence, with some 15,000 protesters throwing stones and yogurt-filled plastic bags and glasses at the provincial authorities' building in what became known as the "Yogurt Revolution," the Vojvodina leaders found themselves besieged by a hostile crowd. In desperation, the head of the party, Milan Sogorov, called Milosevic to save them from lynching. "Submit your resignations, and you will be saved," Milosevic told them. The same recipe—mass media condemnation, a series of street protests, and the threat of violence—was used in attacks against the moderate leaders of Montenegro two days later. They capitulated in January 1989, only three months after the attacks against them had begun.

Anyone who questioned Milosevic's street democracy, billed in his patriotic media as an "antibureaucratic revolution," would immediately find himself in *Politika's* "Echoes and Reactions." This method was also used against leading Slovenian politicians. They were targeted because of their opposition to Serbia's unilateral, aggressive drive to change the federal constitution. Slovenian politicians and media had been the most outspoken critics of the Serbian—and Yugoslav—repression of Kosovo Albanians. The anti-Slovenian campaign started when a Slovenian-born *Politika* journalist wrote a letter covering a whole page, accompanied with his photo, under the double-header, "[Joze] Smole, as a Slovene, I Am Ashamed of Your Politicizing." The journalist lectured the veteran Slovenian politician that "It was not in the interest of the Slovenian people for anyone to start a quarrel with others in Yugoslavia."[28] That letter was followed by dozens of others, reminding the "ungrateful Slovenes" of how the Serbian people had hosted them when they were escaping Nazis in World War II; asking Smole to apologize to the Serbs; congratulating the first writer and stating that they, too, like "the Slovenes from Pula" (in Croatia), were ashamed of him. The campaign escalated against the Slovenes as they opposed manipulation of the public and refused to allow Serb nationalists' planned mass "Meetings of Truth" in their capital city, Ljubljana. In September 1988, when the Slovene representative in the federal party presidency, Franc Setinc, resigned—expressing his concern with the "We Want Arms" banners and the "emotional manipulation of the Kosovo Serbs and Montenegrins" and stating that he no longer felt safe in Belgrade—another avalanche of letters followed. Setinc was accused of being more concerned with what the banners said than with the "separatist terror in Kosovo"; of falsely implying that the Serbian leadership "manipulated the masses" while practicing a Slovene brand of homogenization; and of insulting the "heroic city of Belgrade" and "the whole Serbian people."

"Echoes and Reactions" kept multiplying Serbian "enemies." Any journalist or media outlet anywhere in Yugoslavia that voiced criticism of the "Meetings of Truth" or, even worse, of Milosevic's use of crowds to impose constitutional changes, would get his share of angry letters: the Zagreb weekly *Danas (Today);* the Novi Sad *Dnevnik (Daily);* and intellectuals such as Croatian economist Branko Horvat, who dared to question the official line of "counter-revolution in Kosovo," and Bosnian intellectual Fuad Muhic, who called the street democracy "the masochistic ecstasy of the masses." The biweekly *Duga (Rainbow)* ran an entire special edition on Horvat's book *The Kosovo Question,* accusing the Zagreb professor of "falsifying history, misusing science, misrepresenting the history of the [Serbian] people and ideologizing the past of [the Albanian people] in order to give his politically indefensible thesis and conclusions the mantra of false scientific dignity."[29]

"Echoes and Reactions" gave prominence to letters praising the mass gatherings as the highest form of democracy. "Citizens Are Revealing the Real Causes of the Crisis," "No Matter How Bitter and Awful, the Truth on Kosovo Has to Be Told," "Meetings Are the Expression of Solidarity with Those Threatened," "Gatherings Have Strengthened the Brotherhood and Unity," "They Used Their Right to Speak, Now They Have to Answer"—Minovic's pages echoed with calls for Serb unity in the face of "tolerated genocide." Later in the crisis, with greater international involvement in efforts to avoid a bloody conflict, "Echoes and Reactions" expanded the list of enemies to include virtually the entire world: The headlines screamed, "Is That Europe?" "Catholic Europe Against Serbia," "Dictate Behind the Curtain." The paper that was once well-known and respected for its interest in and superb coverage of international news now devoted the whole front page—and sometimes ten or more subsequent pages—to reporting on mass gatherings throughout Serbia. Nenadovic wrote that *Politika* had accepted its own demise as an objective observer and thus as a professional newspaper, taking instead an "agitator-propagandist role," manipulating readers to uncritically serve "a higher national interest." Indeed, *Politika's* top people delivered even more than was expected of them: "They open almost all political news pages in an unrestrained eruption of not only cheap homely pseudo-patriotism, chauvinism, and uncontrolled political gossip, but also for the eruption of blind hatred towards Albanians, Croats, Muslims, Slovenes, Macedonians . . . and 'Serb traitors.'"[30]

While Nenadovic and many of his colleagues mourned the use of their paper for "a chauvinist offensive not only against political opponents in Serbia but against whole ethnic groups outside it," Minovic received the highest recognition for "making the people the editor of *Politika.*" Receiving the Serbian leadership's recognition on the occasion of the paper's eighty-fifth anniversary, Minovic said, "*Politika* has no right to think differently than the people."[31]

The bitter feeling among *Politika's* veteran journalists that their once-respected paper was being taken over by the highest political offices was confirmed later in the memoirs of the president of the Yugoslav Presidency, Milosevic's close ally Borisav Jovic. On August 2, 1990, Jovic's journal reads:

> I wrote a series of articles, "The Truth About Ante Markovic" [at that time reformist prime minister of Yugoslavia] and forwarded them to Slobodan [Milosevic]. They shall be published in installments on August 5, 6, and 7 under someone else's pseudonym. We have to expose [Markovic], because the people are gravely mistaken about who he is and what he is.[32]

Sure enough, the articles appeared in *Politika* on the days chosen by Jovic and Milosevic. The first, "A Reformer with a Short Memory," tried to prove that it was the Yugoslav Presidency under Jovic's chairmanship that brought inflation down and not Markovic's government; the second article, "Against Yugoslavia by Veto," accused Markovic of using the National Bank of Yugoslavia to clear Croatian foreign debts of up to $800 million and stated that "Ante Markovic was never in the first line of combat for change"; and the third, "Holding Back on His Ustasha Days," claimed that Markovic only worked in accordance with Croatian and Slovenian "separatist tendencies." Jovic's articles were published under the false initials "S.L."

Psychiatrists Mobilize Serbs in Croatia, Bosnia

The Memorandum was even more enthusiastically implemented in the editorial policy of Serbian magazines. *Duga*, for example, carried a regular column "Serbs' Business," written by the satirist Brana Crncevic, evoking, issue-by-issue, Croatian Ustasha genocide against Serbs during World War II. *Duga's* other regular contributor, Dragos Kalajic, distinguished himself through articles of an openly racist nature against Bosnian Muslims. Rajko Djurdjevic's report on Kosovo was entitled "The Savagery of Albanian Nationalists Against Everything That's Serb: They are Burning, Raping, Stoning, Wrecking, Breaking, Vandalizing" (*Duga*, September 17–30, 1988). Much later, in his published reflections Dobrica Cosic provided an insight into the double role of journalist-crusader played by Djurdjevic: It was Djurdjevic who brought a delegation of Kosovo Serbs to meet Cosic in Belgrade, and it was Djurdjevic who drafted their original petition against "Albanian terror" in early 1986, edited by Cosic. Then—two years later—he wrote articles in *Duga* in line with allegations of "Albanian terror" from his own handwritten petition.[33]

With his propagandists in control of the major media, Milosevic was assured of unreserved support throughout Serbia. Even neutral coverage of street protests was enough to incite patriotism or fear. Threatening banners, pictures of Orthodox saints alongside those of Milosevic, Chetnik beards and insignia, uniforms and flags of the past—all of this was broadcast into the homes of Serb families day in and day out. By February 1989, twenty-two months after his historic promise in Kosovo, Milosevic's "revolution" had changed the political landscape of Yugoslavia. With his loyalists now holding key offices in Serbia, Montenegro, and Vojvodina, and with all the other republics silent except Slovenia, Milosevic was ready for the final stroke: changing the Serbian constitution to give Belgrade total control of the two provinces, Kosovo and Vojvodina. Albanians were denied any say in what the future of their province would be. Justification was offered in the form of nationalistic historiography, public statements, newspaper articles, and interviews such as the one with Amfilohije Radovic, a high-level Orthodox priest, who said: "The Shiptars' roots were erased in Albania, and they never had roots here, so they have become a people biologically grown up but with no roots" (*Duga*, Number 388).[34]

While the Serbian Parliament was readying for constitutional changes, stripping Kosovo and already conquered Vojvodina of their autonomy, Albanian miners in the Trepca zinc and lead mine in Kosovo announced a hunger strike in defense of their national and political rights. At that time, at the peak of anti-Albanian reporting in the Serb media, Goran Milic—one of the journalists who, with his New York correspondent exposure, still enjoyed some respect nationwide—went to Kosovo to look for positive stories for Belgrade TV. An Albanian friend told him: "Listen, all they report on us in Serbia is that we are murderers and rapists. But I'll tell you my story. My Serb neighbor killed my cow, and you should know what that means in a Kosovo context. That calls for revenge. But I forgave him the cow, and we had a drink together, and that's how neighbors should live with each other."[35] Milic liked the story, but it did not impress the TV bosses. "You'd better come back home," Belgrade TV told him. "We are very disappointed," agreed Zagreb TV with no further explanation. Another time, Milic asked a young Albanian

TV journalist, Linda Abrashi, to do a report in her native language on the evening TV journal he edited. The story was on a nonpolitical issue, and he ran her story with subtitles in Serbian. "That was a rare, if not the only, occasion that Belgrade TV ran a prime-time report in Albanian. I thought it was a way to show that we can still understand each other, if only we want to," Milic reasoned.[36]

This gesture led to an opportunity. With the hunger strike in Trepca announced for February 20, 1989, Linda Abrashi, who was a daughter of the director of the mine, called Milic to say that her father would like him to come to Trepca. Once there, Milic requested that he and his crew be allowed to enter the underground mine and talk to the miners. They gave him a list of ten demands, including respect for the Yugoslav Constitution of 1974 which granted Kosovo autonomy, and he read it on camera. But Milic knew that Belgrade TV was not likely to let "separatists' demands" be read during prime-time news. Instead of sending his report through regular channels from Pristina TV, Milic went to Skopje and from there sent a report to Bane Vukasinovic, a morning news editor who was less politically briefed. "I am sending you an exclusive. You'll like it," Milic told his colleague. Vukasinovic liked it and ran it, but Belgrade TV bosses ordered Milic to come back immediately. "That was the last time I reported from Kosovo," he said in an interview.[37]

The Trepca miners endured for a week but, after 180 of them were taken to hospitals, they had to abandon their hunger strike. A day later, the Slovenian Committee for Human Rights called for a meeting of solidarity with the Albanians. It was held in a large music hall, Cankarjev dom, where participants strongly condemned Serb oppression in the province. Joze Skoljc, then head of the Slovene youth organization, said, "Albanians in Yugoslavia are in a position similar to that of the Jews in World War II." Milan Kucan, leader of the Slovene Communists, stated, "Yugoslavia is being defended in the Trepca mine. The situation in Kosovo shows that people are no longer living together but increasingly against one another."[38] Once again, the propaganda master Mitevic went to work: He followed the events in Ljubljana through an internal TV exchange channel but postponed its broadcast in Serbia until the late evening news around 10:30 p.m. By then, well-trained crowd organizers were roaming their bases of support—Red Star Soccer Club fans, students in dormitories, workers in the Belgrade suburbs—to make a case for a new huge protest. "Do you see what they are doing to us? We won't take it any longer! Let's go to the Parliament!" All of Belgrade was alarmed by the Ljubljana demonstration of solidarity with the "Albanian separatists." By the next morning, a huge crowd of approximately one million people surrounded the Federal Assembly building. Milosevic let the tension build for many hours before he addressed the protesters. The crowd greeted him by chanting, "Arrest Vllasi, arrest Vllasi!" Already a master of mass manipulation, Milosevic responded, "I can't hear you well," turning his ear theatrically toward the crowd. "Arrest Vllasi!" they repeated louder. "He will be arrested, I promise you!" he said. Azem Vllasi—a younger-generation politician, former president of the Yugoslav youth organization during Tito's time, and perhaps the last Albanian who was still able to communicate the Albanians' concerns— was arrested the next day. His arrest marked the end of hopes for a peaceful outcome.

On March 28, 1989, two years after Milosevic's fateful promise in Kosovo, Tito's Yugoslavia was finally dead. While Serb politicians celebrated the new constitution, which gave them control over the provinces, a state of emergency was imposed in Kosovo, with many dead and wounded in street protests. Three months later, on June 28, 1989, a huge gathering of Serbs took place in Gazimestan, Kosovo, to mark the 600th anniversary of the historic battle against the Turks. Addressing yet another rally, Milosevic made a thinly veiled threat against all those who would oppose his drive for "the restoration of Serb pride": "Six centuries later, we are in battles again. These are not armed battles, though this cannot be excluded yet." *Vreme* journalist Milan Milosevic wrote of the event:

> The commemoration had all the trappings of a coronation staged as a Hollywood extravaganza. Milosevic descended by helicopter from the heavens into the cheering crowd; the masses were the extras. The cameras focused on his arrival. In some vague way, the commentator placed Milosevic at the center of the Serbian ancestral myth of Prince Lazar, the hero and martyr of the Kosovo battle. Exactly six hundred years ago, the voice-over told the viewers, on this very soil, Prince Lazar had chosen the kingdom of heaven over his earthly kingdom, the glory of death over survival in defeat. The relics of Prince Lazar, killed in the battle, had been carried a month previously, in a procession accompanied by unprecedented

media pomp, through virtually all Serb-populated regions where war would later break out.[39]

With Serbia "whole again," Milosevic set his sights on another Memorandum goal: "All Serbs in a single state" or what was better known as "Greater Serbia." The patriotic press now intensified attacks against Slovenes and Croats. The newspapers ran a series of articles on Serbia's economic exploitation. Genocidal Ustasha crimes against Serbs during World War II were carefully interwoven into renewed cries against "discrimination against Serbs outside of Serbia." Individual incidents, like the arrest of Croatian Serb leader Jovan Opacic during the ceremonies in the Krajina region of Croatia commemorating the 600th anniversary of the Kosovo battle, were used to stir up feelings of a renewed threat to the Serbs. "Is it the fate of Serbs in Croatia to suffer genocide in war and discrimination and assimilation in peace?" Dobrica Cosic asked at one of the protest evenings organized by the Serbian Writers Union.[40]

Multiethnic media projects in Yugoslavia came under intense nationalist pressure at that time. Belgrade and Zagreb Radio, for example, had a joint program called "Green Megahertz," which had run for over sixteen years. With Milosevic's "street democracy" in full swing, it became increasingly difficult to maintain ethnic balance in the coverage of sensitive issues. The Belgrade studio insisted on broadcasting long reports on different mass protests at the expense of issues important to Croatian audiences. An open debate broke out in September 1988 when Belgrade insisted on an hour-long interview with Atanasije Jeftic, an Orthodox priest in Kosovo, although the whole segment on the Orthodox church had been planned for just half an hour. For the other half-hour, Zagreb had prepared a report on that year's tourist season in Croatia, the country's most successful exporting business. In the end, "Green Megahertz" did not run the hour-long interview. Another piece of evidence of "Zagreb Radio's extreme indifference toward the suffering of Kosovo Serbs and Montenegrins" was found in the Zagreb studio's decision to cut short Belgrade's broadcast of a street protest in Titograd (now Podgorica). Zagreb editors claimed that the report from Titograd wasn't announced in the regular planning communication between the two studios, and they found it to be "one-sided, irritating, and exaggerated." In his essay "The Turnaround of the Electronic Media," Rade Veljanovski says that, despite nationalist pressures, Radio Belgrade managed to maintain a degree of objectivity, partly because of the exchange of programs with other Yugoslav radio stations, even though there was an increased number of radio stories reexamining Serbia's past with an emphasis on "Yugoslavia as an artificial entity imposed on the Serbian people."[41]

The past, with its glorification of the Serbs' struggle through the centuries and its emphasis on all the evil committed against them, was becoming even more important than the present for Serbian media. For example, on April 10, 1990, Tanjug (the Yugoslav news agency) announced the suspension of two female Novi Sad TV editors, Doda Toth-Isakov and Biljana Vorkapic, "because of the editorial mistake they made in running the report on the 175th anniversary of the Second Serb Uprising [against the Turks] at the end instead of the beginning of the evening TV Journal."[42] The judgment of the chief editor of the current affairs program, Petar Petrovic, was also called into question. The stirring of nationalistic passions in the Serbian media reached a boiling point by the summer of 1990. In order to prepare Serbs living outside Serbia for the redesign of Yugoslavia in a way that would finally ensure the Memorandum goal of all Serbs in a single state with the "Serb parts" of neighboring Bosnia and Croatia incorporated into "Greater Serbia," Belgrade had encouraged the creation of the nationalist Serb Democratic Parties (SDS), first in Croatia and then in Bosnia.

It is interesting that, in both Croatia and Bosnia, psychiatrists undertook the job of fueling fear and hate. In Croatia it was Dr. Jovan Raskovic. In Bosnia he handpicked a colleague, Dr. Radovan Karadzic, as a partner in awakening the feeling among Serbs of being a "threatened nation" that had to organize to "defend itself." That year Raskovic was promoted to the Serbian Academy, and he published a book, *Luda zemlja (Mad Country)* (Akvarijus, Belgrade, 1990), attributing genocidal tendencies to the Croats. In his medical practice, he said, "I found very little feeling of guilt in the Croatians over the genocide committed by some of the Croatian people."[43] Thus the Serbian media suddenly discovered an academic genius in this little-known sixty-one-year-old psychiatrist at a hospital in Sibenik on the Adriatic coast. In his interviews Raskovic paid special attention to his theories concerning the ethno-national characteristics of Yugoslav ethnic groups: "It is not just a matter of opposition between [Croatian] Catholicism and [Serb] Orthodoxy, as I think that this opposition is not as deep as the one between the oedipal Serbs and the castrated Croatians. It is therefore not surprising that a situation of total hatred and paranoia is developing in this country," he said in a September 15, 1989, issue of *Intervju*, a Belgrade magazine published by *Politika*.

The two psychiatrists, Raskovic and Karadzic, with the enthusiastic support of the Milosevic-controlled Serbian media, worked hard to stir up those feelings: hatred and paranoia. At the Serbian Orthodox Church initiative on "unearthing the bones of those killed in World War II in order to give them a decent burial," they undertook a months-long campaign throughout Serb-populated areas in both Bosnia and Croatia. The bones of the Serbs killed by the Nazi-installed Croatian Ustasha regime fifty years earlier were excavated from pits in mostly rural areas, carried through villages, and then reburied in ceremonies as Orthodox priests and Serb nationalist politicians made inflammatory speeches that presented the fifty-year old crimes as a clear and present danger. These events were extensively covered in the Serbian media, and they were often accompanied by serialized stories of Ustasha atrocities that presented the emerging nationalist government in Croatia as "Ustasha followers," threatening the very survival of the Serbian nation once again. In his "Serbs' Business" column in *Duga* magazine's special July 1990 edition entitled "Serbs in Croatia," Crncevic wrote, "The Serbs are not going to allow themselves or others to once again be served [as a meal] at the democratic table. The world shouldn't overlook once again the sacred truth that even Serb-eaters are still only cannibals."[44] Years later, in an interview with Yutel Television in January 1992, Raskovic admitted his role in making the war possible:

> I feel responsible because I prepared for this war even if not in terms of military preparation. If I hadn't created this emotional strain in the Serbian people, nothing would have happened. My Party and I lit the fuse of Serbian nationalism not only in Croatia but everywhere else in Bosnia and Herzegovina. It's impossible to imagine a Serbian Democratic Party in Bosnia and Herzegovina or Mr. Karadzic in power without our influence. We have driven this people and we have given it an identity. I have repeated again and again to this people that it comes from heaven not earth.[45]

Alternative Media Launched

Vreme, a weekly launched in 1990 by a group of liberal Serbian intellectuals, characterized itself as "a magazine without lies, hatred, or prejudice." The name means *The Time* or *Die Zeit*, and the magazine distinguished itself by its independent position, critical of warmongering and the nationalistic mobilization for the upcoming wars. Its founders included some of the most prominent Serbian civic activists: Srdja Popovic, a Belgrade lawyer famous for his defense of dissidents in the former Yugoslavia; Vesna Pesic, a university professor involved in efforts to preserve and strengthen Serbian civil society; Lazar Stojanovic, the movie director who was jailed in the seventies for a movie "Plastic Jesus," which was interpreted by the Communist authorities as an attack on President Tito; and Stojan Cerovic, a writer behind many public pleas for human rights in Yugoslavia. Cerovic explained in an interview how the magazine was born out of their desperation in October 1990:

> At that time, Milosevic enjoyed 100 percent support in Serbia. The press was aggressive, full of hate and poison. We felt that, with a history of fighting for human rights, we had to do something. The initial idea, to form some kind of liberal political party, did not fly: There wasn't any support for something like that either in Serbia or elsewhere in Yugoslavia. We agreed that the main problem was in the media, in the society's state of mind and Milosevic's manipulation of the media, and we agreed that it was even more important to act in the media than in the political sphere. So, we started to think of a newspaper. In the beginning, we thought just of some publication in which we could speak our own minds; then we thought of a paper that would provide just plain information as opposed to official lies; and, finally, we opted for a news magazine.[46]

The founders did not have any problem assembling some of the finest Belgrade journalists. For the true professionals, there was nothing else to do because they could not participate in the prevailing nationalistic media crusade. So *Vreme* was joined by a trio of veteran columnists who were highly respected throughout Yugoslavia: Dragisa Boskovic, Jug Grizelj, and Jurij Gustincic. Additionally, some of the best journalists came from the once reputed weekly *NIN*: Zoran Jelicic, Milan Milosevic, and Milos Vasic. Soon after, Dragoljub Zarkovic from *Borba* joined the team.

With an initial investment provided by Srdja Popovic, *Vreme* established itself right away as a well-written, professional, reliable source of information. "At the beginning, before the disintegration of the country, we could have been labeled pro-Yugoslav, but with Yugoslavia gone, what remained was an antiwar option. I think that *Vreme* was consistently liberal, antinationalistic, pro-Western, pro-European," Cerovic said.[47] But *Vreme*—like *Borba*—couldn't have the influence of Milosevic's large-circulation propaganda newspapers, such as *Politika*, *Ekspres*, or *Novosti*. With a circulation of no more than 22,000 at best, even when a single copy was shared by four to five readers in impoverished Serbia, the magazine was largely ignored by the Milosevic regime. Milosevic even used it, together with some other independent media of limited outreach, as proof that there was a free press in Serbia after all.

The same could be said for the early days of the alternative Radio B92, formed several months before the fall of the Berlin Wall, as founding editor Veran Matic likes to emphasize. In the beginning, the station operated within the elegant Youth House in downtown Belgrade. Matic believed that B92 should serve a dual purpose: to provide unbiased, professional information and to serve as a voice of the newly emerging youth culture, opposed to nationalistic manipulation and open to rock 'n' roll, new technologies, and new ideas. In an increasingly nationalistic environment, B92 developed into an urban alternative culture, expressing itself in a variety of ways—through theater and CDs, radio and publishing, concerts and visual arts, conferences and human rights advocacy. Matic himself remembers running a series of interviews in 1989–90 with until-then banned Yugoslav dissidents "of all colors," even those accused by the Communist regime of belonging to Chetnik or Ustasha movements, and with prominent democratic emigrants like Desimir Tosic in the West. For the first time, these "dissidents" were able to interact with the public in Yugoslavia. Matic recalled in an interview:

> Somehow, I felt that there was a connection between all those [emigrant] people, of what was happening to them—without us knowing anything about it—and what was about to happen to us. There was all that hysteric reinterpretation of our history, with many people—politicians and social scientists alike—involved in endless black and white picturing of the past, with everything good on "our" side and everything bad on "theirs." The history was used to justify daily nationalistic policy, and I believed we needed a more balanced, pluralistic perspective on the past.[48]

But the problem for *Vreme* and B92—as well as for the rest of the independent and opposition media—was their limited outreach, the poor consumption of newspapers in increasingly impoverished Serbia, and the deafening noise of the nationalistic press, radio, and television. In an article published by *Vreme,* Slobodan Antonic of the Belgrade Institute for Political Studies wrote that, in mid-October 1990, the evening Journal of the Belgrade TV was watched by 2.5 million people in Serbia proper and an additional 800,000 in Vojvodina—almost 70 percent of all adults in the republic—while 30 percent of the adults never read the daily press, and 26 percent read it only occasionally. The study concluded that, with the predominance of *Politika* and *Politika ekspres* in the readership of the daily press, Milosevic's control over Radio and Television Belgrade and the *Politika* publishing house amounted to control of nine-tenths of all Serbian media.[49]

While *Borba, Vreme,* and Radio B92 provided oases of sanity in the midst of the nationalism unleashed by the mainstream media, they could not counter the overwhelming outreach of the state radio and television and the large circulation newspapers such as *Politika, Politika ekspres,* and *Vecernje novosti.* Thus, the idea was born to establish an all-Yugoslav television that could offer an alternative to this mainstream ultranationalism. In 1989, Goran Milic—at that time already demoted from being the most popular prime-time news announcer to producing occasional one-hour international specials—first discussed the idea with federal prime minister Branko Mikulic, a Bosnian Croat. But with the fall of Mikulic's government, it took Milic another year to reopen the issue with the new prime minister, Ante Markovic. Milic reflected on the initial motives for Yutel (as the all-Yugoslav television was to be known):

> The idea was to produce one or two hours of news a day and get all the republics to agree to run it on their Channel 2 evening program. They were supposed to appoint the editor-in-chief by consensus in the Federal Parliament, and then—with all the ongoing quarrelling between them—it would be next to impossible to reach a consensus to fire him. Markovic, with his reformist policies and international support, seemed to be the best partner in these efforts to establish a professional television that wouldn't be subject to nationalist manipulation.[50]

The project's appointed director, Nebojsa Bata Tomasevic, who originally suggested the name "Yutel," was a former Yugoslav government

employee who had been sent to London to study English and the
Western way of life. He had fallen in love with an Englishwoman and
refused to return to Yugoslavia. Thus, he had lost contact with the
country for twenty to twenty-five years until he accepted the position
of director of the Yugoslav Review, a publishing house famous for
organizing an annual international publishers' book fair in Motovun,
Istria. Under Tomasevic's supervision, the fair grew from five to a hundred participants, becoming a major cultural event in the former
Yugoslavia and giving Tomasevic easy access to high places. For that
reason, the federal government officials involved in efforts to establish
Yutel considered him the right person to manage the project. Milic
recalled:

> At the beginning, Yutel was an idea attractive to many, and everyone want-
> ed a piece of it. Reformers, nationalists, royalists, you name it. With the
> republics' rising rivalry and mistrust, and the potential for an all-Yugoslav
> television being blocked by the refusal of some of the republics' TV stations
> to carry it, one alternative was to use a system of 18 transmitters that had
> been purchased for the Yugoslav Army in the early 1980s, a system that was
> never used. That system would have provided Yutel with coverage of most
> of the Yugoslav territory.[51]

Yutel's interest in the army's mobile TV system provided the broader
Yugoslav public with a rare glimpse into the secret world of the privileged military: In the mid-1980s, the army had spent some $45 million
to acquire top-of-the-line equipment to produce and transmit messages "in a possible crisis situation." In addition, there were huge
expenses for specially equipped vehicles and infrastructure. But in
negotiations with the federal information ministry, which represented
Yutel, the army insisted on unacceptable conditions, including control
of editorial content. Yutel continued to look for a solution within the
existing Yugoslav television network. Milic explained:

> In the end, only Bosnia—for obvious reasons of being the most multieth-
> nic and thus the most vulnerable to media extremism—was ready to accept
> Yutel, offering it accommodation and airtime within Sarajevo TV. So I
> moved to Sarajevo, together with some forty journalists. They all had a
> healthy dose of reserve towards both Milosevic and Tudjman—some more
> towards Milosevic, some more towards Tudjman. We believed that
> Yugoslavia could survive only as a reformed, democratic country, based on
> equality and a market economy. We agreed that it wasn't our role to support

any of the conflicting nationalist policies. Besides our support for democratic reform, the only agreed upon editorial line was an antiwar position.[52]

Yutel was launched on October 22, 1990, with a reception and the first evening newscast from the Sarajevo TV building. It was near the end of the campaign for the first multiparty election in Bosnia, and even the newly founded nationalist parties in Bosnia—the Muslim Party of Democratic Action (SDA), the Serb SDS, and the Croat HDZ—expected more from Yutel's promise of "equal opportunity" than from Bosnian TV, traditionally suspicious of any nationalist agenda in that multiethnic republic. Milic said:

> Take, for example, (SDA leader) Alija Izetbegovic: He spent most of the eighties in prison for writing his Muslim Declaration, and he couldn't trust the Sarajevo journalists who reported on his politically motivated trial the way he could trust a "new TV." We tried to provide balanced reporting but, being supportive of reformist federal government, we had a hard time convincing the political leadership throughout Yugoslavia that Yutel wasn't "Markovic's TV." He wasn't even on our program that often, except when as the Yugoslav prime minister he met foreign dignitaries. This also gave us an opportunity to interview world politicians, such as Mikhail Gorbachev, François Mitterand, James Baker, and others.[53]

The need for Markovic's reform-minded government to support the idea of a countrywide professional television was underlined by an incident on November 15, 1990: Belgrade TV refused to broadcast the prime minister's speech to the joint session of the Federal Parliament "on the current political and economic situation in the country and . . . economic policy for next year." The government saw the refusal as a continuation of attacks on Markovic's cabinet and an "attempt to impose an information blockade."

In the beginning, there was some hope that Yutel might reach most of the former Yugoslavia. Its one-hour broadcast from Bosnia was accepted in November 1990 in Macedonia, in December in Slovenia, in February 1991 in Croatia, and in May 1991 in Serbia. At that time, only Kosovo remained out of reach except for areas bordering Macedonia that could receive a signal from Macedonian transmitters. "Only Bosnia and Macedonia [two of the more multiethnic republics] accepted a direct broadcast of our news hour," Milic recalls. "Slovenians were able to watch us with a one-hour delay—and their signal reached parts of Croatia too—but the reception in Croatia was the least enthusiastic. Zagreb TV would broadcast Yutel only at 12:30 a.m. when even the most persistent viewers fall asleep after a midnight dose of classical music."[54]

The delayed transmission of Milic's news hour from Sarajevo was not sufficient to counter the Milosevic media's well-orchestrated manufacturing of enemies. The image of a "threatened nation," surrounded by enemies on all sides—projected in all prime-time broadcasts, all state radio news programs, and enforced in headlines screaming on the front pages of the three largest-circulation dailies—moved Serbia toward the "battles" that Milosevic promised at Kosovo Polje. Antiwar sentiments and voices had no public resonance. The Civic Alliance—brave groups and individuals opposing the nationalist warmongering in the early 1990s—could not be seen or heard in the statewide media except as "traitors" and "enemies."

To understand how and why it was possible for Milosevic's propagandists to silence and sideline all those opposing confrontation with the rest of Yugoslavia, it is necessary to understand the Yugoslav concept of "public," "media," and "authority" prevalent at that time. The Yugoslav public—in spite of the fact that it had a more liberal and better edited press than the rest of Eastern Europe—still had only been exposed to one ruling party and its ideology. What once was the Communist-controlled media became the nationalist-controlled media. Milosevic simply renamed his party—from Communist to Socialist—and switched chips in the party-programmed media from "brotherhood and unity" to "hatred toward neighbors." The same media executioners—accustomed to serving the Party—embraced and promoted the new ideology with the same enthusiasm they had had for the old one. Likewise, the public did not have an alternative source of information. In Serbia, even in Belgrade during the late 1980s and early 1990s, people could not even switch TV channels: For the vast majority of Serbs, there was just "Slobovision," as the state TV was called. People with satellite dishes could not get alternative sources of information from international broadcasts—BBC, Deutsche Welle, CNN, and others—because few people in Serbia spoke English or German and because the international media were busy covering the fall of the Berlin Wall and the liberation of Eastern Europe, and they were not paying enough attention to the Balkan tragedy in the making. A

Belgrade colleague and friend told me at the time, "You know, I watch the Hungarian TV Journal every evening: I don't understand a word, just the pictures, so I am spared my portion of state TV poisoning."

Moreover, as Stojan Cerovic of *Vreme* said, not everything was a product of simple media manipulation. "Some people saw Milosevic's rise to power as truly liberating, as a clear break with the Communist old guard, and seized the idea of redesigning Yugoslavia through his 'antibureaucratic revolution' and 'will of the people' as a way to correct some of their grievances from the past. They enjoyed the freedom to criticize, even remove from power, the 'bureaucrats' and 'autonomists' of Vojvodina, Kosovo, and Montenegro; to challenge the Yugoslav constitutional arrangements 'depriving Serbia of its rightful place.' So they didn't have to be manipulated; they joined the 'revolution' wholeheartedly."[55]

Dusan Simic, a longtime foreign correspondent for *Politika*, described the "liberating feeling" aroused by the rise of Serb nationalism in the late 1980s with another reflection on *Politika's* "Echoes and Reactions." "Those pages, announcing an open season against 'enemies of all colors' under the guise of a paper 'edited by the people,' attracted many previously unknown, marginal pretenders to fame. They only needed an opportunity and a framework to express themselves in what was still the most prestigious Serbian paper, often with paranoid, racist ideas and theories," Simic observed in an interview. As for the public's reaction, he explained: "The educated minority was appalled by what was in the paper. For them, it was repugnant. But for large numbers of the silent majority, those manipulations were a revelation concerning whom to blame for all that was wrong. It was through those *Politika* pages that Milosevic managed to channel people's dissatisfaction with their living conditions into challenging and combating Serbs' alleged national inequality in Yugoslavia."[56]

This ideological line—developed fully by Serbia's leading intellectuals in the Academy's Memorandum in 1986, embraced and enforced by the ruthless new regime in 1987, aggressively and systematically promoted by media with an audience of 90 percent of the Serbian public—laid the ground for the mayhem of the 1990s. According to the prevailing ideology, the Serbs were all alone—surrounded by Albanian "Shiptar terrorists," "Croatian Ustashas," "Slovenian separatists," and Bosnian "Islamic fundamentalists"—with no choice but to prepare to defend themselves in wars, none of which would be fought on Serbia's territory.

Serbo-Croatian War: Lying for the Homeland (1990–91)

WHEN FRANJO TUDJMAN BECAME PRESIDENT of Croatia in May 1990, *Oslobodjenje* ran my regular column, "Pages of the Calendar," suggesting that he should send his first letter of gratitude to "comrade Milosevic." It was the Serbian leader's drive for domination that all but ensured the victory of nationalist forces elsewhere: Mobilize Serbs, announce that even "armed battles are not excluded," and that will have everyone else— Slovenes, Croats, Muslims, and Albanians—up in arms. As the new president, Tudjman granted his first extensive interview to Croatia's state daily *Vjesnik*. The elections and Tudjman's rise to power marked the beginning of the decline in that newspaper and in Croatian journalism generally.

Like all other dailies in each of the Yugoslav republics, *Vjesnik* had been controlled by the Communist Party after World War II, but in the dying years of the one-party state, it had gained some measure of independence. In the political vacuum left by Tito's death, *Vjesnik* defied what was known as "Croatia's silence" in Yugoslav affairs in the late 1980s and opened its pages to pluralistic debate, challenging the traditional limits of what was allowed in Communist-controlled Yugoslavia. Other Croatian publications also gained a measure of respectability and, with it, a wide readership. Within *Vjesnik's* publishing company (also called Vjesnik), Croatia had the first magazine in Yugoslavia resembling *Playboy (Start)*; the weekly news magazine *Danas (Today)* replaced the Milosevic-controlled *NIN* as the most respected in the country; Vjesnik's tabloid *Vecernji list (Evening Newspaper)* reached the circulation level of Belgrade's once far more popular *Vecernje novosti (Evening News)*; and there were three successful regional dailies in Croatia, one of which, *Slobodna Dalmacija* in Split, was even more widely distributed and respected than *Vjesnik* itself.

Mirko Galic, a prominent Croatian journalist who spent many years as *Vjesnik's* correspondent in Paris, was the editor-in-chief of *Danas* in the late 1980s, a time when the magazine was among the first media outlets in Yugoslavia to open debate on the future of the country. In 1988, another longtime foreign correspondent in Bonn and New York, Drazen Vukov-Colic, succeeded Galic and continued to maintain the magazine's reputation for open debate on previously forbidden subjects. In a recent interview, Galic remembered the late 1980s as a time of great turnaround in Yugoslav journalism: While the traditionally liberal Serbian media became both instruments and enthusiastic supporters of Milosevic's drive for a "Greater Serbia" at the expense of everyone else, the once strictly controlled Croatian media started to break from the Party's grip. In 1987, while Milosevic's Serbia was obsessed with nationalism, *Danas* printed a programmatic article titled "The Ten Points," in which, for the first time in socialist Yugoslavia, a prominent economist and a publisher, Marijan Korosic and Slavko Goldstein respectively, argued for a market economy and democracy, including a multiparty system, free elections, and the disbanding of the one-party parliament. Galic recalled:

> There were two dominant ideas in our editorial policy at the time: One was to expose the deep crisis in the country and argue for fundamental democratic reform, and the other was to resist the dictate from Belgrade on the future of the country. In that context, *Danas* was from the beginning sharply critical of Milosevic's ultranationalistic policies, to the point that the Croatian leadership—under pressure from Belgrade—accused us of causing "conflicts among the peoples [of Yugoslavia]."[1]

Unfortunately, instead of building on these ideas and embracing the promise of pluralism, immediately following the first multiparty elections in May 1990, *Vjesnik's* leadership showed itself ready to offer its services to the new ruling party, Tudjman's HDZ. Just when it had almost freed itself from the iron grip of the previous one-party monopoly, the paper surrendered its freedom to a new one-party dictatorship.

According to accounts by Zagreb journalists concerning that ritual sacrificing of the paper's independence on the altar of a new ruler, in a ceremonial first meeting, *Vjesnik's* editor-in-chief Hido Biscevic (by background a Bosnian Muslim) told Tudjman: "Mr. President, you know that there are Muslims with a capital M [as a nation] and a small m [as a religion]. I am a Muslim with a capital H [for Hrvat, i.e., a Croat]." Whether this anecdote is true or just a product of the Balkan tendency to characterize everyone through jokes, it is true that *Vjesnik*—and later Croatian Radio and Television—became the first trophies of the new nationalistic government. The key to Tudjman's takeover of the main Croatian media was threefold: First, the character of ownership, the so-called "social property" status of all large companies; second, the character of the leading editors, many of whom grew up without ever questioning the God-given right of the ruling party to control the "means of information," as the media were called in Communist parlance; and third, most important, the character of HDZ rule. Croatia's electoral law made it possible for Tudjman's party—with only 42 percent of the popular vote—to assume total, even totalitarian, control of all of the country's institutions. The new constitution was tailored in such a way as to give Tudjman almost imperial power. The socialist-invented "social property" was translated into state property and even, with HDZ's stranglehold on the country's economy, into Party property. Through the HDZ-run privatization process, all of Croatia's best businesses—including the Vjesnik publishing company—ended in the hands of Party loyalists.

Biscevic, the anecdotally self-declared "Muslim with a capital H," made sure that *Vjesnik* followed the Party line under his leadership. Zivko Gruden, one of *Vjesnik's* most respected commentators, left the paper after Biscevic edited one of his commentaries, deleting an "undesirable" paragraph and adding a paragraph of his own because what was left of the commentary was "too short" for his taste. The paragraph in question concerned Vinko Nikolic, a prominent member of Croatia's Nazi-installed Ustasha government in World War II. During the war, Nikolic had been responsible for a racist educational system and, like many other former Ustasha activists, he had emigrated back to Croatia on the wings of the HDZ victory. Some of these former Ustasha officials received prominent positions in Tudjman's government: Nikolic had been offered the position of chairman of the board responsible for the construction of Croatia's new university library. Gruden had commented that there was nothing wrong with people returning to Croatia after decades of emigration, but it was unacceptable for people with a pro-Nazi past to be honored with prestigious positions. That was the paragraph Biscevic didn't like, and so he wrote a new one instead. "I am not going to accept this kind of editing and am leaving the paper," Gruden told him. "But, why? What's wrong with the editor-in-chief editing a story?" Biscevic asked. "No one has ever edited my comments this way in my thirty years in journalism, not even during the hard-line Communists' time," Gruden said, and he left the paper.[2]

At that time, some forty of Gruden's colleagues had been placed on a list of "unreliables" that HDZ loyalists used to remove them from the editorial process. Some eventually left of their own volition. However, at that time not many journalists in Croatia or Serbia were ready to sacrifice their employment as Gruden had. Some, accustomed to ruling-party manipulation under Communism, embraced the opportunity to serve the new rulers with the same enthusiasm as they had served the old ones, while the majority merely accepted the new reality, resigned to keeping quiet in affairs they felt were beyond their control.

As for Biscevic, he summed up the year 1990 with the following commentary:

> In the previous year, and particularly in the second half of it, Croatia accomplished a task which for its importance and scope belongs to those non-measurable and sublime moments in the life of a nation, to those brilliant take-offs when the historical matrixes and systems of living are changed, when we break out of the boundaries of one model in order to penetrate a new one.[3]

Vjesnik's abandonment of the freedom it had won in the waning years of Communist rule, combined with its now unquestioning loyalty to the new party in power, had devastating consequences for the public trust and the paper's circulation. Between 1990 and 1992, in just two years of service to the HDZ, its readership sank from more than 80,000 to barely 20,000. Nevertheless, Biscevic, once a prominent writer in

Vjesnik's foreign news department, was rewarded for his loyalty to Tudjman and the HDZ with an appointment as Croatia's Ambassador to Turkey and later to Russia.

The promotion of ex-Ustasha functionaries to prominent positions in "Croatia's young democracy" represents a characteristic, symbolic feature of the early days of HDZ rule. Indeed, Croatia's huge, pro-Ustasha emigrant communities in Canada, Australia, the United States, Latin America, and Western Europe supported and financed Tudjman's party. Once in power, the Party was ready to return favors by rewarding some of its most enthusiastic supporters with positions in parliament, government administration, the diplomatic service, and other high-profile public jobs. In its victorious takeover of the country, the HDZ let Croatian ultranationalism run rampant. The Party reintroduced symbols reminiscent of Ustasha times, such as the *kuna* (the currency of the pro-Nazi regime) and the centuries-old checkerboard flag used by the Ustasha. They reduced Serb citizens, the Serb language, and Serb national institutions to ethnic minority status and undertook an ethnic purge. For example, they reduced the Serbs' disproportionate representation in the state services, such as public administration, police, and the media, thus threatening the Serbs' livelihood. They changed the names of streets and institutions—for example, Zagreb's Square of Victims of Fascism was renamed the Square of Great Croats. This Croatia-above-all euphoria was best represented by street vendors at the central Zagreb square: They began selling "fresh Croatian air" in soda cans!

These measures provided perfect material for the Serb nationalist media to spread among Croatian Serbs fear of the rebirth of an Ustasha state. Croatian Serb leader Jovan Raskovic, a master of waking ghosts from the past, orchestrated a hysterical campaign in the Belgrade media calling the HDZ takeover "an attack against the entire Serbian people," initiating a series of articles in Belgrade newspapers on the Ustasha terror against Serbs during World War II, sounding the alarm against "a repetition of genocide," and urging the "protection of Serbs against Ustasha vampires." All of this was a prelude to Raskovic's July 25, 1990, declaration of Serb autonomy in Croatia. At this time, local Serb extremists installed their own governments, police, and armed forces in the regions of Knin Krajina and Eastern Slavonia. "This is a Serb uprising," Serbian media headlines read. As one media analyst put it:

Uncertainty, anxiety, fear, and the instinctive need for self-defense were extensively portrayed among the Serbs in Croatia—Serbs in Croatia 'would not accept the checked flag' because it was 'hoisted by those who had slaughtered them in World War II'—while among the Serbs in other parts of former Yugoslavia (and especially in Serbia) a mass image was produced of the feeling of solidarity with the 'part of our nation' and the need to participate in its defense. Among both groups this also produced hatred.[4]

Each group's nationalism played into the hands of the other. Milosevic's threat of Serb domination awakened the "thousand-year-old dream" of Croatia's independence. Tudjman's takeover, based on his Croatia-to-Croats promise, gave an excuse for the Serbs to rebel and declare autonomy. That, in turn, served as a perfect pretext for the HDZ's mass purge of all public institutions and services of all those considered unreliable or unpatriotic. Galic said in an interview:

> Croatian nationalism—even though it had always existed—would never have assumed such proportions had it not been for Milosevic's policy, which since the beginning had laid claim to Serb-inhabited regions of Croatia and even pushed Croatia toward secession 'without historic Serb territories.' There are documents—such as the diary of [Yugoslav President] Borisav Jovic—on the Serbian leadership's design for two-thirds of Croatia to 'leave Yugoslavia' while one-third would join 'Greater Serbia' in order to have 'all Serbs living in a single state.' This real threat from Serbia, with its drive to redraw the borders, caused an almost natural state of emergency in Croatia, with everything—including most of the central media—being mobilized for the defense of the homeland.[5]

It was in the context of this patriotic call to duty that the HDZ moved to take over radio and television. Immediately after the election victory in May 1990, Tudjman dispatched his trusted associate Anton Vrdoljak, once the director of movies on Tito's liberation struggle, to meet with Radio-Television's editorial board and ask all editors to resign. Otherwise, Vrdoljak threatened them, there would be street protests, violence, and broken windows. His arrogance was underlined by the racist statement that "It was unacceptable for the Croatian TV to have six and a half Serbs running its evening TV journal" (the "half" was the one with "mixed blood").[6] Just two months after the electoral victory, RTV Zagreb was renamed Croatian Radio and Television (HRT); soon afterwards, the HDZ-controlled parliament appointed Party loyalists to top managerial and editorial positions. The first HDZ-appointed director general, Hrvoje Hitrec, marginalized all "unreliable" journalists. The second, Anton Vrdoljak, went to extremes: He pledged to turn HRT into "the cathedral of the Croatian spirit." On September 16, 1991, guards at the entrances to the HRT building told more than 300 employees that their passes were no longer valid. The move was later attributed to "security reasons." Most of those on the security blacklists were fired because of their (Serb) nationality or that of their spouses, or because their father was an officer of the Yugoslav Army, or simply because they did not publicly support the HDZ. In a decade of Tudjman's party control, that negative selection of editors and journalists made the HRT an open instrument that maintained the HDZ in power.[7]

Vrdoljak, who was also a vice president of the HDZ, was so enthusiastic about promoting the party line that even Tudjman grew wary of his ultrapatriotism, according to a prominent Croatian columnist, Danko Plevnik. Plevnik recounts how another columnist, Slaven Letica, Tudjman's former adviser and later an independent candidate to replace him as president in 2000, explained to him why Croatia never had a vice president under Tudjman.[8] It was Vrdoljak who urged Tudjman to amend the constitution in order for Croatia to have a vice president, "just as in the United States": "Think, Franjo, what would happen if something happens to you! Croatia would be decapitated!" Suspicious Tudjman took Vrdoljak's "concern for Croatia" as a potential threat to his rule and even, in the worst-case scenario, to his life, so he decided to rule the country by himself, with no vice president at all.

Miljenko Jergovic, a writer and media analyst working for the independent weekly *Feral Tribune*, saw three waves of purges at HRT: First, it was "ethnically cleansed" of Serb journalists; then of all those who were independent-minded, respected, and thus dangerous journalists; and then, one by one, of those who decided that they could no longer support ultranationalism. Directors and editors would replace those raising "objections of conscience" with new, younger, and—as a rule— less competent journalists. And the newly promoted would try to buy their positions by promoting the party in power, "and the program got worse and worse," Jergovic said in an interview.[9]

By 1991 the media war between Croatia and Serbia was in full swing, helping set the stage for the next phase of confrontation. Milosevic controlled most of the well-tuned state media in Serbia, which called for "the restoration of Serb national pride." To everyone else in the former Yugoslavia, such statements sounded like the threat of Serb domination. Using the Serbian threat, Tudjman made all major Croatian media—above all, radio, television, and the Vjesnik publishing company—a disciplined "frontline of the country's defense" in which there was no place for questioning party or presidential wisdom. In her collection of essays, Croatian writer Dubravka Ugresic describes how the "infernal media campaign" in Serbia and Croatia helped prepare both entities for war:

> In Serbian newspapers articles began to appear about the Ustasha camps during the Second World War (and no one could deny their truthfulness, because they existed and Serbs, Gypsies, Jews, and Croats perished there). More and more pictures of the camps began appearing on Serbian television. Croats began increasingly to be called criminals, "Ustashas." Serbian newspapers were full of horrifying stories about "necklaces of Serbian children's fingers," worn by the Croat "Ustashas," of the "genocide" that the Croats were again preparing to carry out against innocent Serbs.
>   The Serbian media propaganda orchestrated by Serbian authorities finally achieved what it had sought: a reaction in the Croatian media. And when the Croatian media also filled with tales of "necklaces of Croatian children's fingers" worn round the necks of Serbian "cut-throats," the preparations were laid for war.[10]

Foreign correspondent Blaine Harden gave a colorful description of the Yugoslav media war:

> Ethnic scare headlines—"Hellish Police Hunt on Serbs," "Fascist Terrorists Sent to Subjugate Serbs" or "Croatian Police Throw Serbian Infants Around"—are daily breakfast fare in Belgrade, capital of Serbia as well as the Yugoslav federation. An article on the Yugoslav government's attempt to bring market reform to socialist Serbia carried this headline: "Serbian Economy Knifed in the Back."[11]

Noting that according to foreign journalists, ethnic rivalry had eroded the objectivity of journalism across Yugoslavia, the report concluded that "the media that Milosevic controls remain far and away the most hysterical and inaccurate."

With mainstream media in Serbia and Croatia firmly controlled by

Milosevic and Tudjman propagandists, respectively, there was little room for a critical, open-minded, pluralistic journalism. Nevertheless in Serbia, the Belgrade daily *Borba (The Struggle)*, now under the editorial leadership of Manjo Vukotic, fought desperately to maintain its professional independence. Vukotic said in an interview:

> We refused to be another mouthpiece of Milosevic's "antibureaucratic revolution," and—to preserve independence—we had to refuse any political patronage, be it state or party, so we opted to support the economic and political reforms represented at that time by the reformist federal government of Ante Markovic. But there was a price tag attached to independence: We were gradually losing any financial support, enjoyed by all major media in socialist Yugoslavia, including the loss of thousands of subscriptions in the increasingly pro-Serbian federal Army.[12]

Still running interviews with and opinion pieces by those from the "other sides" of the debate on the future of Yugoslavia, and still open to pro and con arguments on the most sensitive issues, *Borba* and its editors were singled out by Milosevic's "patriotic press" as "traitors" to the Serbian national cause.

Yutel Television's one-year existence in prewar Yugoslavia provides a case study of the limits of "objective reporting" in a country engulfed in ethnic rivalry in which ultranationalist rulers used media to stir hatred and mobilize people for war. Whatever balanced reporting Goran Milic and his team tried was doomed to raise objections and criticism. Their support for Markovic's democratic and economic reforms in the still-existing Yugoslav federation made them "Yugo-nostalgics" and "unitarists" in the eyes of independence-minded Croats and Slovenes. Their openness to proponents of different views in a country accustomed to well-filtered "our truths" made them the target of extreme accusations: Serb nationalists called it "Ustasha TV"; Croat nationalists, "Chetnik TV." Even Yutel's antiwar advocacy—culminating in "Yutel for Peace" mass rallies in Osijek and Sarajevo, with prominent artists, folk and rock groups, and civic activists calling for peace—provoked sharp criticism. "Why are they calling for peace in Croatia and Bosnia, the targets of Serb expansionism, and not in Belgrade?" media critics cried. Milic is not apologetic about Yutel's advocacy for peace:

> We were based in the heart of Bosnia, and there was such an antiwar sentiment that one day we received an appeal for peace signed by one million

Bosnian children. They brought it to Yutel, believing naively but honestly that TV could prevent the war. That was the feeling of the majority of Bosnians, except those recruited and driven by nationalism. A decade and 250,000 dead later, I don't know if we should have done even more: Once we had 70,000 people singing for peace in Sarajevo; maybe I should have called on them to march on the Yugoslav Army barracks, asking officers to let us defend Bosnia if they were not ready to.[13]

However, the first serious challenge to Milosevic's rule in Serbia came in March 1991 when Vuk Draskovic, leader of the Serbian Renewal Movement (SPO), called for a protest against the regime's manipulation of the media. Draskovic himself was a victim of the state-run media discreditation campaign, as was anyone else who dared to challenge Milosevic's power. Belgrade Television accused him of plotting with "Tudjman Ustasha" and "Albanian separatists" to undermine Serbia. The clash between Draskovic, who was known as "King of the Squares" for his role in street demonstrations ever since he participated in a Belgrade student uprising in June 1968, and Milosevic, who by then had near-totalitarian control over all major instruments of power, including the police, army, and media, placed both men in uncharacteristic roles. Until then, Draskovic had been known as one of the instigators of Serb ultranationalism; he was the author of *The Knife*, a novel glorifying Chetniks during World War II. Some even believe that his September 2, 1986, letter to the Zagreb daily *Vjesnik* marked the beginning of a drive for "Greater Serbia." "Serbia was, is, and will be everywhere where there are Serb mass graves, execution sites, and graveyards," Draskovic wrote in a clear reference to Serb-inhabited areas of Croatia. He had borrowed the line from his political idol, World War II Chetnik leader Draza Mihajlovic, who in a document attributed to him declared, "Wherever Serbian graves are found, there is Serbian land."[14] Milosevic, on the other hand, had risen to power on the promise to Serbs that "no one is allowed to beat you," and it was he who, four years later, ordered a brutal police response against protesters in the streets of Belgrade, including the deployment of army tanks.

The day after Draskovic's mass demonstration in the Belgrade city center, the loyal *Politika* ran a front-page headline approving the president's action, "Milosevic Says Serbia Must Fight the Forces of Chaos and Rage." *Politika*, together with its sister publication *Politika ekspres*, alleged Draskovic's collaboration with both Ustasha and Shiptar forces. In the week after the demonstrations, Draskovic was jailed and released; Radio B92 and television Studio B were shut down because of their objective reporting on the protests; and the daily *Borba* became the sole voice of opposition, reaching a record circulation of more than 100,000. Protesters, holding a twenty-four-hour vigil called "Terazije Forum" at the heart of the city, forced Milosevic to fire his chief propagandist Dusan Mitevic (the head of Belgrade TV) and forced Serbian police chief Radmilo Bogdanovic to resign. Eventually, however, Milosevic prevailed, taking the country on the path to war.

Victims of "Patriotic Reporting"

By the summer of 1991, the media war had escalated into a real war. Slovenia and Croatia declared independence on June 25, 1991. Two days later, the Yugoslav Army was ordered to "secure the external borders" of Yugoslavia, with tanks rolling through Slovenia toward the Austrian and Italian borders. The Slovenian Territorial Defense and Police were mobilized to defend the republic's independence. In one of the most memorable snapshots capturing the absurdity of the Yugoslav war, Ivica Puljic, a TV journalist from Sarajevo reporting for Yutel, found a young Bosnian conscript in a trench. "What are you doing here, Bahrudin?" the reporter asked. "I don't know. They, like, want to secede, and we, like, won't let them," the soldier said.[15]

Slovenia, with only 2.4 percent Serbs, was not on Milosevic's "Greater Serbia" map, and Milosevic and the army had an agreement to let Slovenia go. So the war in Slovenia ended after only ten days—on July 5, 1991—with approximately seventy dead. Yet, as had been the case ever since ethnic stereotyping began in *Politika's* "Echoes and Reactions" in the late 1980s, the paper was happy to find further "proof" of how bad the alleged Serb enemies—Albanians and Slovenes, Croats and Bosnian Muslims—were. For example, *Politika* carried in three prominent installments an essay written by the internationally successful Bosnian movie director, Emir Kusturica, for the Paris daily *Liberation* in which he denigrated Slovenes and claimed that they had sent "Yugoslav Army boys" into the streets unarmed and then shot them in the back.[16]

The war to fulfill the promise of "all Serbs in a single state" was saved for Croatia (with 12.2 percent Serbs) and Bosnia (with 31.4 percent). As Croatia's drive for independence culminated in a formal declaration, armed incidents provided both the Serbian and Croatian nationalist media with an opportunity to rehearse what would become a vicious propaganda battle.

On March 1, 1991, a story appeared claiming that Serb members of the Pakrac police station had taken over the station, declaring it "Serb only," but the 200-strong antiterrorist unit of the Croatian police chased them away. Belgrade journalist Milan Milosevic gives the following account of the media fabrication of this story:

> Special correspondents of Montenegro TV announced that at least forty people had been killed in the small town of Pakrac in Croatia. Radio Belgrade picked up the report but gave the death toll as six. TV Novi Sad reported eight dead, and TV Belgrade found an Orthodox priest among the dead. The dead priest appeared live on television a few days later with a statement of his own. The Yugoslav presidency finally came out with a communiqué officially stating that nobody had been killed in Pakrac.

In a special edition following the incident, the Belgrade daily *Vecernje novosti* carried three conflicting stories on the Pakrac priest: On the front page it said he had been killed, on page two that he was wounded, and on page three they printed his statement![17]

On March 31, 1991, a busload of Croatian policemen was sent to reassert control over the Plitvice National Park after Serb militia annexed it to the self-declared Autonomous Region of Krajina. They were ambushed by Serb paramilitaries; one policeman was killed, and some were injured on both sides. Two major Belgrade dailies ran predictable headlines: *Politika* called the rebels "the defenders of Plitvice" and their action "a protection against genocide." *Politika ekspres* labeled police action against Serb paramilitaries "an attack on the whole Serbian people." That same day, the Zagreb daily *Vjesnik* praised the police action against "terrorists and rebels," declaring that "peace and order [were] restored in Plitvice." Research of the two dailies during the Serbo-Croatian conflict "established that on both sides there are the same frameworks of propaganda, repeating: 'we' are the victims, 'they' are the culprits; there is no way to save 'ourselves' other than annihilating and vanquishing 'them'; it is 'us' who have been sanctified, while the 'others' have been satanised."[18]

On May 2, 1991, twelve Croatian policemen were killed in an ambush in Serb-held Borovo Selo. The two sides offered completely different versions of what happened. Serbs claimed that on the previous evening, two Croatian police patrol cars had entered the village and opened fire at "innocent bystanders"; the villagers fired back. A day later a 300-strong special police unit attacked the village, and some twenty-five policemen were killed. The Croatian Interior Ministry said that villagers had fired automatic weapons at the policemen, and the local paramilitaries had arrested two patrolmen. The next day, the police chief from neighboring Vinkovci sent twenty policemen to investigate the attack, but their buses were caught in deadly crossfire that left twelve Croat policemen and three Serbs dead. *Politika ekspres* again reported only a "police raid" at Borovo Selo and "several tens of police specials killed." Belgrade TV had its own videotaped version of the story from Borovo Selo. Ejub Stitkovac writes that the segment "was taped by self-appointed Chetnik commander Vojislav Seselj (later the vice prime minister in Milosevic's Yugoslav government) and shown several times: fourteen of Seselj's men had led the battle against 'the Ustasha.' Fighting with Seselj's men were six locals and two members of the National Renewal Party from Nova Pazova, a town just outside Belgrade. According to Seselj, one civilian and one hundred Croatian policemen died."[19]

A few days later, on May 6, 1991, mass demonstrations broke out in front of the Command of the Yugoslav Navy, which was based in Split, a regional center on the Dalmatian coast. The demonstrators protested against Yugoslav military support for the Serb rebellion in Croatia. Heni Erceg, the Croatian TV correspondent from Split, reported that day: "It is difficult to describe what went on this morning in Split. Before a chronology of events, let's state the tragic balance sheet of the Split demonstration: a soldier, 19-year-old Macedonian Sasko Geskovski, has died," she said in an opening sentence.[20] The gruesome scene of a Croat demonstrator strangling a soldier who had just opened the hatch on top of his armored vehicle was shown only once on Croatian TV. It was cut from subsequent reports "because of the sensitivity of the viewers," the editor who assumed the role of censor-in-chief explained to Erceg. In the style of a police investigator he called her to ask how the scene of the strangulation of an innocent conscript had reached the Eurovision news exchange center and become the centerpiece of evening television

newscasts throughout Europe. She told him that she didn't know what
he was talking about because she was a reporter and not in charge of the
Eurovision program exchange. "But you liked that scene being included
in the report," he said. "Of course," she responded. "Any professional
would approve that." "Is your father maybe a general?" the editor continued in his interrogation—one of the first "misunderstandings" Erceg was
to experience by the end of that year.[21]

For Erceg this exchange and censorship marked the beginning of the
brutal "patriotization" of Croatian TV "based on the same criteria
Communists used to ensure totalitarian control over the media: Whoever
is not with us is against us," she said,[22] describing how Tudjman, with his
chief executor Vrdoljak, had created a propaganda machinery mirroring
the Milosevic-controlled Serbian TV in Belgrade. "Hate speech became
a measure of professionalism. They found executioners within Croatian
TV itself, most often using [confidential personal] files opened by
Tudjman's secret services in combination with petty blackmail or corruption [to coerce reporters]," Erceg recalled.

In her analysis of Croatian and Serbian television and their role in the
awakening of ultranationalism, Sandra Basic-Hrvatin reflects on the ways
in which Croatian TV projected itself as "the cathedral of the Croatian
spirit" as promised by Vrdoljak:

> Cultural populism is evident in the revival of undefined folk culture: music
> with extremely nationalistic lyrics and overwrought national sentiments,
> myths, old forgotten customs, publicity for religious practices . . . . On
> Croatian television there is a whole list of programmes made for "the life
> of the nation": *Good Morning Croatia, Croatia: Land and People, Greetings
> from the Homeland, Study Croatia, Croatian Language, Croatian Literature,
> Croatia in the World* . . . . On Serbian television the most popular pro-
> grammes are quiz games whose subject is national history, and pro-
> grammes featuring popular folk music.[23]

The dominant media in both republics—state radio and television as
well as state dailies such as *Politika* and *Politika ekspres* in Belgrade and
Vjesnik and *Vecernji* list in Zagreb—were fully in line for an all-out "us
versus them" showdown. In the newsroom, there was no space for or
interest in "the other's" concern or point of view, not even a pretense of
objectivity or curiosity to hear another side of the story, and no questioning or criticism of what "our side" was doing.

After Croatia's declaration of independence on June 25, the summer of 1991 provided the war propagandists with plenty of opportunities to practice their craft. Serbian paramilitaries, self-styled local militia, and volunteers from Bosnia and Serbia—aided by Yugoslav Army artillery—moved to redraw the borders of "Greater Serbia," attacking and expelling terrified Croatian civilians from large areas of Slavonia and Baranja. The term "ethnic cleansing" became the new name for brutal war crimes. The mainstream media, especially radio and television, in both Serbia and Croatia rallied behind their countries' war efforts. Their job was to convince the public that "we" were engaged in a sacred cause. For Serbian TV, the war in Croatia, including the "ethnic cleansing" of Croats from Serb-inhabited territories, was just the defense of centuries-old Serb hearths and the protection of the Serb people from another genocide at the hands of fascist Ustasha forces. For Croatian TV, the war was the defense of the homeland and a way to realize the thousand-year-old dream of an independent Croatia. In pursuing that dream, there was no place for sympathy for Serb civilians or for public questioning of crimes committed against them. Day in and day out, television on both sides presented the war as a clear case of good versus evil. Enemies were portrayed as the much despised and feared World War II murderers—the Croat Ustasha or the Serb Chetnik forces. Our soldiers were heroes, defenders, and holy warriors, while their soldiers were barbarians, butchers, and beasts. The stories always told of "their" armed-to-the-teeth military attacking "our" defenseless civilians.

There was even a prescribed vocabulary for use in reporting on the war. On August 28, 1991, the Croatian TV management distributed to its regional war correspondents a strict guide, signed by editor-in-chief Tomislav Marcinko and news editor Miroslav Lilic, instructing them on how to report on the war. They had to name the enemy in proper terms: "Serb terrorists" and the "Serbo-Communist army of occupation." Croatian forces were to be called "National Guard and Ministry of Interior units" in order to avoid Serb terms for those forces such as *mupovci* (from MUP, the Croatian name for the Ministry of Internal Affairs). The guide instructed reporters in particular not to show pictures of blown-up, badly wounded, or shot Croatian soldiers, and never to air soldiers' statements or scenes of crying Croatian civilians. Whenever reporting casualties on "our" side, reporters were to use patriotic phrases such as "fell for Croatia's freedom," "gave their lives to defend the homeland," and "heroes in defense of the homeland." Instruction number 11 from that 13-point document warns:

> Do not conceal defeats at the front, but stress the tremendous forces employed by the enemy and his unscrupulousness, and always finish such reports with optimistic declarations and avowals ("but we shall bring back freedom to our Kijevo," for example). Send reports of towns being successfully defended for special programs. Failure to adhere to the above instructions will entail appropriate professional and legal consequences.[24]

The decree also required the editors to preview and approve pictures from the war zones to make sure they followed the script.

Analyzing those days from a postwar perspective, Damir Matkovic, a well-respected Croatian TV journalist, said in an interview that it was a war in which "television was used as a mighty weapon."[25] He acknowledged that the aggression against Croatia was indeed shocking, with pictures of destroyed towns and burnt-out villages, and that there was a legitimate patriotic feeling among Croatian journalists. But, as Matkovic recalls, there were also excesses in "patriotic reporting." Once instruction came from "higher places" to find a village in the war-torn Slavonia region where Croats and Serbs still lived in peace with each other, in order to prove that in Croat-controlled territories, there were also Serbs loyal to their state of Croatia, suffering under Serbian aggression. Matkovic said:

> We found a village and broadcast a story on people resisting the war just a couple of miles from one of the frontlines. That evening a few grenades were fired at the village. People in "higher offices" liked the story, so they insisted it be rebroadcast. The reporter, Ankica Mladenovic, a half-Serb who knew the people in the village, cried and begged the editors not to replay her story. "I know what will happen to them," she warned. But they followed the "instruction from above," and the village was shelled, with people killed and wounded. On another occasion, looking for examples of heroism, we did a story on a village near Vinkovci: It was a report on "only ten brave men defending the village and ready to stay there to the end." Serb commanders saw the story, attacked and "liberated" the village, killing and wounding a number of people in the process. In some cases, while reporting we practically exposed the defense lines. I think that in a war like the one we had in Croatia, with front lines running through peoples' homes, there was a need for some rules, if not censorship—but, of course, not for cheap propaganda.[26]

A similar editorial dilemma, to air or not to air sensitive frontline footage, caused agonizing decision making in Yutel's newsroom in Sarajevo. Milic recounted one such story. "A man brought us a videotape from Vinkovci of a Yugoslav Army jet dropping bombs in a field during an air raid," he said. "I thought: Maybe that pilot was a conscientious young man who didn't want to bomb the city [and its innocent civilians]. The next day he could be replaced by someone who would aim much better. If you used the footage, you might cause destruction and suffering; if you didn't, you wasted a rare opportunity to have a real action picture from the war zones."[27]

Decision making was much easier for those unconcerned about individuals, villages, or towns when there was a "higher cause" to be served. Serbian TV, with four years of experience in reporting on the "anti-Serbian conspiracy"—and with an ever-expanding list of enemies ranging from the Vatican alliance (Slovenes and Croats) to the Muslim threat (Albanians and Bosniaks), from the Western imperialists (Bonn and Washington) to domestic traitors—presented the war in Croatia as evidence of "Ustasha bestiality." In an official note posted on the bulletin board of Novi Sad TV, a Serbian TV affiliate, the management instructed the editorial staff to identify all corpses shown in war reports as "Serb victims." Thus, the station presented the bodies of dead Croat civilians as Serbs. Such manipulations were possible because in television coverage of the war zones—on all sides—the stations showed little footage from battle zones: In an analysis of Serbian TV in 1993, the proportion was 70 percent verbal presentation vs. only 30 percent visual.[28]

Vukovar: The City "Leveled but Free"

Even traditionally reliable international news organizations were sometimes drawn into the Balkan blame game. One of the most memorable incidents involved Reuters. On November 20, 1991, Reuters dispatched a series of reports entitled *Yugoslavia; Massacre, Yugoslavia; Massacre 1, Yugoslavia; Massacre 2.* The reports quoted Yugoslav freelance photographer Goran Mikic, who had told Reuters and Belgrade TV the day before that he had seen and counted the bodies of forty-one children massacred in the backyard of an elementary school in Borovo Naselje near Vukovar. Mikic said he was told by Yugoslav Army soldiers that the bodies were those of Serb children killed by Croat Guardsmen. The news made headlines in Yugoslavia, serving as yet another gruesome example of how important and heroic "the defense of Serb hearths" was in Croatia. Reuters' retraction a day later, based on Mikic's admission that he neither saw nor counted bodies, did not have nearly the same effect as the original report. On November 22, the Croatian daily *Vjesnik* reported prominently at the top of its front page on "The Lie that Circled the World," with Reuters' "correction and apology." The Belgrade daily *Politika*—even though Reuters had corrected its original report—still insisted on its front page that "the crime in Borovo Naselje, in which more than forty children were killed" had not been mentioned at a Yugoslav Army press conference. "Evidence of [this alleged massacre] has not been prepared yet, perhaps because the Ustasha in Borovo Naselje wrapped it in a veil of secrecy," *Politika* said, praising the army for not confirming the story before having the evidence. "The Yugoslav Army cannot do otherwise," the Belgrade daily suggested.

Unfortunately, both *Politika* and the army, which had purged non-Serb officers, were well known for doing exactly the opposite—engaging in war propaganda throughout the war in Croatia. This was especially evident during the two most memorable Yugoslav Army operations in Croatia: the siege of the ancient walled town of Dubrovnik and the siege of the historic city of Vukovar during fall 1991. Reporting on "A Strong Army Action Near Dubrovnik" at the top of its front page on October 3, *Politika* said in the second paragraph that "the war was brought to this area by Croatia's paramilitary, guardsmen and Black Legionaries, and international drifters and murderers, collected by Tudjman to wage a war—for a good salary—against the peaceful people of Montenegro and Bosnia." An official army statement went even further, claiming that "For a long period of time, innocent Croatian and Serbian people, as well as Yugoslav Army personnel, have been subjected to a variety of Croatian paramilitary activities, whose actions are more brutal than any crimes known so far." So the army—in order to protect both Serb and Croat civilians—was "forced" to undertake the action in the Dubrovnik area "aimed at stopping the fascist dictatorship and the terror of the Croatian paramilitary."[29] That same day, *Politika* reprinted an article from *Narodna Armija (People's Army)* magazine, claiming in a headline that "Croatia Is Getting Ready to Produce an Atomic Bomb." It was that type of reporting, provided through the Milosevic-controlled media in Serbia, that led the majority of Serbs to believe that their army was waging a just war even while it was shelling Dubrovnik monuments and terrorizing its people under a blockade. *Politika ekspres* crowned its reporting on the shelling of Dubrovnik with an unsurpassed front-page headline: "Dubrovnik Awaits Its Liberation."

Similar justifications were offered for the three-month-long siege of Vukovar, another historic town near Croatia's border with Serbia. Vukovar was besieged and bombarded for ninety days until its once-picturesque streets were turned into ruins. "Vukovar Finally Free," screamed *Politika's* front-page headline on November 20, 1991, celebrating "victory." Yet the army had entered a ghost city in which, according to *Politika's* page 8 report, the number of dead was measured in the hundreds, probably even the thousands, and "it was not impossible that, among them, unfortunately, the majority [were] civilians." Just days after Reuters' retraction of a "massacre" in Borovo Naselje, the paper continued to insist that the fabricated story was an established fact. In the same report, following the "liberating army" around the ruined city, the paper continued to repeat the false claims: "[I]n front of the kindergarten, where foreign correspondents saw forty slaughtered children, we found a horrible scene: There were dozens of dead, with their throats slit, stabbed by knives through their cheeks, their skulls broken . . . ." In another front-page article the same day, *Politika* reported on "more than a hundred corpses of people killed by torture, whose heads are crushed, and internal organs stolen to serve the needs of foreign clinics."[30] The whole story was aimed at proving "genocide against the Serbs." Later, though, the International War Crimes Tribunal in The Hague indicted three Yugoslav Army officers for—among other crimes in Croatia—the execution of 300 patients at Vukovar hospital. One of those indicted, Major Veselin Sljivancanin, marked the "liberation of Vukovar" on Serbian TV with the following statement: "It's leveled but free!" International TV crews taped Sljivancanin ordering his troops to enter the Vukovar hospital. He shouted at the International Red Cross representative who tried to stop them, "This is my country, we have conquered this. This is Yugoslavia, and I am in command here!"[31]

Stojan Cerovic commented on the contribution of journalists to the regime's war propaganda: "With regard to the media who started and successfully waged this war, their first move was to disregard professional standards. Instead of checking the facts, the quotes, and the sources, [they exercised] full poetic license. The adjectives have become flavor-of-the-month and they are still in high demand, although the repertoire has proved to be quite limited."[32] In the same article, Cerovic cited another example from *Politika*. The once-reputable Belgrade daily reported that, while besieging Vukovar, the army "captured twelve Czechoslovakian women who were fighting on the Croatian side." The Czech ambassador to Belgrade sent his representatives to the Foreign Ministry and then to the Ministry of Defense to inquire and to contact the prisoners, but the Czech representatives were told to "be careful when dealing with the domestic press." Another of so many fabricated stories. No Czech women had been captured.

Patriotism, as defined by the nationalist authorities, was the order of the day for both the Serbian and Croatian media. Any antiwar statements or sentiments met with a barrage of criticism, including the charge of "betraying the homeland." One such example was the attack in *Vjesnik* against *Danas's* music critic, Jasmina Kuzmanovic, for her view that Croatia could make better use of its artists than "sending them with weapons to the front lines." Jagoda Martincevic found this view to hold "a trace of fifth column in journalism," suggesting that it was "bad to think, and even worse to publicize the thought that the participation of Croatian artists on the battlefield was a phenomenon but similar participation by an engineer, a shoemaker, or a vegetable seller wasn't."[33] While Martincevic may have had a valid point on the equality of citizens before the law, labeling a journalist with different views as "fifth column" during the war amounted to a call for her public persecution. Even more persistent in the search for a "fifth column" was the official HDZ publication *Glasnik (Herald)*. It accused independent intellectuals and civic activists such as Zarko Puhovski and Ivan Zvonimir Cicak of being "damaging to Croatia's interests"; it criticized the coalition of opposition parties, Croatian National Alliance (HNS), for "attacking the President of Croatia" in a paid election advertisement in *Vjesnik* in a way that "questions the very dignity of the state"; it attacked the Split daily *Slobodna Dalmacija* for carrying "works of the fifth column" such as articles written by the prominent publicists Igor Mandic and Drago Buvac.[34]

Silencing Opposing Voices

Tudjman's "young democracy" was as ruthless in silencing opposition voices as was Milosevic's "antibureaucratic revolution." A case in point was the Osijek daily *Glas Slavonije (Voice of Slavonia)*. Under the editorial leadership of Drago Hedl, the paper—once an obscure organ of the Socialist Alliance like most of the other papers in the former Yugoslavia—became in the late 1980s a credible witness to events leading to the dissolution of Yugoslavia. Covering a sensitive area near the Croatian-Serbian border, *Glas Slavonije* began to examine once-prohibited issues, and its circulation rose from under 10,000 to a record high of 18,000. With ethnic tensions rising in Slavonia, the regional HDZ leadership increased its pressure to take control of the paper. On June 28, 1991, the HDZ Board in Osijek actually bought a whole page in *Glas Slavonije* in order to call for "a boycott of the so-called independent paper of *Glas Slavonije*" and "the resurrection of our and your daily Croatian newspaper." The HDZ accused *Glas Slavonije* of "undermining the basic interests of the defense of Croatia's internal and external sovereignty" and of "animosity toward the HDZ." The public response was not what the Party had wanted. That day, people bought two copies of the paper instead of one, and it sold out in just a few hours.

But the pressure against the paper's independence became even more severe. In early July, the paper's manager Vladimir Kokeza and editor-in-chief Hedl received official notices to report to local defense headquarters; they spent the night "mobilized for the front" but were released the next day with a warning that the next time they would end up in the trenches. In the second half of July, a radical nationalistic magazine *Slobodni tjednik (Free Weekly)* published a list of "KOS [the Yugoslav Army Counter-Intelligence Service] collaborators in Osijek's media." A dozen *Glas Slavonije* journalists were on the list. By the end of the month, the local privatization agency named a new managing board with regional HDZ boss Branimir Glavas as president. Kokeza and Hedl were forced to resign. That same day, Glavas, escorted by ten armed soldiers, occupied the paper. All "suspected journalists" were fired, and the paper resorted to articles full of hate and incitement for the war. Hedl wrote of the paper he had edited:

Glas Slavonije became a bulletin of the ruling party charged with promoting the activity of the regional authorities and serving in its showdown with
those of different political views. The paper's dependence is best illustrated
by the fact that in some months it carried more than fifty pictures of Glavas,
almost two per day, culminating on March 14, 1992, with a series of fourteen photographs beginning with one showing Glavas in National Guard
uniform holding a white dove and spread over the entire front page, and
ending with three pictures of him on page 12.[35]

Tudjman's Party focused its intimidation efforts primarily on the
statewide Croatian media. Serb aggression provided the best possible
justification for a final onslaught against freedom of the press.
Vrdoljak's purge of Croatian TV left hundreds of personnel on "waiting lists." Some of the purged discovered their status only when the
guards at TV headquarters told them they were not on the list of those
who could enter the premises. Some of the station's most respected
journalists were given early retirement or simply disappeared from the
TV screens. In an interview with *Vecernji list* at the end of 1992,
Vrdoljak justified the purge with a litany of paranoid accusations
against the former employees:

> All editors, even though they went through intelligence training in Belgrade,
> had a chance to continue reporting. But some suspicious things began to hap-
> pen: Our editors, even though they were required to provide accompanying
> commentary, carried official [Yugoslav] Army statements without any editing
> or explanation. It wasn't difficult to discover who was on which side. Or the
> case of an experienced reporter covering the Plitvice incident who advised
> Chetniks over the TV screen that their grenade didn't explode because they
> hadn't removed the safety pin. It sounded like "see how stupid the Chetniks
> are." After his report, they never failed to remove the safety pin. Or a famous
> woman journalist, busy granting interviews, who in the most critical days
> stood in front of the [nuclear powered] Krsko energy facility explaining its
> weak points and what kind of grenade could cause an ecological disaster, and
> so on.[36]

According to Heni Erceg, who covered the war zones throughout
Croatia including the siege of Dubrovnik, things became bad after
Vrdoljak took over HTV: First, an order came requiring the use of new
terminology for naming the enemy, such as "Serbo-Chetnik" or "Yugo-
Communist Army," she said in an interview. Then the journalists were
asked to follow these orders—and some agreed. Finally, the "news" was

produced in Tudjman's Crisis Headquarters. Erceg said that her problem with the authorities began when she refused to use the prescribed language:

> After I came out of Dubrovnik, at the end of 1991, Vrdoljak accused me of handing over a videotape to "someone"—even today I don't know what or who he was talking about—but allegedly it was a tape with "the truth about the Dubrovnik siege" that I gave to enemies, foreign agents, or who-knows-who-else. In short, I was accused of collaborating with the enemy and was placed "on ice." After a couple of months of not getting any assignment, I quit my job. Others were simply fired or put on "waiting lists," mostly because they were "the wrong nationality." The patriotization of the Croatian media was conducted using Milosevic's script.[37]

With *Vjesnik* well under control, the HDZ next set its sights on Croatia's finest newsmagazine, *Danas*. The weekly's two editors, Mirko Galic and Drazen Vukov-Colic, had introduced into Croatian journalism their experiences as longtime correspondents in Western democratic countries—including the United States, France, and Germany. Now *Danas* and its staff were accused by the HDZ of being "anti-Croatian," "sold souls," "fifth columnists," and a "Yugo-nostalgic" breeding-place for "commies." When *Danas* refused to join the Tudjman propagandist machinery, the HDZ moved to crush it economically. First, the Croatian printing company, part of the Vjesnik publishing empire, refused to print *Danas* "because of accumulating debt," even though the paper was seventh on a long list of debtors. *Danas* had to look for a printer in neighboring Slovenia. Then the state privatization agency named a new managing board whose mission was to close the paper down. The editorial staff found a new, private publisher and, in July 1992, started the magazine under the name of *Novi danas (New Danas)*. Very soon, however, the regime imposed a new obstacle: *Vjesnik's* distribution network—which controlled 80 percent of Croatia's newspaper market—cancelled the contract for the distribution of *Novi danas*. After only eight issues, it had to close down.

In a perverse twist of events, HDZ's official *Glasnik* occupied *Danas's* old offices. Soon *Glasnik* ceased to exist and was replaced—in what prominent Croatian columnist Jelena Lovric called "a first class media perversion"—with an HDZ magazine called *Danas*. "People who for two years led a campaign against *Danas* started to publish *Danas!*" Lovric

wrote.[38] In his 1933 unpublished essay "How Free Is Croatian Journalism?" Zivko Gruden sums up the fate of that HDZ publishing
experiment: "The *Danas* that was formed by the transformation of
Glasnik, taking the name of the former and the content of the latter, did
not succeed on the market: It sold only 5,000 copies, which was two or
three times more than *Glasnik* had sold, but a catastrophic circulation
for a newsmagazine and only one-tenth the circulation of *Novi danas*
(the record circulation of the original *Danas* was almost 200,000
copies)."

In both Serbia and Croatia, the nationalist governments—by imposing strict party control and replacing reputed professional journalists
with those ready to serve the cause—managed to degrade professional
standards in all media and to compromise and ruin once well-respected
newspapers such as *Politika* and *Vjesnik, NIN* and *Danas.* Dusan Simic,
one of the *Politika* veterans who had served as the paper's New York
and London correspondent and was the editor-in-chief of *NIN* in its
better days, offered some insight on how Milosevic was able to exert
total control of *Politika* for so many years. According to Simic, Milosevic used the historic shrewdness of the Serbian Prince Milos Obrenovic,[39] who reportedly said, "When you see that people are too
oppressed, loosen up a little." That was what Milosevic did with his
opponents—individuals, parties, and the media. If he felt they didn't
pose an imminent threat, or if he expected strong opposition, he would
leave them some margin of "freedom of action," creating an illusion that
something might be changed. "That was the case with *Politika,*" Simic
recalled. He said:

> In 1991, we organized an Independent Union of Journalists that openly
> challenged Minovic and his editorial policy. We issued petitions and pub-
> lished them in then-liberal *Borba,* we organized protest meetings, and still
> we remained with the paper. We believed we were achieving something,
> and we did achieve something—including the replacement of the top edi-
> tors of *NIN* and *Politika,* Teodor Andjelic and Zivorad Minovic, and we
> even won the right for journalists to elect their own editors. But the expec-
> tation that we could bring substantial and long-term changes from within,
> which kept us with the paper, at the end proved to be just an illusion.[40]

A majority of the editorial staff voted to replace Minovic as editor
with former *Politika* foreign correspondent Aleksandar Prlja, who at

that time served as Serbia's foreign minister. I asked Simic how it was possible that journalists themselves, who had fought so hard for editorial independence, voted for someone from the heart of Milosevic's regime. Simic, who was the Journalist Union's candidate for the position himself, sees two possible reasons for such an outcome:

> One reason is typically Milosevic. Immediately following Minovic's forced resignation, Prlja was sent to *Politika* as the acting editor-in-chief, which gave him enough time to gather his supporters, promising them promotions, editorial positions, foreign correspondents' assignments, and other benefits. A more important reason was that Prlja, with his position and government support, was able to offer the newspaper's silent majority, especially small town correspondents and technical services employees, security while I could offer them only uncertainty; he promised them the continuity of a great national illusion while I in my "campaign speech" argued for a change and for professional standards and values. Our micro-election was just a sad reflection of larger realities in Serbia and its general election outcomes.[41]

On January 2, 1992, Croatia's Minister of Defense Gojko Susak and Yugoslav Army General Andrija Raseta signed an agreement in Sarajevo for an "unconditional cease-fire," leaving Serb-occupied parts of Croatia under army control. But the war left both Serbian and Croatian journalism, with the honorable exception of a few media outlets and dozens of brave individuals, in the deep trenches of extreme nationalism, blinded by hate and ready to continue the war "by other means."

The fate of those still loyal to professional ethics and standards is best illustrated by an open letter written by a suspended Belgrade Radio correspondent from Zagreb, Vesna Knezevic, to her employers on January 31, 1992. Her letter was in response to one she had received from her editors on January 24 after a three-month suspension. They invited her to resume work if she was willing to accept their "editorial policy criteria." In the letter, published in *Vreme*, she asked her editors to let her know what their current criteria were: How, for example, should she report on the United States' and Europe's anticipated recognition of Croatia's independence; how should she now treat Croatian Serb leaders as "undesirable" in the Serb media when they had been treated as heroes for so long? How explain the wave of Serb refugees from Croatia? Who blame for the war's slaughters, the leadership of Serbia or Croatia? Who name as having given Croatia an alibi for a "final solution" to the Serb question? Who orchestrated the Croatian Serbs' rebellion and now treats them only as a nuisance and a burden? And finally she asked, "Who is fundamentally responsible for the fact that Serbia today is alone and lonely in the world, deserted by God and people, with the Serbian name provoking only cold contempt in Europe, or something even worse—a fear of terrorists and unrestrained people in European countries?"[42]

"Patriotic journalism" in Serbia under Milosevic and in Croatia under Tudjman operated on the same simple formula: Yugoslav patriotism was replaced with Serb or Croat patriotism, Communist ideology with nationalist ideology, the old ruling party's dictates with the new ruling party's dictates. The new leaders used the same instruments to control the media: the appointment of the most loyal party ideologists to all top positions in the state-controlled media, especially radio and television and the leading national dailies, leaving them to appoint and control their own loyal editors. In both Serbia and Croatia, dozens of the best journalists lost their jobs resisting the patriotic call to spread hatred and intolerance. They were replaced immediately by others who were eager to serve, national enthusiasts who are perhaps best represented by a young, female Croatian TV journalist who proudly announced on the air, "I am ready to lie for my homeland!"

Bosnia: Ground Zero (1990–95)

MANY OF THE JOURNALISTS, SCHOLARS, AND DIPLOMATS who spent the 1990s trying to understand and explain the Balkan nightmare of that decade themselves fell victim to the following media stereotype: While Belgrade, and much later Zagreb, enjoyed a liberal, free-spirited, open-minded, and critical press, Sarajevo was always behind, true to its anecdotal reputation as "a world of darkness" *(tamni vilajet)*. That judgment was correct until the mid-1980s. It was then that, following the excitement of the Sarajevo Winter Olympic Games in 1984, a new spirit of greater openness in cultural life, the arts, and the media began to weaken the once iron grip of the Party over Bosnia. Generally speaking, the international media experts missed that point.

Under Communism, the media had followed prescribed outlines of permissible public dialogue in Bosnia. After all, the Party's fundamental promise of "brotherhood and unity" had been most severely tested in Bosnia. A mixture of three ethnic groups—43.7 percent Muslim, 31.3 percent Serb, 17.3 percent Croat, 7.7 percent "Yugoslav" and "Other"[1]— the republic was kept under the watchful eye of Party ideologists. They made sure that the Bosnian media followed the script, avoiding the occasional debates on "national issues" such as Serbo-Croat or Serbo-Albanian disputes and quarrels. The Party-appointed director general and editor-in-chief of Bosnia's major media outlets—Sarajevo Radio and TV and the daily *Oslobodjenje*—were charged with upholding strict respect for the Party line. There was no need for open censorship, however. The very nature of the system censored public debate and thus all media. In public life, there was no forum to challenge the Party line. People promoted to any level of the government or any organization within "the front of organized socialist forces"—i.e., the League of Communists, the Socialist Alliance, the Labor Union, and even war veterans and youth organizations—were thoroughly tested for their loyalty to the cause. All public debates were limited to a search for answers "within the system of socialist self-management." And if, on a rare occasion, some of the participants expressed unorthodox, critical views, there would still be that alert editor-in-chief or reliable associates in the newsroom to edit out all controversial content. As for the media, there simply were no opinion pages or radio and television programs to debate or challenge the official line. What passed as commentary was in fact media support for decisions made by the Party or the government—with no room for questioning the wisdom of those decisions.

Bosnia's Short-Lived "Spring"

All of this changed dramatically in the late 1980s. The Bosnian media experienced its years of great hope almost exactly at the time when the previously more liberal Belgrade media began to follow Milosevic's script for "the need to restore Serbia's dignity," which led to the violent overthrow of moderate governments in Vojvodina, Montenegro, and Kosovo; a unilateral change of constitution; and, ultimately, wars in Slovenia, Croatia, Bosnia, and Kosovo. In the summer of 1987—the same summer when Milosevic moved against moderates in Serbia—Bosnia suddenly became engulfed in what appeared to be politically motivated scandals at the top of the Party hierarchy. First, it was the revelation, through a small-town *Borba* correspondent in Serbia, that an "economic wonder," the huge agricultural and trade conglomerate, Agrokomerc, in the small Bosnian town of Velika Kladusa in the Bihac area, was built on false promissory notes totaling $865 million. The scandal shook the very foundations of Party rule in Bosnia. The crime committed by Agrokomerc boss Fikret Abdic, one of those unofficial Party-sponsored governors of Bosnian regions, exposed a web of co-conspirators in the highest Bosnian and federal offices. One of the many high-ranking officials forced to resign was a Bosnian vice president of the Yugoslav Presidency, Hamdija Pozderac. Agrokomerc was based in his hometown area, and he was considered one of Abdic's key supporters.

Many believe that Pozderac was the ultimate target of the whole "Agrokomerc affair." As the country's vice president and—by virtue of annual rotations—slated to become the next year's president, Pozderac would have presided over the commission in charge of constitutional changes. As the conspiracy theory goes, he was considered potentially too hard-headed to give in to pressure from Serbia to abolish the autonomy of Kosovo and Vojvodina and strengthen Belgrade-based central institutions. Thus the story about the promissory notes was leaked to *Borba's* small-town correspondent in order to get rid of Pozderac.

The affair exposed corruption throughout the Bosnian Party hierarchy. The once harmonious meetings of the Central Committee, the republic's Parliament, and the Socialist Alliance now became battlegrounds, with formerly untouchable functionaries accusing each other of all sorts of immoral and illegal activities. Bosnia's media seized the opportunity. Just reporting on what was said in those meetings, Radio and Television Sarajevo, *Oslobodjenje*, and other media in the republic exposed the wrong-doings of those in power. This included the misuse of public funds and favorable credits to build cozy villas at Neum, the only Bosnian town on the Adriatic coast; nepotism; unlawful hometown influences and connections; and the extensive use of police to control political opponents and even to spy on rival factions within the ruling elite. The Party's authority in Bosnia was irreparably weakened. A new, younger leadership wanted to clean house and was much more sensitive to the public image of the Party and state institutions. The media, on the other hand, had helped to weaken the Party and at the same time gained the freedom that until then had been unknown in either Serbia or Croatia. It was the beginning of the short-lived "Bosnian spring."

The pace of change was set, not surprisingly, by the youth media. Radio Sarajevo started a special Youth Program, with a group of young journalists challenging and expanding "the borders of what was allowed" including the editor Boro Kontic and reporters Senad Hadzifejzovic, Neven Andjelic, Senad Pecanin, Mladen Sancanin, Aleksandar Hemon (now a well-known fiction writer in the United States), and Pedja Kojovic. Pecanin—later a founder and editor of the most respected Bosnian political magazine, *Dani*—shared his experiences at the beginning of unparalleled press freedom in Bosnia:

> We opened our program for a free on-air discussion of once prohibited subjects, such as Tito's historic legacy or political trials of the past. In the beginning there was still some harassment, mostly in the form of some of us being invited to the secret police for so-called "informative talks." But those were just the last reflexes of a dying Party monopoly. Very soon, we had regular open-air debates on almost any current political issue of the day, which included comments from some of the most famous Yugoslav dissidents.[2]

Pecanin had his own problems with the police over his reporting for Youth Radio. He was taken in for questioning after he reported that the leading candidate for the Bosnian member of the Yugoslav Presidency, Nenad Kecmanovic, had withdrawn his candidacy because he had been accused of spying. The documents on which Pecanin had based his report had been stamped "state secret."

Indeed as liberalization continued, all three of the most influential Bosnian media outlets—Radio and Television Sarajevo and *Oslobodjenje*—rejected Party-appointed editors and managers, the most efficient instrument of media control, and convinced a new, reform-minded, Bosnian leadership to let them elect their editors on the basis of professional and public reputation. That's how, at the end of December 1988, I became editor-in-chief of *Oslobodjenje*. Our first innovation was to introduce *Oslobodjenje's* own Op-Ed page. The page included regular staff and guest columnists; a daily cartoon by *Oslobodjenje's* cartoonists, who were among the finest in Yugoslavia (Bozo Stefanovic, Hasan Fazlic, Djoko Ninkovic, Midhat Ajanovic); and opinion pieces on issues of the day written by respected authors from all sectors of society including university professors, writers, politicians, economists, artists, and other public personalities. The paper also launched a front-page "In Focus" column featuring *Oslobodjenje's* best writers as well as Bosnian, Yugoslav, and international public figures reflecting on the issues of the day. Our contributors included movie director Emir Kusturica (who later supported the Milosevic regime during its siege of Sarajevo, leaving his fellow Sarajevans feeling betrayed); the republic's and federation's top politicians; widely respected writers such as Abdulah Sidran, Camil Sijaric, and Izet Sarajlic; national soccer team coach Ivica Osim; and even UN Secretary General Javier Peres de Cuellar. Contrary to the prevailing trend in the Yugoslav press at that time, which was to promote exclusively "one's own" political leaders and ideologies, we began a daily, full-page "YU-Press Review" of the most interesting and controversial articles from the other republics' newspapers. On Mondays, we had a page called "YU-Journal," with the editors of evening TV journals in all eight Yugoslav republics and autonomous provinces contributing articles on the dominant issue of the week. Some readers, especially Party functionaries, criticized us for "promoting inter-republic quarrels," but those two pages reflected the realities of a country heading toward a violent breakup and offered the public much-needed information on what others in the country were thinking and saying.

In addition, every day there was a special section, "a paper within a paper": On Mondays and Tuesdays, it was sports; Wednesdays, "Globus" (international issues); Thursdays, "Weekend"; Fridays, "Radio and TV Guide" (the best-selling supplement); Saturdays, "Culture, Science, and Arts"; Sundays, "The Week" *("Nedjelja")*, which later became a separate weekly magazine and was replaced in the paper with "7 Days," including contributions of some of the most respected authors in Yugoslavia. My favorite innovation was the expansion of the "Letters to the Editor" column, which had avoided controversial debate, into a full-page "tribunal." With citizens freely debating the ruling elite's corruption and misuse of political power, the page became an open forum in which we soon had two presidents of the federal Presidency, Bosnian Raif Dizdarevic and Slovene Janez Drnovsek, federal Prime Minister Branko Mikulic, and all of the leading Bosnian politicians responding to letters published on that page. "*Oslobodjenje (Liberation)* is a paper that is beginning to live up to its own name," commented Sidran, once a regular critic of the paper who had become a contributor.

By the end of my first year as editor, *Oslobodjenje* was named Newspaper of the Year in Yugoslavia in 1989 in an annual poll among professional journalists conducted by the Split daily *Slobodna Dalmacija*. But we still needed to change something more. With all the excitement of presiding over "changing the character of the paper," as *Slobodna Dalmacija* explained in giving us its award, I still felt as if I were editing Moscow's *Pravda* from the worst days of Communism. At the top left corner of *Oslobodjenje's* front page was the slogan "Comrade Tito, We Pledge to You . . . [that we will follow your path]," which had been printed there ever since Tito died on May 4, 1980. My generation of journalists at the paper had been raised in Tito's time and learned in school that there was nothing better than "the best of all worlds" in which we lived. Nevertheless, although we appreciated many of the good things he did for the country, we still found the slogan too ideological to allow *Oslobodjenje* to break with its own past as a Party bulletin. We removed it from the first issue of the paper in 1990. To better emphasize the paper's new, market-oriented policy, we sold the space to a Slovenian company, Gorenje from Velenje, best known for producing refrigerators and television sets. "Comrade Velenje, we are Gorenje," read a satirical comment by Ozren Kebo in another Sarajevo daily *Vecernje novine (Evening Newspaper)*. The still-ruling Communist Party also offered criticism, mostly from its municipal committees and local branches of the Labor Union and War Veterans. But the public's response was highly positive. In those few years, *Oslobodjenje* finally halted a steady circulation decline and gained thousands of new readers, advertising revenues grew substantially, and the company was among the healthiest in the Republic.[3]

Oslobodjenje—along with Sarajevo Radio and TV—became a forum for the free expression of different views and ideas on the future of the country, supporting political pluralism and (federal Prime Minister) Ante Markovic's project for democratic and economic reform. Many Balkans media analysts missed that crucial point. The Bosnian media gained its professional independence while the Communists still ruled the republic. The media had carved out its own role in the anticipated pluralistic society without waiting for an uncertain election outcome. Zlatko Dizdarevic, one of the key editors of *Oslobodjenje* in the late eighties and early nineties, said in an interview, "I was extremely happy to belong to a generation of journalists, at that time mostly at *Oslobodjenje*, who managed to fundamentally change the practice of journalism in Bosnia. We also changed the public's long-standing perception of Bosnian journalism as rigid, controlled, and ideological throughout the decades of one-party rule."[4] Dizdarevic said that changing the character of the paper and of Bosnian journalism involved "swallowing some bitter pills" in printing the statements, opinions, and views of people opposed or even hostile to the tradition and culture of ethnic and religious tolerance. "But that was the price to pay for promoting professional standards, such as looking for the 'other side of the story,' and being an open-minded, pluralistic, liberal newspaper," he said. His list of *Oslobodjenje's* "bitter pills" was substantial: during the war in Croatia, printing a lengthy, two-part interview with Yugoslav Army Chief of Staff Blagoje Adzic that lacked all the appropriate, challenging questions; printing the highly nationalistic views of Serb writer-turned-politician Vuk Draskovic (respecting his right to reply to some previous criticism in *Oslobodjenje's* pages); or publicizing in the weekly *Nedjelja* an article by Radovan Karadzic, now an indicted war criminal, laying out the political platform of the still-to-be-founded Serb Democratic Party (SDS). Dizdarevic recalled:

> One day Karadzic came to our editorial office offering us an opinion piece. "We wrote it as a platform for a new party," he told me. I asked him who is the "we" who wrote the piece. "A group of my colleagues, Sarajevo friends who contemplate forming a political party," Karadzic said. The party was to become the SDS, not yet "Serbian" but "Socialist Democratic Party." That was his first appearance in public as the future president of the Serb party in Bosnia.[5]

Through public debate and working with the new reform-minded political leadership, Bosnian journalists made it a law that the three major media would be nonpartisan; their staff would select the editors and managers based on professional achievements and reputation; their journalists would not actively participate in any political party; and those who accepted a nomination for any public position had to put their work as journalists on hold. With the Serbian media under the "iron fist" of Milosevic's regime and bracing for confrontations with everyone else in the former Yugoslavia, and the Croatian media increasingly heeding the "patriotic call of duty" issued by the nationalist-totalitarian Tudjman regime, Sarajevo—once "the heart of darkness"—became a safe haven for freedom of expression. Yutel, the all-Yugoslav TV network, was forced to leave Belgrade and settle in Sarajevo. Belgrade journalists Dragan Babic, Aleksandar Tijanic, and Mirjana Bobic-Mojsilovic ran their call-in political talk show, "The Art of Living," from Sarajevo. They debated issues forbidden in Belgrade with their guests, political and civic leaders from throughout Yugoslavia. Sarajevo Radio, and later Television, produced a widely popular political satire show, "The Top List of Surrealists," poking fun at nationalist hysteria. Such freedom stimulated the culture more broadly. For example, some of the best Yugoslav movies and rock music of the time were produced in Sarajevo.

Media analysts and journalists failed to perceive or report that dramatic turnaround in which the Bosnian media liberalized while the Party took control of the Serbian media, turning it into a propaganda organ. Why? Most foreign reporters and media experts were based in Belgrade, the Yugoslav capital and center of the ensuing crisis. They were fascinated with the once-respected Serbian media's sharp decline into war propaganda. Some of those who wrote on the Yugoslav media without spending much time in Zagreb or Sarajevo picked up the stereotype, classifying the Belgrade media as "traditionally liberal" and the Bosnian media as "always controlled" without bothering to check on the changes in Bosnia. Some accepted the "media-are-all-bad-and-nationalistic" theory prevalent in Belgrade intellectual circles among those who needed a convenient excuse for not challenging the rising tide of nationalist propaganda in the Serbian media. Only those foreign correspondents based in Yugoslavia for a significant period of time noticed the change. Roy Gutman, who received a Pulitzer Prize in 1992 for his reporting on Serb "death camps" in Bosnia, reported in *Newsday* on May 1, 1991, that "in most of the republics, particularly in the two biggest, Serbia and Croatia, the press took up the fervent nationalism of leading politicians, fueling the ethnic tensions that have pushed the country far down the path to dissolution, if not self-destruction. . . . But Bosnia-Herzegovina was a different world. 'The air in Sarajevo was freer than anywhere else in Yugoslavia,'" Gutman reported, quoting Hari Stajner, a *Vreme* editor.

Encouraged by the relative prosperity of the reformist "Markovic years" (the late 1980s), a stable national currency, blossoming small private businesses, and a vibrant civil society, Bosnia seemed to be immune to the nationalist tensions developing between its two neighbors, Serbia and Croatia. The Bosnian mainstream media stood solidly behind the reformist policies of the federal government, supporting political pluralism and a market-oriented economy, and they were critical of both Milosevic's drive for Serbian domination and Tudjman's unilateral moves toward Croatia's independence. However, the pressure mounted on Bosnian Serbs and Croats to follow the "sacred national cause" as Belgrade called for "all Serbs in a single state" and Zagreb promoted Tudjman's Croatian Democratic Union (HDZ) as the "planetary party of all Croats." Squeezed between Serbia and Croatia, which were bracing for confrontation, Bosnia—with its multiethnic population—was vulnerable to the tensions in the region. Although the Bosnian media remained loyal to the tradition of inter-ethnic tolerance and refused to be drawn into nationalist propaganda, they couldn't protect Bosnians from the calls to arms coming first from Milosevic's Serbia and then from Tudjman's Croatia. The Bosnian media market was free and open to all. Sarajevo Television, in addition to its own prime-time news journal, regularly broadcast evening news from Belgrade and Zagreb on its second channel. Bosnian kiosks carried alongside *Oslobodjenje* all the newspapers from Belgrade and Zagreb, already deeply engaged in the "media war."

As Bosnian Serbs were increasingly intimidated into expressing loyalty to the "threatened Serbs" in Kosovo and Croatia, and as Bosnian Croats became more and more engaged in "the defense of the motherland," Bosnian Muslims, with no outside republic to view as their "other homeland," had to decide how best to protect Bosnia. Centuries of coexistence—a tradition and culture of living together in appreciation of differences—came under increasing pressure from nationalist movements with opposing and soon-to-be irreconcilable goals. With the Serbo-Croatian confrontation looming on the horizon, Bosnia's first free, multi-party elections in November 1990 became a kind of ethnic census: The vast majority of Muslims voted for the Muslim Party of Democratic Action (SDA), Serbs for the SDS, and Croats for the Croatian Democratic Union (HDZ). The three nationalist parties—united in their determination to win at any cost and worried that Bosnians might vote for Markovic's Alliance of Reform Forces (SRS) or the Social-Democratic Party of reformed communists—went so far as to encourage voters to vote for any one of the ethnic parties in order to generate a winning coalition against their major opponents.

Their strategy paid off, but once the three parties were in power, they immediately engaged in endless quarrels, with representatives of one or the other nationalist party walking out of parliamentary and cabinet sessions in protest over majority decisions. Yet there was one issue on which all three displayed perfect agreement: to take control of the republic's media. In March 1991, the three parties adopted a law under which they could appoint the editors and managers of all Bosnian media based on an agreed-upon "ethnic key." One party would have the position of editor-in-chief, the other of director general, the third of news desk editor, and so on—all the way to the editor of photography. Bosnian journalists realized that implementation of such a law would deprive them of the freedoms they had enjoyed even during Communist times. Together with radio and TV editors and the vast majority of journalists, *Oslobodjenje* opposed the law, publishing hundreds of letters from all parts of Yugoslavia in support of media freedom. We challenged government representatives to radio and TV debates, arguing in public that media organized by the nationalist parties would function exactly as their government did, with editors walking away in disagreement, unable to reach consensus on what to print. We staged a mass protest in front of the Bosnian Parliament and—most important—we challenged a new law in both the Yugoslav and Bosnian constitutional courts. The Yugoslav court granted us a stay of implementation until the case was considered before the Bosnian court, where I represented *Oslobodjenje*. On October 3, 1991, the court finally ruled in our favor, finding that the new law was not in accordance with the constitution of Bosnia and Herzegovina.

Thus, the Bosnian media—Sarajevo Radio and Television and *Oslobodjenje*—faced the events leading to the violent disintegration of Yugoslavia under entirely different circumstances than their colleagues in Serbia and Croatia. They fought and won two battles for independence, against both the departing Communist regime and the newly arrived nationalist parties, and they had no affiliation with either the government or the ruling nationalist parties. The SDS regularly charged that we were anti-Serbian, HDZ that we were anti-Croat, and SDA that we were anti-Muslim. "We wouldn't be so good if we were not so bad!" *Oslobodjenje* answered the criticism, borrowing from an ad for a controversial New York radio station and finding the attacks by nationalists in power the best investment in our credibility.

Covering the 1991 war in Croatia seriously tested both our professionalism and our objectivity. The war zones controlled mostly by the Serbs were off-limits for journalists of other ethnic backgrounds.

Oslobodjenje was blessed to have on its editorial staff veteran reporter Vlado Mrkic. He earned a reputation as a writer of deeply human, eloquent, captivating stories on the tensions between Serbs and Albanians in Kosovo in the 1980s. Mrkic confirmed that reputation while reporting on the Yugoslav Army siege of Vukovar and Dubrovnik in Croatia, and on an attack on the Croat village of Ravno in Bosnia Herzegovina in the fall of 1991. Mrkic's reports from the war zones differed sharply from anything in the Serbian or Croatian press: They weren't about "bloodthirsty Chetniks" or "genocidal Ustashas" but about people on the receiving end of the horrors of the war, their losses and suffering. While *Oslobodjenje* couldn't have reporters in all of Croatia's war zones all of the time and often had to depend on propagandistic wire services, Serbia's Tanjug and Croatia's Hina, we printed their conflicting claims and counterclaims side by side (instead of using just one of the services, as was the case with the media in the two republics at war).

If the Bosnian media had one constant line in the months leading to the war, it was their opposition to war. That's why the Serb nationalist party in particular took extreme measures to silence us six to seven months before the outbreak of war in Bosnia in April of 1992. With increased polarization in the country and within the republic on the future of Yugoslavia, Bosnia faced a no-win dilemma: to join the drive for independence by Slovenia and Croatia or to remain within Serb-dominated "Yugoslavia." The SDS in Bosnia aggressively promoted the ideology of "all Serbs in a single state." The HDZ also moved to take control of "historic Croatian lands" in Bosnia. Ironically, while a brutal Serbo-Croatian war raged, the two sides had reached a mutual understanding on plans to carve up "Serbian" and "Croatian" territories in Bosnia during the Milosevic–Tudjman talks in Karadjordjevo and elsewhere in the spring of 1991.[6] On October 14–15, 1991, in an endless session of the Bosnian Parliament debating Bosnia's options, SDS leader Radovan Karadzic issued a televised threat against any move toward Bosnian independence. "This might lead Bosnia into a hell and [cause] one people to disappear," he said in a direct threat to Bosnian Muslims.[7]

With two out of three ruling nationalist parties preparing the ground for both "Greater Serbia" and "Greater Croatia," Bosnia's multiethnic, tolerant, antiwar media became a major obstacle. More and more frequently, drivers distributing *Oslobodjenje* in Serb-majority areas were stopped at illegal checkpoints and the papers seized. Even though Sarajevo TV made it possible for Bosnian Serbs to watch the Belgrade TV Journal through regular broadcasts on its Channel 2, that didn't satisfy a party bracing for war. The SDS wanted Serb-only programming, with no opposing points of view, so they moved to take over the Bosnian TV transmitters by force. On August 1, 1991, eight months before the war in Bosnia began, Serb paramilitary supported by the Yugoslav Army seized a transmitter on Kozara mountain between Banjaluka and Prijedor. This effectively cut off from the Sarajevo TV signal a wide territory that included ethnically mixed towns; instead, viewers were directed toward Belgrade. After that, it was all Milosevic all the time. Constant war propaganda divided Serbs and Muslims who had lived together peacefully in Banjaluka, Prijedor, Sanski Most, Bosanski Novi, and dozens of other neighboring communities. Belgrade TV rhetoric concerning "threatened people," "the reawakening of the Ustasha," "national survival," "the Croat–Muslim conspiracy," and "the Islamic threat" replaced the traditionally balanced reporting of Sarajevo TV, gradually separating long-standing neighbors and even close friends. "This is a terror," my mother, Sena Kolonic, who lived in Prijedor with my stepfather, Kemal Kolonic, told me over the phone. "Even older people feel marked as enemies just because of their religion or name. We miss our TV so much." She was abruptly interrupted by the voice of a woman who had obviously been monitoring her telephone: "We'll soon send all of you Ustasha where you belong!"

Soon after Kozara, the paramilitary took over other transmitters—Pljesevica, Doboj, Trovrh, Velez, Vlasic—reducing Sarajevo TV coverage to less than half of the Bosnian territory. In the spring of 1992, during the takeover of the Vlasic transmitter, Sarajevo TV engineer Bajram Zenuni was killed and the rest of the crew taken prisoner. Thus, when a referendum on Bosnian independence was called for February 28–March 1, 1992, the voice of the Bosnian media supporting a democratic way of deciding the republic's future was not heard in the SDS-controlled territories. Nevertheless, 64 percent of Bosnians opted for independence. The SDS, supported by the Yugoslav Army, set barricades and checkpoints, blocking Sarajevo and reducing movement throughout the republic, and paraded artillery and armored vehicles through Bosnian towns, demonstrating its readiness for war. It seemed that war was imminent.

I joined a desperate last appeal for peace with the editors-in-chief of Bosnia's main media including Goran Milic of Yutel, Nenad Pejic of Sarajevo TV, and Milenko Vockic of Sarajevo Radio. All four of us made a short, personal statement, urging the people of Bosnia to refuse any party's call to attack their neighbors. Prime-time radio and television news as well as *Oslobodjenje* carried the appeal just before the outbreak of war.

Criticism followed from ruling nationalist parties and, less predictably, from some media analysts claiming that we contributed to "pacifying Bosnians in the face of imminent aggression." Nevertheless, peace was on the minds of most Bosnians. On April 5, 1992—ironically on the eve of the date forty-seven years earlier when the city had been liberated from the Nazis—Bosnians took to the streets of Sarajevo celebrating international recognition of Bosnia's independence. They chanted, sang, and danced for peace in front of Bosnia's Parliament. Tens of thousands of people came from Sarajevo neighborhoods chanting "Bosnia, Bosnia." Miners from Tuzla and Zenica came carrying pictures of Tito and posters calling for peace. The crowd of Bosnian Muslims, Serbs, Croats, and Jews sang in a single voice, "Let them hear in Serbia and the whole of Croatia that our Bosnia is a community of brotherhood." The demonstration was suddenly interrupted by sniper fire from the Holiday Inn, where the SDS leadership had their offices. While people ran for cover, a female medical student from Dubrovnik, Suada Dilberovic, and a clerk in the Bosnian Parliament, Olga Sucic, were killed by a Serb sniper at Vrbanja bridge. They were the first of more than 10,000 victims of the ensuing three-and-a-half-year siege of Sarajevo.

Still, the republic's mainstream media not only advocated but also represented, by the composition of its editorial staff, the tradition and culture of ethnic tolerance. Some of the best journalists at *Oslobodjenje* were Serbs: deputy editor Gordana Knezevic; assistant editor Branko Tomic; frontline reporters Vlado Mrkic and Rajko Zivkovic; the paper's best columnist Gojko Beric; cartoonist Bozo Stefanovic; and photographer Danilo Krstanovic, to name just a few. Knezevic, who came back to Sarajevo in August 1991 after a four-year stint as a correspondent in Cairo, admits that for a long time she felt like a foreign correspondent within the newsroom. In an interview, she discussed her early encounters with the war:

> At that time I knew more about political life in the Middle East than about the new political parties in Bosnia. I am not proud of my lack of knowledge, but with my friends and neighbors I shared the illusion that no one would dare to shell Sarajevo because he couldn't know who he is killing, since we were so mixed together. I didn't know that, in Milosevic's kitchen of evil, it was declared not only allowed but even desirable to kill not only non-Serbs but also Serbs mixed with non-Serbs. I believe that at the root of that concept was the intention to commit crimes that can't be forgotten, kill even the possibility of living together, so that borders drawn in blood between ethnic groups couldn't be erased ever again. Karadzic was a spokesman for apartheid based not on race but on ethnicity.[8]

In the early days of the terror, Radio and TV Sarajevo and *Oslobodjenje* kept their prewar editorial line of respect for Bosnia's diversity, but with one crucial difference: key RTV people left the city, while all key editors and managers of *Oslobodjenje* remained in Sarajevo. The sudden departure of RTV director general Nedjo Miljanovic, TV director Besim Ceric, and editor-in-chief Nenad Pejic soon left the now SDA-dominated Bosnian Presidency in a position finally to appoint people of their choice to all top positions. Sarajevo TV, renamed TV of Bosnia and Herzegovina, still abstained from spreading ethnic hatred and followed the official Presidency's Platform calling for the maintenance of a multiethnic state. But they nevertheless got too close to the ruling party, giving the SDA-dominated government uncritical support.

Pale TV's Satanic Jokes

In the early stages of the siege, with top managers and editors gone and new ones appointed by the SDA, Bosnian TV began to disintegrate along ethnic lines. By the summer of 1992, a number of its Serb editors and journalists had left the city, joining the newly established "Serb Radio and TV" in Pale, a mountain village some ten miles away from Sarajevo. Pale became the "capital" of the self-styled "Serb Republic," housing SDS headquarters from which its leadership coordinated the siege and shelling of Sarajevo. Pale TV Journal, anchored by some of the former Sarajevo Radio and TV journalists such as Risto Djogo, Ilija

Guzina, Dragan Bozanic, and others, was full of praise for Serb "liberating forces" that took over vast areas of Bosnia, from towns along the Drina River to Bosanska Krajina and Eastern Bosnia, in a campaign of terror that saw some of the worst atrocities in Europe since World War II. What was soon to be known in Western media as "ethnic cleansing," with concentration camps, mass executions, rape, looting, and the expulsion of hundreds of thousands of people from their homes, was celebrated on Serb TV as a "liberation."

Pale TV editor Risto Djogo was most memorable for his primitive hatred of Bosnian Muslims. People who watched his Journal day in and day out remember him sporting a long knife and saying, "And this is what we have for our former neighbors Balije [derogatory term for Muslims]." He would keep his bare feet in a pan of water, ridiculing a Muslim ritual before prayer. He accompanied a news report on a meeting in Geneva attended by a member of the Bosnian Presidency, Tatjana Ljuic-Mijatovic, with footage from a pornographic movie suggesting the immorality of her remaining, as a Serb, loyal to Bosnia. On the occasion of the massacre of civilians in the Sarajevo marketplace in February 1994, he finished his report by lying on the studio floor beneath the editorial desk, posing as a fake victim of shelling and exhibiting a traditional Serb three-finger salute as a symbol of "Serb victory."[9]

Miljenko Jergovic, a Bosnian writer working for the Croatian weekly *Feral Tribune*, remembered Pale TV in an interview: "Djogo was definitely the most evil media figure of that war. He was the only one who tried to make Serbs believe that shedding other people's blood could be a subject of fun, something even joyous. No one else was doing that. He disregarded death, projecting it as something positive."[10] Years after the war, *Oslobodjenje* columnist Gojko Beric remained puzzled as to why Sarajevans—while there was still electricity in the besieged city— regularly watched the Pale TV Journal, which was broadcast immediately after the Bosnian TV news at 8 p.m. Beric said in an interview:

> People were waiting for Djogo's evening Journal, like in some masochistic ritual, expecting to see how low it could get. In the beginning, there was still some disbelief that the war—with the killing of people in their homes, in the streets and parks, with Djogo and all the evil he represented—would last long. But later it became almost a need to see what kind of people were behind all that terror. I think that Djogo's primitive hatred produced an

unintended reaction among the Sarajevans—defiance and superiority against the evil—and I believe that, in the end, it contributed to the survival of the city.[11]

When Djogo's body was found in the water at a dam near Zvornik on September 13, 1994—following his "disappearance" in that town most probably at the hands of some of his "Serb heroes"—Jergovic wrote an essay listing some of his most memorable "Satanic jokes."[12] In one of them, in the winter of 1992–93, when Sarajevans were literally freezing and starving, Djogo said that they were the luckiest people in the world: While everyone else plays Lotto and gets nothing, they all have seven accurate "hits"—on their homes. Nor did he hesitate to make racist comments. Ridiculing horrifying stories of the mass rape of Bosnian women in Serb-held detention centers, he said, "Those converted Turk women claim that we are raping them and yet one of them just gave birth to a black baby in a refugee center." Telling that racist "joke," Djogo appeared with a black mask over his face. In his essay Jergovic wrote, "He was the first one who openly told Croats and Muslims, with a smile on his face, that Chetniks don't aim to subjugate them but to exterminate them."

Sarajevo TV journalists had not been surprised when Djogo or Guzina joined Pale TV: They both belonged to a group that, like the Bosnian Serbs' wartime leader Karadzic, lived and made their careers in the city but never fully accepted its cosmopolitan, multicultural spirit. Guzina enjoyed his sudden superiority over his former colleagues. Whenever another grenade exploded at the RTV building, he would call them at the newsroom, asking triumphantly, "How are you, *Balije?* Aren't you scared to death?" Much more shocking for them was to see people like Dragan Bozanic—a child of the city, a former track and field star, a foreign news editor, and fluent in English—leaving Sarajevo and joining the Pale war propagandists. Bozanic was seen following Serb General Ratko Mladic's troops on their "victory march" through the looted and torched Bosnian countryside, being warned on the air by the arrogant general, "If you don't report well, you might end up at the front lines."[13]

Pale TV did not need Mladic to tell them to "report well." In their coverage, they always went further than expected and often further than what actually happened. They specialized in inventing "terror against Serbs" in Muslim-held Sarajevo. On one occasion, they said that Serb children were being fed to the lions in the Sarajevo Zoo. On another occasion, they reported that "in last night's terror against prominent Serbs in Sarajevo," former soccer star and director of the Sarajevo Football Club Svetozar Vujovic had been killed. Vujovic appeared in public the next day. When he died of terminal illness a couple of months later, hundreds of Sarajevans of all ethnic backgrounds congregated at the Holiday Inn to pay their last respects to their fellow citizen.

Pale TV was routinely quicker than Karadzic's headquarters to deny any responsibility for shelling of the city by Serb forces. Ever since the breadline massacre in Vase Miskina Street on May 27, 1992, which claimed the lives of more than twenty Sarajevans and maimed dozens, Djogo and his staff would automatically claim that it was "Muslims killing their own people in order to provoke international intervention." One of the most notorious fabrications, attracting international attention, occurred in April 1995 when 17-year-old Maja Djokic was killed by shrapnel from a Serb-fired grenade at Sarajevo's city center. On April 11, two days after she died, Pale TV showed her body in the city morgue, stating that she was not a victim of Serb shelling as the "Muslim media" had said, but a victim of followers of (Bosnian President) Alija Izetbegovic. "On Friday night the Mulsims raped her, killed her, and threw her out on the plaza in front of the stadium. They had caught this unfortunate girl as she was trying to escape to the Serb part of Sarajevo," Pale TV claimed.[14]

But this time the lie was immediately uncovered. There was a witness to the murder, a Serb, Aleksandar Lucic, who had been selling flowers in Titova Street near the Bosnian Presidency building when he heard the familiar sound of an incoming shell and saw a flash, then a girl falling. He ran to help, taking her to the Kosevo Hospital in his car, but she was already dead of shrapnel wounds. The dead girl was also a half-Serb. She had been killed on her way home from volleyball practice. Roger Cohen of the *New York Times*, reporting on the tragedy, quoted her father, Branko Djokic: "There are perhaps 10,000 dead in Sarajevo, of whom perhaps 1,700 are children. So we cannot think that Maja's death was anything special. But of course she was our Maja, so we think it is special."[15]

Mladen Vuksanovic, Bosnian TV's award-winning author of documentaries before the war, provides rare insight into the workings of the Serb propaganda headquarters in Pale. Born in that town and residing there since 1984, he spent the first 110 days of the war isolated in Pale, refusing to join the nationalistic Serb TV. He eventually escaped with his family to Croatia taking with him his diary, which was later published as a book.[16] Vuksanovic chronicled, day by day, the intimidating pressure of his former colleagues who had left Sarajevo TV and who had been put up in Pale hotels by the SDS and tasked with creating a "Serb Informational Television Center." A woman journalist who had a close relationship with a doctor-politician who had first been an enthusiastic communist, then an enthusiastic reformist, and was now an enthusiastic Serb, called Vuksanovic from the Bistrica Hotel at the Jahorina ski resort, asking him not "whether" but "when" he was going to join them. After trying to find some excuse, he finally told her, "I am not an ethnic, but a professional journalist."[17] He describes late-evening visits by a former Sarajevo TV director, who had enjoyed all the freedom he wanted in Sarajevo but now claimed that he had been "threatened and thwarted" in his work. He was enjoying generous pay for his propagandistic services. Vuksanovic writes about an encounter in which the former director accused him of being a traitor: "I don't drink anything, he drinks brandy. With each new glass he is more and more angry with me and the 'Turks' who should be exterminated. He pulls a gun from his belt threatening me for not agreeing to work with them."[18] On Tuesday, April 14, 1992, Vuksanovic noted, "I am listening to my former colleagues calling 'their people' over Serb Radio to a final showdown with 'Islamic fundamentalism.' Only last year they were calling 'their communists' to a final showdown with nationalists."[19] On May 2, 1992, he wrote the following note: "Serb Radio is just announcing that 'no single grenade was fired from Lapisnica (near Pale) at Sarajevo.' While listening to that, I hear a thunder of cannons from Lapisnica. These people are the substance of lie, their substance is lie."[20] And he wrote of the breadline massacre on May 27, 1992 : "On Serb TV in Pale, my former colleague Rada Djokic says that [the attack] was done by Muslims, 'green berets,' to shock the world. I am beginning to hate my profession from the bottom of my soul. They are not journalists, they are professional murderers."[21] Vuksanovic left Pale on July 12, 1992. He settled on Croatia's island of Cres, working as a night guard, rather than serve the nationalist propaganda. He died of heart failure in exile in Croatia on October 24, 1999. He was 57.

Tolerance Under Siege

Covering the war in their own city and country presented Bosnian journalists with the ultimate personal and professional challenge. On a personal level, regardless of whether they were Muslim or Serb, Croat or Jew, they experienced the same terror: Their apartment buildings and neighborhoods were shelled from Serb artillery positions in the hills surrounding the city; their families were deprived of basic needs, from bread and milk to water and electricity; and yet they never blamed "Serbs" because many Serbs suffered the same as they. On a professional level, they still wanted to publish a daily with their editorial office building under constant artillery and machine-gun fire, without newsprint, without water or electricity, and without a phone/fax line to communicate or a kiosk to sell their paper.

The journalists at *Oslobodjenje* were a case in point. After the first shots were fired at *Oslobodjenje's* once elegant glass-and-aluminum building in early April 1992, I said at an editorial staff meeting that I wanted the paper published "as long as Sarajevo exists." I cited at least three reasons. First, we had a responsibility to the paper's tradition. *Oslobodjenje* had been started as the anti-Nazi movement's paper during World War II, and we couldn't just close it in the face of a new racist ideology. Second, we had a responsibility to the profession: If hundreds of foreign journalists could cover the war, how could we whose families, city, and country were at stake abandon the duty to report. And, finally, we had a responsibility to our readers: In the years preceding the war, *Oslobodjenje* had gained new respect in the eyes of the public for its fight for pluralism and against nationalism, and we couldn't leave our readers during the worst days of their lives. This last point proved to be the engine that kept us going.

On June 20, 1992, the *Oslobodjenje* building was set afire by incendiary bullets from Serb positions in Nedzarici, just 200 yards away, and—because Sarajevo still had electricity—people could see the paper's twin towers in flames on the late evening news. No one expected a paper out of that flame. But we moved the newsroom to an atomic bomb shelter underneath the building. While firefighters fought the flames, a sniper killed one of them, Avdija Aksamija. Undeterred, the paper hit the streets early the next morning, causing joy among desperate Sarajevans.

With no regular newsprint supply, we reduced the press run and the size and number of pages, printing during the worst periods just 3,500 copies in tabloid format. With telephone connections down, we installed radio equipment and communicated stories through a network of ham radio operators. With no electricity, we needed 100 liters of diesel fuel to type and print for just four hours a day, using candles the rest of the time. With no drivers or kiosks to distribute and sell the paper, journalists themselves volunteered to drive the paper through the sniper-covered streets and to sell it in their neighborhoods.

In the process, some of our staff members were killed. Kjasif Smajlovic, *Oslobodjenje's* correspondent in Zvornik, a town on the Drina river separating Bosnia from Serbia, was the first journalist killed in the Bosnian war. On April 9, 1992, Serbian paramilitaries entering the town found him in his correspondent's office, writing his report on the fall of the town, and killed him. According to an eyewitness, a woman who talked to his wife and son who had escaped the town the day before it fell: "They dragged him out of the office by his legs."[22] Later that summer, veteran photographer Salko Hondo went to take pictures of people waiting in line for water in Sarajevo's Ciglane neighborhood. As with many lines of Sarajevans waiting for water, bread, or the distribution of humanitarian aid, the people were shelled and Hondo killed. The next day the paper carried both his last picture, Sarajevans filling their canisters with water, and his obituary. The paper's accountant, Zuhra Besic, was killed by a sniper while on a company bus on her way home from work. Some *Oslobodjenje* employees and their loved ones were killed at home or on the street—as civilians—and dozens were wounded.

But others continued to work at great personal risk. One of *Oslobodjenje's* editors, Mehmed Husic, was trapped with his family in the besieged "Olympic Town" of Dobrinja on the outskirts of Sarajevo. In the spring of 1992, he reported the suffering of his neighbors both for *Oslobodjenje* and for Bosnian Radio and TV. From his apartment window he was able to see the barrel of a Serb tank trained at his building. Serb snipers made sure Husic and his neighbors knew they were within reach: They would fire at their balconies and occasionally into their apartments. Finally, on June 18, they came to the building's entrance, threw a hand grenade into the entry hall, and then forced their way into Husic's apartment: They took Husic, his wife Hana, and his children—

Melika, 13, and Omar, 7—to the neighboring prison known as Kula. While they were kept in prison, Pale TV sent a crew to interview Husic, who was obviously not free to say what he wanted to say with his loved ones in Serb armed forces' hands. "But I couldn't tell them what they wanted to hear either," Husic said in an interview.[23] Together with his wife and children Husic was later exchanged in one of the prisoner swaps for some captured Serb soldiers.

Despite all the threats and challenges, the paper never missed a day of publication throughout three and a half years of the siege. More important, it remained true to its tradition of respect for citizens of all ethnic and religious backgrounds. Even though some of the Sarajevo war stories, such as the crimes committed by renegade units and commanders of the Bosnian Army operating at the outskirts of the city, did not get full coverage, we did report individual crimes that we knew about. For example, in the first summer of the siege, we reported the murder of five members of a Serb Ristovic family and the "disappearance" of prominent SDS member Milutin Najdanovic, who was taken from his home and executed. That summer columnist Gojko Beric and I both editorialized against routine searches of apartments that most frequently targeted Serbs. Beric recalled:

> My front-page comment was one of the first to react against some of the self-styled "heroes of the city's defense" who took the law into their own hands, looting all remaining stores and committing the occasional murder in the process. Just one year later, I was afraid of my own comments. Any of those 'heroes' could have sent someone to just take me away or kill me. I didn't write that out of bravery, I wrote it as an act of civic protest, maybe naively.[24]

Knezevic, who replaced me as acting editor when I was hospitalized for a war-related injury, incurred during a high-speed car crash while escaping from a sniper-covered intersection, agrees that a dose of self-censorship was practiced at the paper. "One of the analysts, who spent just a couple of days in Sarajevo, cited an unpublished story on one of the renegade commanders, Musan Topalovic-Caco, taking people from the street to dig trenches as an example that *Oslobodjenje* 'wasn't entirely independent,'"[25] Knezevic recalled in an interview. She explained:

> It is true that I decided not to run that story since our rented downtown office was in the Stari Grad municipality, Caco's jurisdiction, and his soldiers—

Above left: On April 9, 1993, the author greets U.S. Senator Joseph Biden (D-Del.), right, at the entrance to the *Oslobodjenje* building, which had been repeatedly set on fire and destroyed by Serb incendiary bullets, mortars, and tank fire. The staff improvised a newsroom-bedroom in an atomic bomb shelter beneath the building and continued to publish every day during the three-and-a-half year siege of Sarajevo. (Photo: *Oslobodjenje*)

Below left: Another view of the author in front of the destroyed *Oslobodjenje* building shows the elevator shell of the newspaper's collapsed twin towers in the background. (Photo: *Oslobodjenje*)

Above: With the *Oslobodjenje* twin office towers destroyed, the staff continued to publish the paper daily from an underground atomic bomb shelter. They never missed an edition. Working on a new issue are, left to right, Slavko Santic, Branko Tomic, Boro Simic, and Amira Sehic. (Photo: *Oslobodjenje*)

engaged in open armed conflict with police in those days—could have just walked in and taken us all to the front lines, if not doing something even worse. Of course we were not totally independent of the circumstances of terror and siege.

Also, very few people in the besieged city were willing to tell reporters on the record about their personal experiences of mistreatment at the hands of lawless, armed "city defenders." In one instance, a well-known Sarajevo actor told an *Oslobodjenje* reporter about being taken from the street by Caco's men to dig trenches. The day we reported the story, he came to the office asking us to print his denial. "Please print that I never told you that I was forced to dig trenches," he pleaded. At the end, we printed a "clarification" stating that the man had asked us to print that he had never told us that story. On October 26, 1993, the Bosnian Army and police killed Caco and arrested dozens of other officers and soldiers, charging that they had conducted "a campaign of murder, robbery, and rape." Only then was it revealed that members of the two brigades had held dozens of people—mostly Serbs—in illegal prisons in the hills around Sarajevo and executed some of them.

Oslobodjenje wasn't the only newspaper operating in wartime Sarajevo, but it was the only one publishing every day of the siege. The other Sarajevo daily, *Vecernje novine*, struggled to keep publishing, facing all the obstacles *Oslobodjenje* faced. When they ran out of newsprint, *Oslobodjenje* devoted one of its eight pages to the paper, and *Vecernje novine* staff printed whatever they considered most important on that single page with their logo on it. The magazine *Dani (Days)* was first printed in the fall of 1992 under the name *BH Dani*. Published irregularly, depending on the availability of newsprint, the magazine distinguished itself for critical, in-depth coverage of the most delicate issues of the country at war and the city under siege, including criticism of Bosnian authorities and even army commanders. Led by publisher and editor Senad Pecanin, the magazine brought together some of the finest Bosnian writers including Ivan Lovrenovic, Miljenko Jergovic, Aleksandar Hemon, and Semezdin Mehmedinovic, as well as a score of young journalists such as Ozren Kebo, Vildana Selimbegovic, Karim Zaimovic, and Mladen Sancanin. Zaimovic, who had published since he was fourteen and was one of the most talented cartoonists in Yugoslavia, was killed at the age of twenty-four during the August 1995 shelling of the city. Well-written, unafraid of engaging issues that were sometimes too controversial for the mainstream media, *Dani* established a reputation as "the most independent medium anywhere in Bosnia."[26]

Another influential wartime magazine was *Slobodna Bosna (Free Bosnia)*, which, for some time during the siege, published on free territory in the Zenica region, smuggling some of its copies into besieged Sarajevo. Its editor, Senad Avdic, established a reputation for fearless criticism of the Bosniak authorities, and his often anonymous investigative team competed with *Dani* in trying to examine the most controversial issues in Bosnia. The Sarajevo media scene, even during the worst days of the siege, was also enriched by a number of independent electronic media. TV Studio 99 was known for editor Adil Kulenovic's extensive, open-minded late-night interviews with Bosnian personalities, including those critical of the government. Radio Zid (The Wall), founded by law professor Zdravko Grebo, offered a combination of the best music, international news, and its own lively call-in shows with citizens freely airing their anger and frustration with both those shelling the city and the Sarajevo authorities. There were also dozens of regional newspapers, radio, and TV stations throughout Bosnia, most often controlled by local authorities propagating their political agenda.

One TV news story broadcast on May 7, 1992, at the very beginning of the siege of Sarajevo captured everyone's attention. A tall, strong, seemingly boorish man left his home only to buy an increasingly rare commodity in Sarajevo, a loaf of bread. His unsuspecting three-year-old daughter ran after him. Suddenly, the familiar whistle of sniper bullets filled the air, and the child cried: "Daddy, I'm hurt." Moments later, while doctors were tending little Sanida's injury, fortunately not serious, a Sarajevo TV reporter asked her father, Rifet Bajrovic, "What would you do to the person who just shot your child?" "I'd like to meet him over a cup of coffee and ask him why he did this to me," the man replied. For a long time thereafter, this story stood as a symbol of the spirit of the city suffering in dignity.

The story is symbolic in another way too. A year later, Sarajevo TV invited the man to a studio, and he was still the same forgiving person. But the reporter, Rasim Borcak, insisted, "Who was it that shot your child?" "I don't know," the man said. "Your neighbors?" "Maybe my neighbors."

Afterwards, a Bosnian Serb journalist in Sarajevo, who supported his country's and his city's struggle for survival, pointed to that episode in which the reporter insisted on the neighbors as the ones who shoot, kill, and rape as the beginning of the subtle destruction of what was left of multiethnic tolerance in the city under siege. While only a few of the people interviewed for this book could remember any incident in which Sarajevo TV incited hatred the way Pale TV did throughout the war, many said that the station's close ties with the SDA made it less sensitive to the feelings of non-Muslims. The more Izetbegovic's party moved away from the official Bosnian Presidency's Platform, adopted in summer 1992 and advocating a single, multi-ethnic, all-inclusive Bosnia, the less Sarajevo TV felt obliged to provide a diversity of views and, sometimes, news.

Part of the problem was that all three top executives left the station in the early weeks of the war, giving the SDA a free hand to appoint editors of their choice—an outcome Bosnian journalists had fought so hard to avoid in 1991. Coupled with nationalist pressure for journalists to join "their people's" media, which caused some twenty Serb journalists to flee to the "Serb Republic" and ten Croats to Croatian "Herzeg-Bosna," the traditionally balanced ethnic makeup of the newsroom began to deteriorate. With each new round of personnel changes, the competence level of Bosnian TV decreased. The ruling party interfered more and more in running the program. In an interview with *Slobodna Dalmacija*, Ivica Puljic, a member of the first managing board who later left Sarajevo and settled in Washington, D.C., where he began working at the regional service of the Voice of America, pointed to one form of interference. TV editors would sometimes find out that one of their journalists had gone to cover one of the many peace talks in Geneva, London, or Lisbon only by watching footage from the airport showing a journalist, who had been handpicked by a politician, boarding the plane. "We couldn't figure out how the journalist got there, and no one in the office knew that he was traveling. What is worse, [he had a reputation as a poor journalist who] had no idea how to file a good story," Puljic said.[27]

To the credit of the remaining professionals, TV Sarajevo maintained a daily program throughout the siege. However, because of the loss of nine out of eleven transmitters, their broadcast barely reached outside the besieged capital, and it was almost impossible to get any footage from Serb- or Croat-controlled areas, which constituted more than 70 percent of Bosnian territory. Just covering the front lines of Sarajevo was a gigantic task. In the process, fifty-two employees of Bosnian TV lost their lives—some on assignment, some as conscripted soldiers, and some as innocent civilians—and many more were badly wounded. The program was usually reduced to no more than two hours daily, with archival material broadcast another ten hours. The mass exodus of staff could only decrease the quality of programming.

Senad Hadzifejzovic, who served as the editor-in-chief of Bosnian TV, said in an interview:

> I researched my files and found that since 1990 when I first edited the evening TV Journal, ninety people had performed that top role in the newsroom. Can you imagine, ninety people in a single decade serving as prime-time news editors on national TV? Regardless of the circumstances, it was a big mistake. Some of the young people grew with the experience and became good journalists, but you can't really promote someone into the most demanding position in the newsroom without a basic knowledge of journalism. Sometimes it was embarrassing to watch your own inexperienced reporter being fascinated just by the fact that he was at some exciting assignment. They tell you, "Good evening, we are at The Hague [War Crimes Tribunal]" or "We are at Pec [in Kosovo]," and they are happy just to establish their presence there without telling you the real story.[28]

The government, or SDA, interfered with the program routinely—before, during, and after the war, Hadzifejzovic said. "And they played on our key weakness: individuals, immature journalists, who just love to be close to political parties. They interfered through these individuals who voluntarily became moles in their own institution."

At the beginning of the siege, Sarajevo TV's coverage of the war was complemented by Yutel, which was housed in the same building. Goran Milic, Yutel's editor-in-chief, remembers those first months of the siege as, plain and simple, "a struggle between good and evil."[29] At that time, he said in an interview, it was still a fight to save the cosmopolitan city from the barbaric siege. But Yutel was increasingly marginalized. There was some sense in producing their own Journal as long as Sarajevo TV used the first channel and Yutel used the second. But with the siege, they were supposed to use exactly the same footage on the same channel on the same evening. Yutel was reduced to reporting to Sarajevans on what was going on in their neighborhood. "They knew it better than we," Milic said, adding:

> On one occasion, our rush to uncritically report the news as we received it from the Sarajevo Center of Public Safety, on the Bosnian Army liberating the Karadzic-held suburb of Ilidza, had even deadly consequences. People rushed toward Ilidza in celebration of the announced victory, but the report was not true, and Serb forces fired at them, killing two. Then we realized that it was one thing broadcasting reports from faraway war zones—for example, broadcasting reports from Vietnam in a comfortable Washington studio—and an entirely different thing to report the war on our own streets, under our own windows.[30]

Milic decided to offer all Yutel reports to Sarajevo TV and, soon after, the television station that had started with high hopes as an all-Yugoslav network closed down as Yugoslavia itself was disappearing in the deadly breakup.

The Bosniak Brand of Nationalism

With the Bosnian Serb and Croat nationalist parties carving up their own "ethnically cleansed" territories, inspired and supported by Serbia and Croatia, the Bosnian Muslims—who during the war adopted the historic name Bosniaks to differentiate between their religious identity (as Muslims) and their ethnic identity (as Bosniaks)—gradually developed their own brand of nationalism. That trend was very much encouraged by the European-led peace initiatives. From the beginning, Europeans tried to solve the Bosnian crisis through a traditional, colonial divide-and-rule model. They based all their proposals on the partition of the country, which was for all intents and purposes indivisible: Muslims, Serbs, and Croats lived together not only in the same towns but on the same streets and in the same apartment buildings; they attended the same schools and worked in the same companies. In March 1992, when the European Community negotiator from Portugal, José Cutileiro, introduced his proposal for a Bosnia divided into three ethnic cantons, there was no sizable town in the country that could be claimed as Muslim, Serb, or Croat. The proposal nevertheless gave Serb ultranationalists an excuse for "ethnic cleansing" in the territories they claimed belonged to the Serbs. When in January 1993 British Lord David Owen and former American Secretary of State Cyrus Vance introduced the next set of maps dividing Bosnia into ten ethnically-based provinces, Croat ultranationalists undertook a "cleansing" of their own in Herzegovina and Central Bosnia. By the summer of 1993, with Owen and Norwegian Thorwald Stoltenberg introducing the idea of Bosnia as the confederation of three ethnic states, the Bosniak political leadership abandoned—in deeds, if not in words—any effort to preserve a multiethnic Bosnia. Squeezed into barely 25 percent of the Bosnian territory along the Sarajevo–Tuzla–Zenica corridor and in surrounding enclaves between large parts of the country controlled either by Serb or by Croat forces, the Bosniak nationalist SDA began to create its own Muslim mini-state.

It is within that geopolitical context that those still supporting the tradition and culture of tolerance in multiethnic Bosnia—in the state institutions, in the Bosnian Army, in the media and the broader civil society—lost any realistic hope for their cause. The mood in the summer of 1993 among Serb and Croat journalists at *Oslobodjenje* was somber. We were all concerned about the future of a multiethnic newspaper in an ethnically divided country. We held a series of editorial staff meetings, agreeing on one point and printing it as a promise to our readers: No matter what kind of "new realities" might be imposed on us, there were still certain values and principles worth fighting for. From that point on, however, the voice of tolerance was not heard in any of the peace talks where proposals leading to the de facto partition of the country prevailed. Serbs and Croats were increasingly marginalized in all walks of life in territories under the SDA-dominated Bosnian government control. The Bosnian Army and police, which at the beginning of the war had prided themselves as the multiethnic force fighting for their country, became increasingly Muslim-only, and the deputy commander of the army, Serb general Jovan Divjak, resigned because, as he put it, he didn't want to be "just the ethnic flower arrangement." The time was ripe for the rise of Muslim extremism. With tens of thousands of Muslims already killed, tortured, raped, and humiliated at the hands of Serb and Croat armed forces— and with hundreds of thousands expelled from their homes and towns—the Muslim population became easy prey to a well-financed campaign of radicalization.

The campaign began, not surprisingly, with *Ljiljan,* a magazine affiliated with a Zagreb mosque, gradually infiltrating Bosnia's Islamic community. Asked why the paper began to call the Croats "Ustasha," one of the editors, Nedzad Latic, told a reporter, "Well, I had to do something to force my people to wage war and think with their own heads."[31] Soon there were other publications, such as *Zmaj od Bosne (Dragon of Bosnia)* in Tuzla and the weekly *Bosniak,* calling for revenge against Serbs and to a lesser extent against Croats, not making any distinction between the guilty and the innocent. "Every Muslim should have his own Serb to kill," Zilhad Kljucanin wrote.[32] The Zenica office of the Islamic Religious Community issued its own "Instructions to a Muslim Fighter" by Halil Mehic and Hasan Makic, suggesting that it was "up to the military command to decide whether it was more beneficial and more in the interest of the cause, to liberate, exchange, or liquidate an enemy prisoner."[33] Emir Imamovic, writing about the worst examples of incitement to hatred in the Bosnian media on all three sides lists a number of similar examples in the writings of Kljucanin and other authors in Muslim newspapers.[34] In an editorial in *Ljiljan* on February 23, 1994, Kljucanin wrote: "In Ugljevik there are 500 Serb orphans. Mashallah! The Army of Bosnia Herzegovina has sent to hell around 50,000 chetniks so far. Eyvallah! Serb mothers will be giving birth in the future, as Ibrisim would say, to ice cubes instead of children. Insallah! A Serb approaches being a man only when he is dead or imprisoned."

Adnan Jahic, who would later become the official spokesman for the SDA, contributed to the increasing insecurity of Serbs remaining in Bosnian Army-controlled territory when he wrote in *Zmaj od Bosne:* "The vast majority of Serbs who have remained in the free territory controlled by the Bosnian Army have done so only because until this very day they did not have an opportunity to go to 'their' territory or because they are performing certain tasks for their masters. There is no third reason [for their staying]."[35] Jahic was also the author of an article laying the ground for a strictly Islamic state "after the war when we, Bosnian Muslims, remain alone with ourselves in our own state."[36] He argued for a state based on "authentic Islamic values." In such a state, he wrote, "Muslim ideology will dominate the entire state-political system, from the state and national symbols, through national policy to education, social, and economic institutions and, of course, family as the nucleus of the whole state." The fact that he later became a spokesman for the ruling Bosniak party seriously undermined its claim to represent the ideals of a tolerant multiethnic Bosnia.

This a priori suspicion of Serb neighbors became a regular feature of the extremist Muslim media. It was then used as grounds for apartment searches and other kinds of intimidation, including the takeover of Serbs' "abandoned" apartments and businesses by well-connected rogue elements of the Bosniak armed forces. Even the president of the Alliance of Journalists of Bosnia Herzegovina, Enver Causevic, joined the chorus. In an article in *Ljiljan* on February 9, 1994, he listed a number of Serb and Croat journalists who allegedly crossed "to the other side," which included many who had upheld journalistic standards and ethics and had left the country for personal reasons. In this way, Causevic only replicated what the Serb ultranationalist media had been doing all along: They constantly attacked all Serb journalists still working for Bosnian media in Sarajevo as "traitors" and "Alija's [Izetbegovic] servants." On one occasion, in the summer of 1993, Serb Television in Pale ran a commentary by Dragisa Cosovic, himself a former Sarajevo journalist working for the tabloid *AS*, in which he listed by name Serb "journalist-traitors" from *Oslobodjenje*. For some of them whose families lived in Serb-controlled areas, this amounted to a clear threat to the safety of their loved ones.[37]

Even the most symbolic and most intimate expression of the culture of tolerance, the so-called "mixed marriages" so common in Bosnian cities, became a target of ultranationalist attacks. In a series of articles written by close Izetbegovic associate Dzemaludin Latic and then-Bosnian minister of culture Enes Karic, *Ljiljan* denounced those marriages as the result of "ideological abuses" of the Communist era and in plain racist language called the children of such marriages "disoriented."[38]

Karic also suggested in his *Ljiljan* article that *Oslobodjenje* was in the service of the West, asking a question aimed at compromising the paper's position among the Bosniaks: How was it, he wrote, that *Oslobodjenje* had newsprint at a time when Sarajevo children didn't have powdered milk? I responded in *Oslobodjenje* that, first, everywhere else in the world, the government is responsible for people's basic necessities, including milk, while newspapers only conduct their own business;

and, second, if his cheap logic equating newsprint and milk should be accepted, was his luxuriously produced translation of the Koran a higher priority than powdered milk in the besieged city?

Ljiljan's systematic campaign against anything still multiethnic in Sarajevo culminated in attacks against non-Muslim intellectuals still supporting an all-inclusive Bosnia, including poet Marko Vesovic and journalist Gojko Beric, and against all secular Bosniaks who challenged the rising Islamization of public life. It was increasingly difficult to be a non-Muslim in Sarajevo. But as my colleague Gordana Knezevic pointed out, it was almost unbearable to live in Sarajevo at all, regardless of your ethnic background. As a Serb in Sarajevo, she was afraid of the same grenades as her Muslim, Croat, or Jewish neighbors, or those who did not even care about their ethnic background. She survived on the same humanitarian assistance as all her neighbors in Kosevsko Brdo (the Sarajevo neighborhood where she lived). She recalled in an interview:

> Since I spent most of the day at *Oslobodjenje* and my husband Ivo—who, as you know, is a Croat—worked for the Bosnian government, our son Boris was at home, but he wasn't hungry because our Muslim neighbor Kana Kadic took care of him. He couldn't go to school for three years because of the siege, but with Kana and her family he learned more than they teach at colleges. My life in Sarajevo was a life in two surreal ambiences—my neighborhood and *Oslobodjenje*—where no one was marked by his nationality. You didn't have to be of a certain nationality to know that the Muslims were the prime target of that war and that they were supposed to be eliminated by Milosevic–Tudjman design to destroy multiethnic Bosnia. Until the war, I was not even aware of the meaning of multiethnicity, but once it was denied by terror, when what was the best in our lives became a curse, I realized that [multiethnicity] was my identity, and I wanted to preserve it. That's how I became a "traitor" to the Serb national cause.[39]

Another Sarajevo journalist and writer, Miljenko Jergovic, a Croat, expressed similar feelings when asked to compare the media environment he left behind in Sarajevo and the one he found in Croatia when he went to Zagreb after almost sixteen months of the siege. He said in an interview:

> It was a very strange feeling. Sarajevo was bombarded and there was that everyday terror of grenades. On the other hand, on the level of the media, I felt completely protected, in my own world. At least, until that point of the war—early summer of 1993—there was nothing in the Sarajevo media that would make anyone feel threatened because of their ethnic or religious back-

ground. Then I went to Zagreb and experienced a shock of a different kind. I felt personally threatened by almost all the media, by their perception of the war. There was an indifference toward the suffering of Sarajevo—in the media, but not among ordinary people I met—and I felt the media systematically shaping the feeling that would lead to direct aggression against Bosnia, a feeling that I perceived as aggression against me personally.[40]

Serbia: Media Propagandists Fuel Bosnia War

The Serbian media were already veterans of war propaganda by the time the international community recognized Bosnia's independence on April 6, 1992. That very day, Serb paramilitary forces supported by the Yugoslav Army attacked the new country. During the months preceding armed conflict, the Belgrade daily *Politika* carried a number of reports aimed at raising the fighting spirit of Serbs. A December 1, 1991, headline boldly declared, "Serbs Are Not Scaring Anyone, But They Are Not Scared by Anyone," on a report about the unveiling of a bust of Serb King Petar the First Karadjordjevic[41] in the Bosnian town of Mrkonjic-Grad, a ceremony charged with nationalism. On that occasion, Bosnian Serb leader Radovan Karadzic compared the Serb people to "a good giant just waking up," and his close associate Nikola Koljevic warned the Serbs "to think with whom they want to live in the same state." The next day the paper headlined a report on the Bosnia Presidency's call for peacekeeping troops as Alija Izetbegovic's "Hellish Plan with the 'Blue Helmets.'" The article reported a threatening statement issued by the self-styled Serb province of Bosanska Krajina that Serbs were ready to oppose the deployment by all means, "including armed struggle." On December 6, under a headline "The Future of Bosnia Will Not Be Decided by The Hague," *Politika* quoted Karadzic as insisting on talks between Bosnia's "three ethnic communities" to begin the following week; otherwise "we are not going to accept responsibility for what might happen." The report on the Bosnia Presidency's request for independence was printed under the front-page headline "Bosnia at the Edge of an Abyss." In reaction to the Presidency's request, sent to the European Community within the established criteria for the dissolution of the Yugoslav federation, the Serb leadership announced their unilateral decision to declare a "Serb Republic" within Bosnia. By the end of December, the paper blamed both Muslim and Macedonian politicians who also had opted for independence for making a "fatal mistake." In an interview with Milosevic's party vice president, Mihajlo Markovic, published on December 25, *Politika* announced "the beginning of the creation of a new Yugoslavia" saying that, in addition to Serbia and Montenegro, it would comprise "Serb republics" in both Bosnia and Croatia. With the Bosnian referendum on independence approaching, *Politika* stirred anti-Muslim sentiments by claiming that "Muslimania"—their name for an independent Bosnia—would be created just in time for the Muslim holiday of Eid-el-Fitr. The stage was being set for armed confrontation.

The last American ambassador to Yugoslavia, Warren Zimmerman —reviewing Mark Thompson's book *Forging War: The Media in Serbia, Croatia and Bosnia-Herzegovina*—writes that Milosevic had skillfully used the press to justify "unspeakable atrocities." He notes that in both the Croatian and Bosnian wars, the Serbian strategy involved five consecutive stages:

> First the Serbian leaders would accuse the enemy of dreadful ethnic crimes, some true, most false. Then, borrowing from the Vietcong, they provoked violent incidents in ethnically mixed villages, causing the escalation of violence and numerous deaths, which could be publicized with the appropriately horrifying pictures. The next stage brought in the Yugoslav Army, which is controlled by the Serbs, ostensibly to "restore order" but really to consolidate Serb territorial gains. The fourth step was to set up Serbian "states" within the territory of Croatia—as in the Krajina—or Bosnia; this step was accompanied by strong support from the mass media for the "principle of self-determination." Finally, Milosevic arranged for direct Serbian assistance to Serbs in Croatia and Bosnia across international borders, proclaiming in the press that all Serbs have the right to live in the same state.[42]

With the mainstream media firmly in his hands, it was easy for Milosevic to sell his version of the war in Bosnia. Even long after the first Serb grenades exploded in Sarajevo, the Belgrade media reported only on some "fighting in Sarajevo" and "Serb forces successfully resisting Muslim fanatics-green berets-fundamentalists-mujahadin-jihad warriors' attacks." The breadline massacre in Sarajevo's Vase Miskina Street in which nineteen civilians were killed and 157 wounded was not reported on Serbian TV until four days later when the Serbian government issued a statement condemning the shelling of Sarajevo by the Bosnian Serb forces. The statement, hastily read at 6 p.m., was targeted more to an international audience than to local viewers as a last-ditch effort by the Milosevic regime to defuse the outrage and, more important, to escape imminent UN sanctions.[43]

Even much later, the Belgrade media still favored the Pale TV version of what had happened, accusing Muslims of staging the massacre in order to provoke international sympathy and intervention. Both Bosnian Serb politicians and Serbian media used that line, that Muslim forces had bombed their own civilians, throughout the deadly Sarajevo siege, April 1992 to November 1995, that left more than 10,000 people dead—1,800 of them children—and much of the city's cultural heritage and business and social infrastructure destroyed. All subsequent killings of Sarajevans were followed instantly by the Serb media claim of "Muslims killing themselves"—including the marketplace killing of sixty-eight people on February 5, 1994, and another forty-one on August 28, 1995; the shelling of a school in Alipasino Polje in which the teacher, Fatima Gunic, and three children were killed; and numerous incidents of civilians killed while waiting for water. Former Sarajevo TV reporter Rada Djokic gave the most memorable description of the siege of Sarajevo: "The Muslim authorities are holding Sarajevo under siege from within. The Serbs continue to defend their centuries-old hills around Sarajevo."[44]

In those days there was no room for professional journalism in Serbia's state-controlled media. Anyone still advocating minimal professional standards or ethics risked not only being taken off the air but also off the payroll. In January 1993, some of the most respected Serbian TV journalists—including Cedomir Mirkovic, Mihailo Kovac, Danka Novovic, Ivan Brzev, Dragan Nikitovic, Jarmila Celovic, and others—were sent to "compulsory vacation" and effectively removed from work. Hundreds of people in both radio and TV were "temporarily dismissed" without notification or the option to appeal the dismissal. Some of them discovered that they were no longer welcome only when they came to the entrance of the TV building where a computer installed next to the guard's office listed people whose work IDs were still valid. Those not on the list were required to turn in their IDs and could enter only as a visitor. Approximately fifty radio journalists, some of them with more than twenty years of experience, also made the list of "undesirables" including Rade Radovanovic, Slobodan Stupar, Olivija Rusovac, and Branislav Canak. One of the dismissed, Milica Pesic, told a *Borba* reporter that she was honored to be on that list: "I've never been in better company."[45] For the next year, Pesic and another former TV journalist, Branka Mihailovic, wrote a column for *Borba*, analyzing Serbian TV coverage of the war in Bosnia. "For a whole year, there was just one piece of footage on the Sarajevo siege in the prime-time news at 7:30 p.m., one Sarajevo building on fire. One picture in one year. That was all. People who were watching Serbian TV had never seen [the siege of] Sarajevo," Pesic said in an interview.[46]

On the fiftieth anniversary of the Yugoslav news agency, Tanjug, Serbian TV ran an exceptionally long interview that Milosevic had granted to eleven handpicked media editors in Belgrade: Slobodan Jovanovic, director of Tanjug; Dusan Zupan, Tanjug's chief editor; Zivorad Minovic and Hadzi Dragan Antic from *Politika;* Mile Kordic from *Politika ekspres;* Rade Brajovic from *Vecernje novosti;* Slavko Curuvija from *Borba;* Dragoljub Milanovic from Belgrade TV; Momir Brkic from Belgrade Radio; Dragan Kojadinovic from NTV Studio B; and Aleksandar Tijanic from Television Politika. One of the highlights of the interview was Kordic's question: "Why is Europe so afraid of Great Serbia when there is a Great Britain and a Great Germany and other great countries? What is, in your opinion, the role of the Vatican in all this?" Milosevic answered:

> Europe consists of Greece and Great Britain, but also Germany and, in a way, Turkey. So this is a question of the strategic interest not of Europe but of those powers that want to control this region and use it as they please, the powers that came up with that Carrington plan to break up Yugoslavia into bits and pieces, and then break up Serbia in the next phase in order to establish, through various puppet authorities, a situation in which there would be no serious, independent, free, and militarily significant state in this region. That is the reason, and not because they are afraid that we will attack them. They know that this nation has never waged a war of conquest. It has always fought defensive wars.[47]

There was no one to ask the president—if not in honest disagreement, then just for the sake of livelier discussion—"How can you fight defensive wars in other countries' territories?"

Vreme magazine was among the rare exceptions in the Belgrade media, offering not-quite-official versions of the war. For example, it carried an article challenging the prevailing explanation of the war. It was written by Stanko Cerovic, head of the Radio France International Serbo-Croatian service in Paris. Cerovic wrote:

I don't know when exactly during the war I became aware that political explanations were ridiculously inadequate for the degree of violence. I counted the causes: mentality, the Communist heritage, the secret police, a pampered army, Serb nationalism, a corrupt intelligentsia, a perfidious bureaucracy, Serbian President Slobodan Milosevic, television, folklore, the moral and intellectual crises, the Greater Serbia project, a set of incredible circumstances, and when all this is added together and the explosive power of such a mechanism built into the head of a weak person, it is still difficult to understand or find an explanation for the cold-blooded slitting of throats, the kicking of people, the dismembering of children and girls![48]

Vreme also exposed one of the most outrageous fabrications of the "news," aimed at inciting hatred through the Serbian media. The magazine discovered that *Vecernje novosti*, a paper that once prided itself on being the largest-circulation newspaper in Yugoslavia, had published a 115-year-old painting, exhibited in the Belgrade National Museum, claiming that it was a photograph of a Serb orphan boy whose parents had been killed in a Muslim offensive in Bosnia. "The boy has been adopted by a family in Zvornik and he's now enrolled as a ninth grader in a military school," *Vecernje novosti* stated in an article on children as the greatest victims of the war. The paper failed to report the boy's name or the names of his parents, but *Vreme* knew that the real "father" was Serb painter Uros Predic, who had painted the watercolor entitled "Orphan on His Mother's Grave" in 1879. The paper's fabrication "was just like the stories about the thirty babies in Vukovar and the necklaces made from the eyes and bones of Serb children," Nenad Stefanovic wrote.[49]

But the independent, antiwar media such as *Vreme* and Radio B92 were limited in their outreach and unable to seriously undermine the government's propaganda campaign. Veteran *Politika* foreign correspondent Dusan Simic recalled in an interview an interesting story about how the government took care to close any loopholes in the uniform presentation of the Bosnian war. Simic was a correspondent in London. In 1992 and 1993 he was able, by quoting the British media, to add to his reports at least some facts concerning what was going on in Bosnia. Early in 1993 during the first Serb blockade of the town of Srebrenica, he sent an article quoting the United Nations High Commissioner for Refugees' representative

Larry Hollingworth, who said that "those who shelled the town, wounding women and children, should burn in the hottest part of hell."[50]

"It was a pretty emotionally written report, and I was glad and even surprised to see it printed almost in its entirety in the first evening edition of *Politika* that I was receiving as a correspondent," Simic said. It was only later that he was told the rest of the story. *Borba* journalists, who regularly checked the rival's first edition to see if there was something worth quoting, used Simic's *Politika* report in their morning edition. But in *Politika's* morning edition, the report from London had disappeared. Simic told me: "That was the end of any possibility to report objectively on the Bosnian war. Very soon we correspondents received a letter advising us 'not to deal with those issues,' since that would be covered by Tanjug [the state news agency], while we should cover events only in the countries we report from."[51]

Borba, which under Stanislav Marinkovic's and Manjo Vukotic's editorial leadership in the late 1980s to early 1990s became a respectable daily, presented a challenge that Milosevic's government did not want to tolerate for long. The paper did not have direct access to the war zones and relied heavily on Serb propaganda machinery such as Tanjug and the Bosnian Serbs' wire service SRNA (Serb News Agency), but it was more open to printing different views either through guest columnists or through its own interviews and a more balanced use of international sources. The government decided to take the paper over by challenging the legality of its privatization in Markovic's time. Claiming that the process had been illegal, authorities decided that *Borba* still belonged to the federal government. The timing of the takeover was carefully planned, as was everything else in Milosevic's silencing of the opposition.

On Christmas eve 1994, a time when *Borba's* international supporters and foreign media usually took their holiday break, the phone rang at the desk of then editor-in-chief Gordana Logar. Federal Minister of Information Dragutin Brcin asked her to meet him at the paper's office early that evening. Logar recalled:

He came at 7 p.m. with two men I didn't know. Later I was told that one of them was former *NIN* editor Teodor Andjelic, and the other the editor of Radio Yugoslavia and one of the key figures in Mira [Mirjana] Markovic's

[Milosevic's wife] YUL party. Brcin told me: "Mrs. Logar, I have come to inform you that you are no longer the editor-in-chief. From now on, it will be me, that's how the Business Court ruled at 3 p.m. today." I told him, "Welcome, Mr. Brcin, come in. Do you want a cup of coffee?" Then I asked the man behind him, "And who are you?" He said, "I am Ivan Markovic, a new director." I told him I couldn't help him, since I didn't know enough about management, so I could talk with Mr. Brcin only. "You should leave us alone," I told him and he left.[52]

Brcin asked to use her phone, and she left the office, telling people in the newsroom that she was no longer their editor. Brcin called Tanjug to say the agency could release the prepared news of his taking over *Borba*, and while he was still in the office talking with Logar, dozens of foreign correspondents as well as other Belgrade and *Borba* journalists congregated at the paper's offices. Brcin asked Logar, "How did you manage to invite all these people?" "It wasn't me, it was you, with the release," she replied. "They all read wire dispatches." News of the takeover became an instant international scandal, bringing an outpouring of support for *Borba*. The presence and support of Serbian opposition figures such as Nebojsa Popov and Mile Isakov, as well as dozens of university professors and other intellectuals, encouraged Logar and most of her staff to defy the government. For the next five days, two papers appeared in Belgrade with the same name: *Borba*. The government's *Borba* was offered at kiosks, while Logar's *Borba* was printed in the smaller Glas printing house in some 5,000 copies and sold in the streets by volunteers that included some of Serbia's finest intellectuals. "Is that *our Borba?*" people buying the paper from the hands of prominent citizens asked, and that's how the new daily—*Nasa Borba (Our Struggle)*—was born. "There was such enthusiasm for our struggle to preserve an independent voice that on New Year's eve dozens of citizens brought us all sorts of food to make a memorable celebration of our last days in the old *Borba* building," Logar said. *Nasa Borba* was printed in Novi Sad, using newsprint donated by the European Union, but by the end of 1995, the paper ceased to exist following a dispute between the editorial board and the paper's majority owner and publisher, Dusan Mijic, over his decision to appoint a new editor without consulting the board.

Kostunica Defends Srebrenica Massacre

The last year of the Bosnian war, 1995, was marked by Milosevic's effort to present himself as a peacemaker. With Serbia exhausted by economic sanctions and the exertions of war, he decided to leave both Croatian and Bosnian Serbs to their own fate, letting the former capitulate to a Croatian Army offensive and pressing the latter to accept the international peace proposal. The Serbian media, which had already reprogrammed from war to peace mode, did not give much attention to the last and the ugliest barbarity of the war in Bosnia, the Serb takeover of the supposedly UN-protected "safe zone" of Srebrenica with the mass execution of more than 7,000 people in a matter of days. Even the televised statement of Serb General Ratko Mladic, "The moment has finally come to take revenge on the Turks,"[53] did not prompt any interest in Belgrade for the fate of the thousands of men from Srebrenica. *Politika* carried a statement by the president of the Democratic Party of Serbia, Vojislav Kostunica, entitled "Srebrenica— A Defensive Action." Borrowing the favorite Serbian propaganda line throughout the Balkan wars of the nineties, Kostunica defended the takeover of Srebrenica—which would become internationally known as "Europe's worst massacre since World War II"[54]—by calling it "a counteroffensive and defensive action against the activities of Muslim forces in an area that was supposed to be a protected zone."[55] The International Criminal Tribunal for the Former Yugoslavia, in announcing the indictments against Serb political and military leaders Radovan Karadzic and General Ratko Mladic, gave the following description of what happened in and around Srebrenica: "The evidence tendered by the Prosecutor describes scenes of unimaginable savagery: thousands of men executed and buried in mass graves, hundreds of men buried alive, men and women mutilated and slaughtered, children killed before their mothers' eyes, a grandfather forced to eat the liver of his own grandson. These are truly scenes from hell, written on the darkest pages of human history."[56] The most comprehensive international report issued on Srebrenica dismisses all the major points Kostunica had made in defense of that crime: First, the UN had repeatedly expressed its satisfaction with the demilitarization of Srebrenica prior to the Serb takeover; second, it found that the Bosnian army in Srebrenica "posed no significant military threat" to Serb forces; and third, contrary to Serb claims that Muslim forces conducted terror from within the "safe zone," it was established that in the month before the takeover there was first an attack in which "a Serb raiding party entered the enclave, ambushed and reportedly killed a number of Bosniak civilians," and then a raid by Bosniaks against the Serb village of Visnjica on June 26 in which "several houses were burned, and according to Bosniak sources, two people were killed, or according to Serb sources, four."[57]

By that time, the state-controlled media in Serbia had been instructed to ease up on their support for the "brothers" in Croatia and Bosnia. Consequently, they remained ignorant of the exodus of Serbs from Croatia and of the losses the Bosnian Serbs suffered in the closing months of the war. While Milosevic was enjoying a major role in the final negotiations leading to the end of the Bosnian war, his cronies were busy getting rid of the man who had been too closely associated with war propaganda, *Politika* director Zivorad Zika Minovic. "On Sunday, October 5, at an odd time—5 a.m.—two inspectors from the Belgrade police arrested Minovic in his office, pushed him into a 'Fica,' the smallest Fiat car, and took him for a 'brief conversation.' Some fifteen hours later, when he was eventually released, Zivorad Minovic no longer held any position," *Vreme* reported.[58] Minovic was not needed anymore. A chapter in the history of Milosevic's manipulation of the Serb media had been closed—with more to come.

Croatian Media Set the Stage for War

By the time Serbian forces attacked Bosnia in the spring of 1992, the mainstream media in Croatia—with the war in their own territory behind them—were already solidly in the Tudjman government's hands. While well-trained in "patriotic reporting," even in "lying for the homeland," their initial reporting on Bosnia was largely influenced by conflicting attitudes at the control center itself. On the one hand, Serbs were the enemy, still occupying large parts of the Croatian areas of Kninska krajina and Slavonija. On the other, they were also tacit allies, as Tudjman even before the war had conspired with Milosevic to divide Bosnia for the mutual benefit of both "Greater Serbia" and "Greater

Croatia." The conflict was evident in the Croatian daily *Vjesnik's* coverage of the internationally sponsored peace talks on the future of Bosnia in 1993. The paper almost triumphantly reported on international proposals to partition the country.[59]

Croatia's media reports on Serb atrocities in Bosnia were uneven in the first year of the war. The media used "Chetnik crimes" in the neighboring country mainly to prove the bestial nature of the enemy in the still unsettled dispute in Croatia. The coverage also reflected some level of denial of Bosnia's statehood, which could later justify Croat claims to Bosnian territories they considered "historically Croatian." The media underreported the Croatian troops' surrender of the Bosnian towns of Bosanski Brod and Jajce, widely suspected to have been part of a previously agreed-upon Milosevic–Tudjman plan. Reporting on Serb and Croat nationalist policies within Bosnia also showed a double standard: While the "Serb Republic" and "Serb Army" were referred to as "self-styled" and "so-called," their ideological twins—the "Croat Republic of Herzeg-Bosna" and its military wing, the Croatian Defense Council (HVO)—were treated with full recognition and respect.

This slanted reporting helped to set the stage for a full-scale Croatian onslaught against Bosnia in 1993. With Serb forces occupying almost 70 percent of Bosnia, and international mediators coming up with yet another design for ethnic division of the country—this time the Vance–Owen plan for ten provinces, three of which would be Croat-majority—Tudjman moved to take control of "his territory." "Herzeg-Bosna" authorities issued an ultimatum to the Bosnian Army and police to submit to Croatian authority in a somewhat expanded "Croatian territories." Bosniaks who had been "ethnically cleansed" from Bosnian territories occupied by Serbs refused to obey the order. By spring, a full-scale conflict broke out with the direct involvement of neighboring Croatia's forces. Some of the most gruesome scenes of the Serb campaign of "ethnic cleansing" were replayed in "Croat territories," with the massacre of more than a hundred Bosniak civilians in Ahmici village in Central Bosnia on April 16, 1993, and with Bosniaks from Mostar, Capljina, and Stolac herded to concentration camps in Heliodrom, Dretelj, and elsewhere in Herzegovina in May. One victim of the Croat "ethnic cleansing" of Mostar was *Oslobodjenje's* longtime senior correspondent Mugdim Karabeg, at that time sixty-three years old. In his memoirs he describes the moment when the Croatian militia broke into his apartment, one of them screaming in a drunken voice, "You, journalist, your whole life you wrote against the Ustasha, and now they have come to get you. Get up! F... your *balija* [derogatory term for Bosniaks] mother! Go down to the front yard!"[60] Karabeg was taken, along with hundreds of others, to the Dretelj concentration camp where he underwent weeks of torture before being allowed to go first to the refugee center in Croatia and then to settle permanently in Chicago.

By the time of the Croatian attack, Bosnians had developed some fighting forces, almost nonexistent in the year of Serb terror, so they managed to defend selected areas, inflicting heavy losses on Croatian forces. In some cases, as in Grabovica (near Mostar), Uzdol (near Prozor), and possibly Bugojno and other locations, the Bosnian forces also engaged in revenge against innocent Croat civilians, committing war crimes of their own.

Reporting by the mainstream Croatian media on the Bosnian conflict degenerated to the level of Serbia's worst reporting on the war. While the media remained completely silent on the causes of the conflict, Croatia's attempt to carve out Croat-only territory within Bosnia, and Croatian war crimes, *Vjesnik* headlines screamed anti-Muslim hysteria, alleging "attacks by the Muslim aggressor" in some Croat-seized areas; accusing the Bosnian Army of crimes of "Holocaust proportions" in the area around Travnik; reporting attacks, killings, and looting in Central Bosnia; and claiming that, after an unsuccessful offensive, Muslims took revenge against innocent civilians.[61] The only mention of the Ahmici massacre of Bosnian civilians came in articles trying to put the blame on either international mercenaries or a Muslim jihad that had prompted the Croats' "defensive" response.[62] Croats' "ethnic cleansing" of Mostar, with international observers reporting the systematic expulsion of Muslim civilians taken to concentration camps around the city, was reported in *Vjesnik* on May 10 through 12, 1993, under headlines suggesting a heroic Croat defense of the city: "Muslim Forces Attacked Mostar," "HVO Prevented the Occupation of Mostar," and "Street Fighting Continues."

Vjesnik's "personal best" at inciting hatred was achieved in a report on the alleged hanging of 35 Bosnian Croats in Zenica in summer 1993. In the first two paragraphs, the "report" said:

According to the testimony of Croats who fled Zenica, at the square in front
of the Catholic church in that city, 35 Croats have been hanged because they
refused to wear the uniform of the Muslim army. That crime is only one of a
series experienced every day by the Croats in a "Bosnian Tehran," where they
are subjected to mistreatment and torture. They are forced to convert to Islam
and to carry IDs with Muslim names while Muslim authorities require all
non-Muslims to pay 900 German marks per person for permission to leave
the city and escape that hell.

Women are forced to cover their faces with veils and dress according to
Muslim tradition, while in Kakanj, Muslim military police beat women and
children who gathered to protest the unbearable living conditions.[63]

The report, signed by *Vjesnik's* Mostar correspondent, Mario Marusic,
represents a case study in the fabrication of news, blatant war propaganda, and incitement to hate. To begin with, not a single Croat was
hanged in Zenica, not to mention in front of a Catholic church. The
report was designed to cause maximum outrage and hate, suggesting
both ethnic and religious persecution. Reading the story, even using the
most flexible professional standards, with an understanding of the diffi-
culties of reporting from unfriendly war zones, one can see immediately
that it doesn't meet even the lowest criteria of credibility. First, the only
source given is "the testimony of [unnamed] Croats who fled Zenica."
The story doesn't give a single name or professional affiliation of any of
the alleged victims or perpetrators. Finally, the paper does not mention
efforts to authenticate the story with alternative sources such as the
United Nations or nongovernmental organizations (NGOs) operating in
Central Bosnia or with commanders of neighboring Croat forces. The
paper did not need to. Incitement to hate was the order of the day.

Sarajevo writer Miljenko Jergovic, criticizing the anti-Muslim hysteria in the Croatian media, wrote:

> Anyone who reads all those papers with his morning coffee and who has
> never seen Bosnia, nor (like most of the journalists who write about it) taken
> pains to learn anything about its nationalities, and who believes those news-
> papers implicitly, is going to get right up and go find two or three Muslims,
> give them a good beating, and then send a telegram of greetings to the
> Bosnian Serbs to thank them for everything they are doing for the Croats.
> At the same time, such a reader probably will be a bit confused about the
> Bosnian Serbs being so good and the Croatian Serbs so bad.[64]

Analysts of the Croatian media coverage of the Bosnian war agree that one reporter, Smiljko Sagolj—who in Communist times was one of the top editors of Bosnian TV—stood out for his anti-Muslim bias. During the months of the Croat–Bosniak fighting, this journalist, who was remembered for promoting brotherhood and unity and being extra-sensitive in condemning Croat nationalism in Communist times, suddenly became a leading promoter of hate. His reports were a direct call to violence, Heni Erceg said in an interview.[65] For example, Sagolj said on prime-time TV news that "while Muslims kill our boys," their refugees have been given shelter in Makarska on the Croatian coast. A similar implied threat to the safety of Bosnian refugees was issued in *Slobodna Dalmacija*, in an article entitled "A Rebellion of *Dimije*" (traditional ankle-length pants worn by Muslim women), in which the author reminded his readers that while Muslims were killing Croats in Bosnia, their mothers, wives, sisters, and children were enjoying Croatia's hospitality at the island of Brac. "That was an indirect call to lynch Bosnian refugees in Brac," Jergovic recalled.[66] The inspiration for such reports came from the Croat ultranationalist party, HDZ. Its leader in Bosnia, Mate Boban, issued a statement saying that, instead of gratitude for the hospitality Bosniak refuges enjoyed in Croatia, "Croats are given a knife soaked in Croat blood, a knife in the hands of mad husbands and fathers, whose wives and children found a safe refuge in Croatian towns and hotels on the Croatian coast."[67]

The Day "The Old Bridge Fell"

Two events in the fall of 1993 offer the best insight into the workings of Croatian war propaganda: the destruction of the famous, four-century-old bridge in Mostar and the massacre of Muslim civilians in the village of Stupni Do. One only needs to compare the reports published on November 9, 1993, in the leading American and leading Croatian dailies.

☐ The *New York Times* reported: "Croatian gunners destroyed the renowned Old Bridge in the Bosnian city of Mostar today, sending one of the most graceful examples of Ottoman architecture crashing into the Neretva river."[68]

☐ *Vjesnik* reported ("Old Bridge Downed!"): "The famous Mostar Old

Bridge fell into Neretva river on Tuesday morning around 9 a.m. In artillery battles Monday evening and Tuesday morning between Muslim forces and HVO, the bridge was repeatedly hit, and it was hit previously even though it was protected by scaffolds, old tires, and sandbags."

That explanation, "the-bridge-simply-fell," characterized much of the reporting in the Croatian press. *Vjesnik* lamented a day later, on November 10, that the bridge was brought down "by the world that didn't do anything to stop the war."[69] Jergovic recalled the agonizing in Croatian Radio and TV news:

Croatian Radio reported at first that Muslims had dynamited the bridge in order to blame Croats. Then, that same evening—thanks to a French cameraman who had taped the moments of the destruction—international TV reported that Croatian forces had done it. Late that night Croatian TV's "Frame on Frame" program showed the footage that forced the propagandists to look for new excuses. General Slobodan Praljak's "explanation" was that the bridge had to be destroyed because Muslims used it to bring ammunition with which to kill Croats. It was more than obvious to the public that there were a lot of lies in all of that.[70]

In the case of the Stupni Do massacre, the *New York Times* again offered a thorough, on-the-spot report, describing some of the most gruesome scenes of bestiality:

Shining a flashlight behind sacks and barrels filled with potatoes, beets, and squashes, reporters found a wooden trapdoor opened to reveal a shallow crawl space. Sitting upright through the opening, their arms intertwined as if for comfort from their terror, were three women in their late thirties or early forties, their bodies blackening. One had had her throat cut. All three had been shot several times, in the face, throat, and chest. Elsewhere in the village, reporters saw another thirteen bodies. United Nations officers said they had counted nineteen, and more were turning up by the hour.[71]

In contrast, *Vjesnik* insisted on the "Herzeg-Bosna" version of the story, first denying that the HVO had committed the massacre and then claiming that there were no Muslim civilians in the village and suggesting that Muslim forces tried to break through Croatian lines by attacking from Stupni Do, all of which was denied by the international observers. With strong international condemnation of the massacre, *Vjesnik* ran a commentary expressing—more than anything else—concern for the "damage it causes to the Croats' position in the world."[72]

Lantern in Darkness

Very few publications were left in which people could voice their antiwar feelings. At the beginning of the war, *Slobodna Dalmacija* in Split still sought to voice a possible "other side" of the story. But the Split daily was perceived to be a threat to the patriotic harmony of the Croatian press because it was widely read and respected even in Zagreb, so the Tudjman government moved to take it over. Croatia's new privatization agency simply declared the previous privatization of the paper illegal and made it possible for one of the founding members of Tudjman's HDZ, newly enriched tycoon Miroslav Kutle, to buy *Slobodna Dalmacija* and install party propagandists in the editorial positions. Formerly one of the finest dailies in Yugoslavia, *Slobodna Dalmacija* became yet another mouthpiece for war propaganda. Only a group of young journalists—Viktor Ivancic, Boris Dezulovic, and Predrag Lucic, who had founded the paper's weekly satirical supplement, *Feral Tribune*—escaped that unfriendly takeover and, together with respected TV reporter Heni Erceg, started a weekly under that name. *Feral* ("lantern") remained the most consistent voice against war propaganda, the totalitarian nature of the regime, and the misuse of power. The Tudjman government tried to destroy the paper by imposing enormous taxes, attempting to block its printing and distribution, and opening court cases against its editors and reporters. Ivancic was summoned to the Croatian Ministry of Culture for his "persistently crude, grossly personal attacks" on Tudjman and, in early 1994, even though he had already undergone mandatory military training as a reservist, he was confined to barracks for several weeks for "failing to respond to military call up."[73]

Novi list and *Feral,* later *Erasmus* and *Nacional,* and occasionally *Nedjeljna Dalmacija* and *Globus,* were all still far from able to counter the Tudjman party line, promoted primarily through Croatian Radio and especially TV, as well as through the state-controlled dailies *Vecernji list, Vjesnik,* and now *Slobodna Dalmacija.* For a long time there was an honorable exception even on state television: a late-night show, "Frame

on Frame" ("Slikom na sliku"), edited by Dubravko Merlic. The show
presented an objective review of international daily broadcasts and held
nightly open-air debates on the issues of the day. In his book about the
program, Merlic lists the following five guiding principles of his editorial policy:

> (1) Don't neglect the real events of the day for any non-professional con-
> sideration since viewers know what the events are and you have to meet
> their expectations; (2) Look at events from different perspectives, using your
> own as well as international material; (3) Don't try to impose your own
> views on the audience; let them make their own judgement; (4) Make sure
> your guests are competent, either by their position or expertise, and ask
> questions of public interest; (5) Offer the audience material they are not
> "ready for" if it is relevant. [74]

Merlic adds: "The program went through the most trying times during the tragic conflict between Muslims and Croats. We never lost trust
in the possibility and the need to resolve that conflict, and we insisted
on our principles, covering it through all available sources."

But Tudjman's Croatian TV prime-time news was no better than
Milosevic's Serbian TV. Functioning on the same follow-the-party
wavelength as *Vjesnik*, Croatian TV engaged in the same stereotypi-
cal presentation of the enemy in Bosnia: Bosnian President
Izetbegovic was referred to as a "Muslim leader" and the Bosnian
Army as "Muslim forces, mujahedin, jihad warriors" and "the aggressor," while Croat forces were "heroic defenders." Damir Matkovic,
who joined Merlic in 1993 as one of the "Frame on Frame" editors,
remembers two examples of news fabrication on the prime-time
evening Journal at that time. Tudjman went to Sarajevo in June 1994,
among the first foreign heads of state to visit the city as Sarajevo was
still under siege. On the 6 p.m. news, viewers could see original
footage of him in Sarajevo, with some people screaming "Murderer!"
and booing, Matkovic recalled. Some were also clapping but it was an
obvious minority. The same day he visited the Croatian community
in Sarajevo and was greeted with applause and cheering. That
evening on the prime-time news, the soundtracks had been switched
with applause and cheering accompanying his visit to Sarajevo,
Matkovic said. "I criticized this at a media roundtable in Dubrovnik,
and the editor called me and said, 'Write a denial!' [of what he had

said in Dubrovnik]. I refused, and he threatened to fire me, but then did not follow through."[75]

Matkovic said that the government prohibited "Frame on Frame" from promoting the views of those prominent Bosnian Croats who objected to the war, such as Franciscan leader Petar Andjelovic and social democrat Ivo Komsic. "We managed to present their views only by using footage of them from some international programs," Matkovic said.

In their patriotic pride in serving the cause, Croatian TV editors admitted their censorship in an official statement, saying they had interviewed Bosnian President Alija Izetbegovic three times and censored him only once "when he said that he was in favor of a confederation with Croatia and also with others, including even Serbia."[76] They believed and announced on air that it was perfectly legitimate to censor an "unacceptable" point of view.

Bitter End

With increasing international pressure to stop the Bosniak–Croat war, and the creation of the Bosniak–Croat Federation in March 1994 in Washington, D.C., the Croatian media's anti-Muslim campaign subsided, leaving deep scars in the public on both sides. Goran Milic, Belgrade TV's most popular news anchor in the late 1980s and then founder and editor of Yutel, left Sarajevo in the summer of 1992 as Bosnia's national team spokesman at the Olympic Games in Barcelona. He then settled in Zagreb, the city of his birth. That way he closed the "Balkan triangle" as a journalist who had lived in the capitals of all three countries at war in the late eighties and early nineties—Belgrade-Sarajevo-Zagreb. In Croatia, which was still bitter at both Serbia and Bosnia, and with a public believing that the country would never again have anything to do with either "Serb Chetniks" or "Muslim mujahadeen," Milic was initially received with a high degree of animosity. He recalled in an interview that some people identified him as the Yutel editor-in-chief who had supported the failed effort to "save Yugoslavia" (at the expense of Croatia's thousand-year-old dream of independence). Others could not forgive him for failing to join the chorus in the anti-Muslim campaign and for maintaining his strong Bosnian ties and friendships.[77] Well-known in Zagreb, easily noticeable in any crowd—both as a familiar TV face and a tall figure—Milic felt strange: The city of his birth gave him the cold shoulder.

Trying to avoid unfriendly encounters, he definitely did not want to meet Marinko Bozic, at that time owner and publisher of the "yellowest" of all "yellow tabloids," *ST*, known for a series of campaigns aimed at compromising all prominent Croats deemed "unpatriotic" by ultranationalists' standards. Bozic's *ST* had attacked Milic as "a Yugoslav secret service agent" and "a Croat working for Milosevic and the Yugoslav Army." Milic was shocked when Bozic approached him on a Zagreb street. "He hugged me, kissed me, and said, 'I want to explain something to you. All I wrote against you was based on strong feelings in Croatia against anyone associated with the 'enemy,' and you who could cross the lines—like [actor] Rade Serbedzija, [singer] Tereza Kesovija, [actress] Mira Furlan, you and all those perceived as 'Yugoslavs'—were traitors, worse than enemies themselves.' Then he suggested that I write a column for his paper. Not having a job and being free to write the way I felt about things, I accepted," Milic said.[78]

Milic didn't want to work for some of the international organizations involved in helping promote civil society and an independent media because, as he understood it, their mission was to bury the recent past, making "all of them" look equally guilty. Milic, who chronicled the Serb destruction of Vukovar, Dubrovnik, and Sarajevo and knew firsthand the bitterness of the Croat-Bosniak conflict, said he did not want to participate in efforts aimed at equal distribution of blame. "As someone fluent in English, French, and Spanish, I was invited to a couple of internationally sponsored conferences, and I soon realized that they didn't want me to remember that, after all, there were guilty people and innocent people, perpetrators and victims of war crimes. I simply couldn't participate in those everyone-is-guilty rituals, and they did not call me again anyway," Milic said.

Back in Sarajevo, years of terror and concerted propaganda for Milosevic's "Greater Serbia" and Tudjman's "Greater Croatia" finally gave a historic excuse for a Muslim brand of ultranationalism to awaken. The only major difference was that Serb and Croat nationalism had been aimed at expansion of those states, while Muslim ideology was the best way to legitimize claims to Serb- and Croat-occupied areas of Bosnia (leaving Bosniaks in what was left). With the Bosniak public's rising perception of Serbs and Croats as enemies, those in Bosnia still respect-ful of the tradition and culture of tolerance became increasingly isolated. Their defense—in what remained of the free media—of a multiethnic, multireligious, and multicultural Bosnia was openly ridiculed in the Bosniak nationalist media as multi-confused. Unfortunately, the voices of tolerance not only could not reach the vast majority of Bosnians but also could not be heard in the closing rounds of the internationally sponsored peace talks in Dayton, Ohio.

Balkan Media Post-Dayton: Missed Opportunities

THE AMERICAN-BROKERED Dayton Peace Agreement, initialed on November 21, 1995, in Dayton, Ohio, and signed on December 14 in Paris, ended the three-and-a-half-year war in Bosnia, which left more than 200,000 people dead and more than one and a half million driven from their homes. The agreement itself was implicit recognition of the international nature of the conflict, as opposed to theories of a "civil war" among Bosnians who had been "killing each other for centuries." It was signed not by the Bosnian "warring factions" but by the presidents of the three neighboring states. In addition to Bosnian President Alija Izetbegovic, the signatories and guarantors were Yugoslav President Slobodan Milosevic (representing the Bosnian Serbs) and Croatian President Franjo Tudjman (representing the Bosnian Croats). The war could end only when those two, who had initiated, commanded, armed, and controlled the forces intent on destroying Bosnia, were hard pressed finally to stop. But a peace acceptable to Milosevic and Tudjman couldn't be much more than a compromise that "guys with guns" would accept. While formally preserving Bosnia as a "single state with two multiethnic entities—the Bosniak–Croat Federation and the Serb Republic

(Republika Srpska) in 51 and 49 percent of Bosnian territory, respectively"—Dayton amounted to a thinly veiled partition of the country. The two entities were given much more power than the state, including their own armies and police, and they retained veto power over any meaningful decision in the weak joint institutions. More important, and almost deadly for Bosnia: Both Milosevic and Tudjman remained in firm control in Belgrade and Zagreb with their power boosted by their internationally accorded status as peacemakers. Their surrogates in Bosnia, the SDS and HDZ, gained legitimacy without denouncing their primary war goals of creating exclusive ethnic parastates in Bosnia in order to make them, at some later date, a part of "Greater Serbia" and "Greater Croatia." (Even though the federation was supposed to be a single entity, it remained deeply divided into Bosniak-held and Croat-held areas with separate parallel institutions, from elementary schools to public companies and law enforcement agencies.)

Thus, in the same decade in which the world celebrated the end of apartheid in South Africa and the removal of the Berlin Wall in Germany, a new apartheid and new walls were created in Bosnia. Some corrective elements of the Dayton agreement, such as the arrest and extradition of some of the leading indicted war criminals, including Radovan Karadzic and Ratko Mladic, to the International War Crimes Tribunal at The Hague and the right of return to their homes of those expelled, have not been implemented, contributing further to the ironic outcome of the Bosnian war. Focused on the main task at Dayton, "to end a war"—as the book written by the main negotiator, Richard Holbrooke, is entitled[1]—international mediators almost completely neglected the role of the media in the peace process. The media were mentioned only briefly, in Annex 3 of the agreement, giving the Organization for Security and Cooperation in Europe (OSCE) a mandate for media issues as part of its role in organizing and supervising elections. The signatories are obliged by that Annex to "ensure that conditions exist for the organization of free and fair elections, in particular a politically neutral environment . . . [and] shall ensure freedom of expression and of the press."[2]

Bosnia: Nationalists Control Postwar Media

Thus Dayton left the Balkan media in the hands of those who had used them to stir ethnic intolerance in the first place. Yugoslav media remained in Milosevic's hands; Croatian in Tudjman's; and Bosnian in the hands of the three nationalist parties. Serbian, Croatian, and Bosniak leaders of the 1990s—Milosevic, Tudjman, and Izetbegovic, respectively—tried their best to shape different, even opposing images of themselves in the media under their control. For Milosevic, the "protector and unifier" of all Serbs, Tudjman was an "Ustasha fascist" and Izetbegovic a "Muslim fundamentalist." For Tudjman, the "father of European Croatia," Milosevic represented the Serb eastern-barbaric–primitive-Balkans culture he didn't want to have anything to do with, and Izetbegovic represented the threat of Islam's expansion from which Tudjman was defending both Croatia and Europe. For Izetbegovic, a "victim of aggression," Milosevic and Tudjman were both enemies united in their mission to expand their territories by partitioning Bosnia and committing even genocidal crimes in the process. Yet all three had one thing in common: They despised independent, critical media. Milosevic tried to silence the media by brutal force, Tudjman by a corrupt privatization process that landed some of the most influential newspapers in the hands of his cronies, Izetbegovic by moral disqualification of all those who criticized him as blaming equally victim and aggressor. All three used almost identical rhetoric in their condemnation of criticism by the media. It was always labeled as a betrayal of the national cause, service to foreign enemies, or selling souls for a handful of dollars. In all three countries, media receiving international aid were attacked as traitors, while those dependent on government privileges were "doing their patriotic duty." And in all three, the George Soros's Open Society Institute supporting democratic change in former Communist countries came under attack at one time or another for its support of free media: In Belgrade, it was declared illegal; in Zagreb, it was attacked by Tudjman himself for an anti-Croatian conspiracy; in Bosnia, its early support for the new Open Broadcast Network (OBN) TV was questioned and obstructed.

    The post-Dayton media landscape in the Balkans could not have been more unfavorable for the development of a free and pluralistic media. On the one hand, the international institutions fully realized that the media had played an instrumental role in creating and maintaining the war mentality, a fact that had been established in reports, memoirs, and debates on the Balkans in the 1990s. On the other hand, the agreement left the "bad guys" in control not only of their by now "ethnically pure" territories but also of the media in all three states as well as Bosnia's two entities and ten cantons. There was a built-in obstacle to the stated goal of the international intervention in the post-Dayton years: While supporting the Dayton agreement might have been the price to end the war, leaving control of the area in the hands of those most responsible for the war made it extremely difficult to develop the institutions of a functioning civil society, including the media. Following the Dayton script, most of the international postwar media efforts in the Balkans contributed to the apartheid-like partition of the area. In the process, the few independent media voices that supported a multiethnic Bosnia remained not only under attack by the nationalist parties that had an interest in fostering ethnic separation, but also marginalized by many in the international donor community who chose to work with the ethnic separatists in support of Dayton.

The initial results were, predictably, tragic. For example, the president of the council controlling the most influential media in Republika Srpska—Serb Radio and Television (SRT)—was Momcilo Krajisnik, the closest associate of wartime Bosnian Serb leader Radovan Karadzic. Krajisnik himself was later indicted and arrested for war crimes. Under his direct supervision, Serb TV treated Republika Srpska as a state, actively undermining any effort to reintegrate the country. The station reported on events in the federation only in its "From Abroad" news program. Immediately following the agreement, Serb TV called Dayton—in a Milos Pribic commentary on November 30, 1995—"a defeat of the Serb national body." Pribic lamented:

> The Serbs did not set out to create a smaller or greater Serbia in the early nineties. They wanted to create their own national state, just like other nations, simply for the sake of their own survival. A part of that same nation, which happened to be outside of their mother country, wanted finally to unite with their mother country and nothing more.

In this way he gave the exact rationale for the war that he tried to deny: the creation of a "Greater Serbia." Everything the SRT did following the signing of the Dayton agreement was aimed at proving that there was no possibility of coexistence among the three Bosnian ethnic groups. The international community's first High Representative in Bosnia, Carl Bildt, was quoted as saying: "They put out propaganda that even Stalin would be ashamed of."[3]

Bosnia's postwar media landscape mirrored the image of that devastated country. In Serb- and Croat-controlled territories, all media—newspapers, radio, and television alike—preached ethnic apartheid. Both areas were blanketed by Belgrade and Zagreb (i.e., Milosevic and Tudjman) television, and in both one could easily find all the nationalist publications from Serbia and Croatia. The opposition press and the press from Sarajevo, still in favor of a functioning Bosnian state, were strictly prohibited. In the Bosniak-controlled areas, the prewar mainstream multiethnic media such as *Oslobodjenje* and Radio and TV of Bosnia Herzegovina continued to exist under a double burden. They had suffered heavy losses in their struggle to operate under the siege—with their facilities and assets bombed and looted, dozens of the most experienced journalists gone, and millions of German marks in debt—all of which would be difficult to recover under even the most favorable conditions. But there was an additional burden: the international community's acceptance of Bosnia's "new realities" of partition. While internationals still paid lip service to the media that maintained the spirit of inter-ethnic tolerance under the most adverse conditions, they didn't see a role for them in a country organized strictly along Bosniak–Croat–Serb lines.

By early 1996, on the heels of a 60,000-strong NATO-led peacekeeping force, dozens of international NGOs and hundreds of mostly well-intentioned enthusiasts—journalists, media practitioners, and trainers—converged on Bosnia with a mission and, in some cases, a respectable amount of money to help establish free media in the country. Unfortunately, they made some strategic misjudgments as well as some regrettable mistakes. Strategically, they were instructed to operate within the Dayton framework, making the Bosnian media a party to all compromises with the ultranationalists instead of encouraging and supporting them to break free and become independent observers and critics of nationalist manipulation of the past and present.

Why was it necessary to "daytonize" the Bosnian media, making them part of the "deal with devil," when that issue had not been regulated by the peace agreement? Carl Bildt said in an interview that when he came to Bosnia, he found the media as divided as the country. The first postwar effort, for peaceful reintegration of Sarajevo and the establishment of confidence between "the Serb and the Muslim communities," failed partly because of the role played by the media, he said. He noted:

Pale and Sarajevo TV were effectively working together to scare the Serbs away from Sarajevo. And the result was that we got nearly 100,000 new refugees [afraid to return to their homes], which very significantly complicated the entire issue of refugee return in the coming years.[4]

There was never any decision on the part of the international community to "daytonize" the media, Bildt said. He explained:

There was great international reluctance to do anything that could be seen as interference in the media. SDA had a very strong constituency in Washington, and I remember that any slight move that might be interpreted as undermining Bosnian state TV had to be handled very carefully in light of this. With Pale TV the problem was different. I argued for us to use our military instruments to force it to behave less virulently, but this came up against the fears of "mission creep" in NATO, and it was not until General Wesley Clark took over European command that NATO agreed to take direct action against the Pale transmitters. Although I had argued vigorously for that action, it happened only after I had left.[5]

Regardless of their intentions, the international organizations legitimized the nationalists' control over the media by accepting the idea that they had to deal exclusively with the ultranationalists. The newly established OSCE's Media Experts Commission, for example, in addition to international representatives included the designated representatives of the three Bosnian governments (Joint, Federal, and Serb) as well as "qualified media specialists appointed by each of the parties." Of course, these "parties," the same ones that presided over the war, were not likely to appoint independent-minded, tolerant, antinationalist individuals to the body controlling the media. As a result, Bosnian journalists were pressured simply to forget the immediate past, to offer a "sanitized" version of what had happened during the war. Any attempt to examine war crimes, "ethnic cleansing," and responsibility for the atrocities risked offending these very people who had become partners in the peace process.

So, with the war over, some of those who had propagated "ethnic cleansing" and intolerance were put in control of Bosnia's postwar media such as, for example, Republika Srpska's Minister of Information Dragan Bozanic, the wartime Pale TV editor and later Deputy Foreign Minister and Bosnian Ambassador to South Africa. Consulting, appeasing, and relying on "the three parties to the agreement" (the nationalist SDA,

SDS, and HDZ), most of the international institutions for media development in Bosnia accepted these parties' criteria and logic. Every journalist and all media had to be compartmentalized into one of the three existing categories—Bosniak, Croat, or Serb—with no room for anything all-Bosnian, multiethnic, and non-national. When I was invited to participate on a panel debating the war in Bosnia, the international moderator insisted, "To clarify your position, we'll identify you as a Bosnian Muslim." I answered: "You might do that, if you also think it's appropriate to identify yourself as an American Catholic or Protestant, or whatever your religious background is. Does that make you less qualified, or less credible, in discussing international issues? You need to understand that there are Bosnians—as there are Americans, Europeans—whose 'position' is not determined by their ethnicity or religion and who can freely criticize positions of their own government the same way they criticize the others."

This need among international mediators always to have clear ethnic representation with people appointed by "the parties" or "acceptable to all three sides" favored either solid nationalists or mediocre journalists with no name or reputation. It was a criterion that sidelined, in media rebuilding efforts, those who belonged to "the fourth party": the party of professional journalism.

One notable exception in supporting early efforts to establish a free media in Bosnia was George Soros's Open Society Fund. Open Society had two distinct advantages over all other media donors: First, the organization had extended its helping hand to the struggling Bosnian media even during the siege of Sarajevo, well aware of what Bosnia used to be; and second, it relied on Bosnian media professionals with a deep understanding of local values and priorities. Soros's Fund not only supported deserving Bosnian media outlets, directing them toward gradual self-sustainability, but also started a journalism school in Sarajevo in cooperation with the BBC to address the shortage of educated professionals. What distinguished the Open Society from more official efforts in the media field was that from the beginning it relied on the expertise of Bosnian professionals such as Zdravko Grebo, Boro Kontic, and Hrvoje Batinic and later Mehmed Halilovic, Jakob Finci, and others who were all Bosniaks, Serbs and Croats, or Jews, but none of whom was appointed by or supportive of nationalist parties in power.

The importance of local initiatives in the media field has been underlined by the experience of another Sarajevo institution, the Media Plan Institute, which started in early 1995. Founder Zoran Udovicic defined the institute's mission in terms that reflected the Bosnian media's most pressing needs: "Think of the future so the peace does not surprise you."[6] The institute focused its activities on educating journalists and monitoring the media, becoming a reliable partner to many of the international institutions operating in postwar Bosnia. The institute's High College of Journalisim, developed in cooperation with the School of Journalism in Lille, France, brings dozens of journalists from the region to Sarajevo for a ten-month course of study, awarding scholarships to out-of-town students to cover their expenses. The teachers at this school include some of Bosnia's best journalists as well as visiting scholars and practitioners from abroad.

The country's media scene presented both Bosnian journalism and international "media interventionists" with a variety of challenges. For example, Bosnian Radio and TV, which compromised its prewar reputation for independence by accepting SDA-led government control during the war, was still the best equipped, most professional and to some extent multiethnic broadcast outlet, with the best prospect of being rebuilt as a statewide public broadcasting station. But instead of cutting off the instruments of SDA control and restoring its countrywide outreach, complemented by the development of regional electronic media, the international community practically legalized the wartime looting of its assets, transmitters, and equipment, leaving them in the hands of "Serb TV" and "Croat TV," and accepting hard-line Serbs' and Croats' claim that anything coming from Sarajevo was "unacceptable." No wonder then that, in the months leading up to the first postwar elections held in September 1996, nationalist Serb and Croat TV continued to insist on wartime partition, treating the territories under the control of nationalist parties as states completely separate from Bosnia-Herzegovina.

In his report "Monitoring Media: The Bosnian Elections 1996," Mark Wheeler cites two examples of openly anti-Bosnian, and thus anti-Dayton, commentaries carried by Serb and Croat nationalist media. He reports that on June 29, 1996, SRT director Ilija Guzina commented in a "News at 8" prime time broadcast:

Eight, yes, eight political parties from the Muslim-Croat Federation have entered the elections in Republika Srpska! The history of European and world democracy, going back to the time of Pericles, has probably never recorded that parties from one state entered the elections of another.... Serbs are presented with two possibilities at the polls. The first is to cast their votes for parties that stand for a united and whole Republika Srpska and for unification with Serbia one day. The second possibility is to give their votes to all those good-for-nothings who have now or somewhat earlier declared themselves as fighters for this or that right, and who are ready to surrender practically the whole state into [Muslim SDA President] Alija Izetbegovic's hands.[7]

A month later on July 29, Veseljko Cerkez, the editor of Croatian Radio Mostar, read an editorial against the "ever-more frequent crimes" of Muslims "against everything Croat" and the "dirty frauds" perpetrated by the international community. Cerkez said, "Not one Croat on this territory and beyond, conscious of the penalty, has the right to remain silent and look on while foreign and domestic hyenas from this space tear piece by piece at our body of freedom, land, and future." Wheeler commented that "Cerkez's stomach-turning editorial was far worse than Guzina's, constituting, in fact, not only an incitement to racial hatred [of Muslims and West Europeans] but an incitement to violence against Croats disloyal to the HDZ."[8]

In both cases, the international reaction was too late and too weak to challenge the hostile pre-election coverage. The SRT even made it clear that they considered themselves a television station on patriotic duty. On July 31, they issued an editorial board communiqué declaring their loyalty to the party in power: "Like Republika Srpska, Srpska Television is a product of the nation. It is a fact that the SRT took on the responsibility of presenting political parties and reporting from campaign press conferences. But it is also a fact that the general national interest is older than the narrow interest of any political party."

Ultranationalists enjoyed the full support of the Serb Radio and TV, firmly controlled by the closest associates of indicted war criminal Radovan Karadzic, such as Momcilo Krajisnik as the SRT council chairman and Velibor Ostojic as the head of the managing board. Michael Maclay, then chief spokesman for Carl Bildt, told Chris Hedges of the *New York Times* that Pale TV "keeps the political atmosphere fetid. It prevents daylight and oxygen from getting through. In the last couple of weeks it has become worse, as Stalinist as any of the old Communist regimes."⁹ In that article, Hedges also reported that "several themes are hammered home each night, but the most important one is the duty of Serbs to defend Radovan Karadzic, the Bosnian Serb political leader, and Gen. Ratko Mladic, the military commander, both of whom were indicted on war crimes charges by the United Nations Tribunal at The Hague." Karadzic's daughter, Sonja Karadzic, had an officially sanctioned role in the media field: She became the director of the International Press Center in Pale and founded her own Orthodox St. Jovan Radio station. In a letter to OSCE chairman Flavio Cotti on September 5, 1995, William A. Orme, Jr., executive director of the Committee to Protect Journalists (SPJ), complained about the dangers facing journalists who try to cross from one to the other Bosnian entity. He noted that Karadzic's daughter charges "unbelievable sums of money" for press credentials for foreign journalists and makes them travel with unwanted "bodyguards."¹⁰

Both the SRT in Pale and Croat TV Herzeg-Bosna in Mostar continued to obstruct the peace process long after Dayton. The Media Plan and Institute for War and Peace Reporting's *Monitoring Report* recounted two incidents in 1997 that underline this point.

☐ On February 10, on the occasion of a Muslim holiday, a crowd of Bosniaks expelled from the Croat-controlled part of the divided city of Mostar wanted to visit the cemetery on "the other side" to pay their respects to loved ones. Leading the crowd were a local imam and local political leaders. As they walked toward the cemetery, Croat extremists attacked and shot at them, killing one of the Bosniaks and injuring twenty others. Croat TV reported that a "Muslim terrorist march" on West Mostar had been stopped. When an international investigation proved that the attack against the civilians visiting the graveyard was organized and led by the Croat police, the station followed that report with a commentary accusing the international community of "blaming Croats for everything in order to maintain good relations with oil-producing Muslim countries." Following the Mostar incident, Croatian TV continued to insist on Croat ownership of the area. In a documentary entitled "Herzeg's Land," notoriously nationalistic Smiljko Sagolj claimed that historic Bosnian *steci*, headstones from the pre-Islamic period, prove the presence of the Croatian people in Herzegovina since ancient times and that the towns of Pocitelj, Capljina, and Stolac "belong to

Croats." Croats who moved to the area from Central Bosnia told Sagolj: "The most important thing is that this is Croatian land with Croatian authorities and a Croatian president." As usual, Croatian TV had nothing to say about Bosniaks expelled from those towns in the ethnic cleansing campaign of spring–summer 1993.[11]

☐ In mid-July 1997, when British commandos serving in Bosnia killed Prijedor police chief Simo Drljaca and arrested wartime town leader Mico Kovacevic in an operation aimed at arresting indicted war criminals, SRT exploded with hysteric anti-NATO rhetoric. Brcko commentator Nedjo Djurevic called the Stabilization Force (SFOR) soldiers "Al Capone mobsters" and "dogs of war," while the station's reporter covering the local protests asked, "Why and for what reason are they killing only us, without trial, without any possibility of defense?" As with all war crime indictments and arrests, SRT never bothered to inform its viewers of what those "Serb heroes" were accused. In the Drljaca-Kovacevic case, the charge was the systematic "ethnic cleansing" of almost all non-Serbs from the Prijedor area and the killing and torture of hundreds of them in Omarska, Keraterm, and Trnopolje concentration camps in 1992.[12]

Throughout the summer of 1997, *Monitoring Report*, published by the Sarajevo-based Media Plan in cooperation with the Institute for War & Peace Reporting, provided plenty of examples of nationalist manipulation of the media on all three sides in post-Dayton Bosnia.

☐ In Republika Srpska, the decision by that entity's president, Biljana Plavsic, to split from her former hard-line SDS colleagues, accusing them of corruption, prompted an avalanche of "patriotic media" attacks against the woman who until then had been glorified as a Serb hero. She was attacked as "a tool of the international community," her decision was called "dangerous and unconstitutional," and her appearance on the balcony of her Banjaluka office to address the crowd was compared to "[Italian fascist leader] Benito Mussolini addressing the people from Roman balconies." Plavsic was called a "renegade president" who "surpassed all Serbian quislings up to now." At the same time, Karadzic and Mladic were called "leaders and heroes of the Serb nation" who "have become the most hounded figures in recent European history."[13]

☐ Denial of war crimes was a constant line in SRT broadcasts. Announcer Marinko Ucur stated on August 11, 1997: "The hunt for Serb
crimes has also been influenced by the so-called mass graves, in which
who knows how many Muslims are buried. . . . When the ground
around Srebrenica was dug up, in the unsuccessful search for Muslim
bodies, not even a dog's skeleton was found."[14] The truth is that more
than 7,000 men from Srebrenica "disappeared" following Gen.
Mladic's "liberation" of the town, with skeletons of hundreds of them
found—some with their hands tied behind their backs with wire—
refuting Serbian propaganda that they had been killed "in fighting."

☐ The showdown between the Pale and Banjaluka leaderships resulted
in at least one consequential change for Republika Srpska's media: The
media also split, unfortunately not so that some of them became independent or professional, but into two opposing blocks—some loyal to
the hard-line leadership in Pale and some to the newly emerging center of power in Banjaluka. *Monitoring Report* (Issue 6, September 21)
offered a striking statistical analysis: "The independent TV Banjaluka
mentioned Momcilo Krajisnik nine times, always in a negative context, and Biljana Plavsic twenty-seven times, always positively. The
SDS got fourteen negative appearances, the RS Socialists fourteen
positive. . . . The independent Banjaluka daily, *Nezavisne novine,* had
fifteen positive items on Plavsic, and fifteen negative on Krajisnik. . . .
The SDS-approved daily, *Glas srpski,* mentioned Plavsic and Krajisnik
twenty-one times, but his appearance was positive, hers negative."
Independent TV went as far as having one of its news announcers
declare: "Let God Bless our President. We are all with her" (July 5,
1997).

By September 1997, the anti-Dayton rhetoric had escalated in the
Pale-based media to the point that the NATO-led SFOR troops seized
their transmitters to prevent them from "throwing kerosene on fire," as
State Department spokesman James Rubin characterized their "inflammatory and threatening language" (AP, August 21, 1997). A *New York
Times* editorial agreed that the Karadzic-controlled television and radio
broadcasts "are poisonous." "What passes for news on Srpska Radio and
Television is hateful propaganda designed to incite ethnic conflict and
mob attacks against NATO forces," the editorial said.[15] But the paper

questioned the wisdom of handing over control of the media from one Serb faction to another, which would end up "merely changing the propaganda message rather than replacing it with unfettered news." According to an Associated Press report, the international supervisors also accused the HDZ-controlled Croat media of "fomenting national hatred."[16] The report stated that Livno's Radio Levnia, for example, called the international peacekeepers "foreign mercenaries [who] come to interfere with our internal politics and . . . [who are] earning money by how many Croats they kill and how many Bosniaks and Serbs they save." The OSCE demanded that Croat TV in Mostar and Livno radio read a public apology five days in a row, with the explicit statement: "We deliberately wanted to divide the peoples of Bosnia and spread national hatred." AP reported that "Mostar TV manager Milan Sutalo refused to read the statement, telling a Zagreb radio station that he feared an apology could be taken as an admission of guilt that could lead to his prosecution on war crimes charges."

Bosnian TV, condemned to continued SDA control, contributed to the picture of three tribes having nothing to do with each other. Its main program, as Wheeler noted, "tended to lend substance to the notion, promoted by the SDA, that it, the state, the army, and the Bosniak nation are one."[17] *Monitoring Report* also registered the "slavish dedication" with which Bosnian state TV in Sarajevo followed the Bosniak member of the state presidency, Alija Izetbegovic. On June 26–29, 1997, on the occasion of the traditional Muslim Ajvatovica pilgrimage, Izetbegovic's participation and his party's flags dominated the news three evenings in a row.[18] On the eve of the electoral silence—the election day when, by the election law, media refrain from any campaign reporting—TV BiH carried an hour-and-a-half-long interview with Izetbegovic. At the end, editor-in-chief Senad Kamenica asked him whether he had a message for voters. Izetbegovic replied, "Vote for the Coalition for a United and Democratic Bosnia, for this is where the SDA is. You will find the Coalition in the last place on your voting list."[19]

Looking for alternatives, the international community opted for a TV and radio program of its own. Just before the elections, it launched TV-IN, later renamed OBN (Open Broadcast Network), and FERN (Free Elections Radio Network) Radio. OBN started on September 7, 1996, with a credibility problem. It was called "Carl Bildt TV,"

suggesting it was under the control of the Office of the High
Representative (OHR), and was dismissed by all three nationalist parties.
SDS and HDZ dismissed it because it had been established in Sarajevo
and was carried predominantly through the Bosniak TV network; the
SDA labeled it "unpatriotic," a competition to "our Bosnian TV."

OBN faced both technological and professional limitations. Tech-
nologically, it needed a network of local TV stations to carry its signal
to the Bosnian audience. Initially, there were five stations: NTV 99 and
Hayat in Sarajevo, TV Mostar, the Zenica-based Zetel, and TV Tuzla,
with NTV 99 withdrawing from the project as soon as it received its
share of the internationally supplied equipment. OBN was largely
understaffed in its central studio while member-stations were not able
to contribute news programming at a level expected in the countrywide
network. Affiliation with local partners, some of which were clearly
Muslim-only, hurt credibility. For example, throughout the month of
Ramadan, Hayat TV broadcast long hours of religious programming
produced in Iran, playing into the hands of both Serb and Croat
nationalists who wanted to undermine anything all-Bosnian.

The international community proved, once again, that it had the ability to raise money for its Bosnian democratic experiment—investing
some $20 million over a period of five years in this new network—but
not a clear understanding of the best ways to achieve its stated goals. A
fraction of the money invested in the project would have been enough to
bring together some of the best Bosnian journalists to produce a high-
quality prime-time news journal and an issue-oriented weekly political
magazine instead of relying heavily on imported foreign programming.
Instead of bringing in a whole team of tested professionals, however,
international sponsors tried to solve the problem by hiring just one top
news executive. In the beginning, they brought former Yutel editor
Goran Milic from Zagreb, but even with all the money invested, they did
not give him personnel capable of carrying out the mission. Milic discussed his short-lived return to Sarajevo in an interview:

> They [the internationals] were obsessed with reaching the audience in
> Banjaluka, in Republika Srpska, while there was no interest in covering
> Croat-controlled territories. When I found a way to penetrate that area,
> with two to three young people who wanted to work for us, the interna-
> tional sponsors still insisted on Banjaluka, to the point that they—the

British Army—supplied us with "news" from Republika Srpska, bringing us their own tapes. In the absence of the regular countrywide coverage, I proposed a mobile TV studio to cruise Bosnia, sending us pictures and stories from "ethnically cleansed" towns such as Visegrad and Capljina and many others, that people expelled from there hadn't seen for four to five years. That mobile studio, which wasn't used at all before I came up with that idea, was suddenly sent to London. There were limits on what one could do.[20]

After Milic left, another prominent TV journalist, Konstantin Jovanovic, a Bosnian Serb who had never accepted the pressure to join the "patriotic media," was brought in to head OBN. He was soon fired for, among other things, refusing to project watered-down versions of responsibility for the war.

With all of its shortcomings, OBN did contribute to the gradual pluralization of the Bosnian media scene. With most of the other television stations controlled by the three nationalist parties, preaching day in, day out that "our side" is right and everyone else wrong, OBN provided a voice of moderation. Unfortunately, it was limited not only in its area of coverage, as it was for a long time unable to penetrate Serb- and Croat-held territories, but also in content. Jadranko Katana, who assumed the position of news director in May of 1998, said in an interview that his team inherited all the original problems the network faced:

> The quality and journalistic standards of the associated local stations were poor. Some of the stations' owners had other businesses, so news production wasn't their priority, and they were either too closely associated with or afraid of the local authorities. I couldn't get them to participate, for example, in our coverage of corruption in Bosnia—that was too hot a potato for most of them—so we could do it only by sending a team from Sarajevo. Of some seventy journalists employed by the member stations, there were hardly two or three who would meet higher professional criteria.[21]

With all of its generous investment, OBN was never given the most precious asset: an "A" team of editors who would shape a program focused on priorities in the peace process. After all, that focus was missing in international policy toward Bosnia as well.

Another electronic media effort—the launching of FERN on July 15, 1996—was hailed as "the media success story in Bosnia and Herzegovina."[22] With an investment of two million German marks from Switzerland and an initial staff of twenty, including stringers, the International Crisis Group (ICG) reported that "FERN has evolved into a powerful medium producing constantly high-quality programming."[23] The report noted, however, that FERN was "concentrated in Bosniak-controlled Federation territory, the part of Bosnia Herzegovina where media are generally the most open."

Postwar Bosnia saw an explosion of new media outlets. According to a study by Zoran Udovicic, president of the Media Plan Institute, in mid-1991 there were 377 newspapers and other publications in Bosnia, 54 local radio stations, four TV stations, one wire service, and state Radio-Television with three channels. At the end of the war in 1995, there were 272 active media outlets: 203 in the Federation and 69 in Republika Srpska. In March 1997, there were 490: 270 in the Federation and 220 in Republika Srpska.[24] The problem was that—with the wartime exodus of hundreds of journalists, the absence of educated young professionals in both newsrooms and management, and the lack of a functional economy—most of the newly started media depended either on international donors or on local war profiteers with dubious political agendas. In the absence of a strategy, which could have included the creation of a high-quality national public broadcast system and support for the establishment of a respectable daily, much of the donors' money was wasted on media projects of no relevance. "A cost-benefit analysis of media investment in 1996 indicates a poor return. The problem is lack of overall strategy and absence of expertise," an International Crisis Group report of March 18, 1997, stated. The report cites as one example USAID's DM 18,400 (about $9,000) support for Bijeljina-based *Ekstra* magazine whose owner, Jovica Petkovic, "was the head of the Bosnian Serb Army's press center and one of Republika Srpska's most chauvinist propagandists [during the war]."[25]

In a country deeply divided into three nationalist-controlled territories, there was little room left for media still advocating inter-ethnic tolerance. A case in point was the fate of *Oslobodjenje*. Internationally praised as "the paper that refused to die," and awarded all of the most prestigious prizes in world journalism—Newspaper of the Year, The Consciousness and Integrity in Journalism Award, The Sakharov Award for Freedom of Thought, The Freedom Award, and The Golden Pen of Freedom, to mention just a few—*Oslobodjenje* faced the challenge of surviving the peace. With almost all prewar assets destroyed and looted, with a huge wartime debt, and more and more senior journalists leaving after years of heroic unpaid work, the paper was also exposed to constant attacks in the newly established nationalist Bosniak media. The paper's balanced reporting on the war was billed as "equalizing the victims with the aggressors"; its multiethnic staff ridiculed as "lost in space"; its advocacy of tolerance as "nostalgia for a Yugoslavia that disappeared without Bosniaks' guilt." The Muslim SDA, unable to control *Oslobodjenje*, backed a new daily—*Dnevni avaz (Daily Voice)*—giving it generous financial support, exclusive access to information, and even police and army support in distribution. A prominent former *Oslobodjenje* columnist Vlastimir Mijovic, in an interview with the Bosniak nationalist weekly *Ljiljan*, said:

> *Dnevni avaz* was launched after the end of the war, when it was possible to work in more or less normal conditions. From the start, it was favored by the ruling party. *Avaz* boasts that the paper is distributed by the police and the army. Naturally, such favors don't come for free. *Dnevni avaz* is a very pro-regime paper, embraced by the ruling party and partly dependant on its finances. . . . They simply have a monopoly with the ruling party for information that draws attention. . . . Naturally, the public has realized that *Avaz* has better access to information, consequently, *Avaz* has been winning over our readers.[26]

Avaz was winning for a number of reasons. First, there was a sharply reduced readership for *Oslobodjenje*, a paper representing multiethnicity in a country torn apart by war terror. Once tolerant, multicultural cities within *Oslobodjenje's* reach—Sarajevo, Tuzla, Zenica—had experienced the exodus of intellectuals, non-Bosniaks, and those in so-called "mixed" marriages, and the influx of tens of thousands of Bosniaks expelled from their homes elsewhere in Bosnia just for being Muslim. These new residents brought with them the memories and bitterness of genocide, becoming an easy prey for extremists preaching radical Islamization of the Bosniak-majority territories. Second, it was much easier to start a publishing operation from zero than to continue running one under the burdens of destruction and war debt. And third, in the absence of a functioning economy, ruling party favors—such as the police and army distribution of the paper, privileged access to delicate information, and exclusive advertising from companies in the hands of government cronies—helped *Avaz* become the most prosperous publisher in postwar Bosnia. *Dnevni avaz* started with a spectacular defection of about forty experienced journalists from the prewar, best-selling Bosnian daily *Vecernje novine*. The reason was simple: While *Vecernje novine*, like most publishers in postwar Bosnia, couldn't regularly pay even symbolic salaries, *Avaz* was able to offer regular and higher pay. *Avaz's* owner, Fahrudin Radoncic, a prewar Montenegro correspondent for the Zagreb weekly *Danas*, claims that it wasn't SDA support but the editorial vision that made *Avaz* the most successful media enterprise in postwar Bosnia, with a range of new magazines, a new, modern building, and its own printing press. "While our competition was producing a war newspaper, we ran a political one. When they began to practice political journalism, we moved to the family-oriented political concept of *Dnevni avaz*," Radoncic said in a *Dani* report.[27]

Oslobodjenje, while antinationalist and independent of the ruling parties, was losing the battle for readers. The paper lost some of its best journalists, partly because it was unable to pay them, partly because of an increasing divide between the management and editorial board over how to survive. In that struggle for day-to-day survival, the paper failed to reenergize and to develop a clear long-term strategy for regaining its central place in Bosnian journalism. *Oslobodjenje* did manage, even during the siege, to print first a weekly and then a daily special edition for Bosnians abroad and, at the end of the war, to start its own weekly, *Svijet (The World)*. Edited by internationally recognized *Oslobodjenje* veteran Zlatko Dizdarevic, *Svijet* was an attempt to offer Bosnians a postwar perspective, not in neglect or denial of the legacy of the war, but with a view to a more normal life. With *Oslobodjenje* unable to pay its bills, *Svijet* tried to survive as an independent weekly, but it eventually had to close down. Dizdarevic's regret was that, among all the media donors that had come to Sarajevo, there was no strong interest in supporting a magazine that offered a clear antinationalist perspective. "For some of the donors, maintaining their own bureaucracy in Sarajevo—with expensive offices, high salaries, drivers, translators, and secretaries—was a higher priority than investing in a magazine that represented values they had come to promote," Dizdarevic said in an interview.[28] His bitterness needs to be understood in the context of the generous international support given to a number of media outlets of far less relevance and integrity.

David DeVoss who directed a $2.5 million print-media development program in Bosnia in 1999 noted in a *Los Angeles Times* interview that media development was big business in Bosnia. "The European Union, Holland's Press Now, the Helsinki Committee for Human Rights, and the Soros Foundation's Open Society Fund all have budgets to develop electronic and print journalism [in Bosnia]. By far the largest donor is the United States, which spends an average of $9.5 million each year to nurture politically independent journalism," he said.[29] In an interview with Mensur Camo of Radio Free Europe/Radio Liberty (RFE/RL) in early October 1999, Senad Avdic, editor-in-chief of *Slobodna Bosna* magazine, said that international donors were trying to create an "artificial media scene" in Bosnia modeled after other countries' experiences, with no chance of succeeding there. "I had an argument with the Deputy High Representative (in charge of the media) Simon Haselock, regarding a TV series financed by the OHR during the last election campaign. Some team of producers, journalists, and cameramen came from abroad to film a dozen irrelevant pieces. That project, Haselock admitted, cost more than a million DEM (half a million U.S. dollars), more than the total assistance provided to all print media in Bosnia last year," Avdic said.

Nevertheless, the lively and somewhat chaotic media scene in Bosniak-majority territories proved to be the most pluralistic in Bosnia with the battle between "the most read" and "the most respected" dailies (*Avaz* and *Oslobodjenje*, respectively), as well as the rivalry between the two independent weeklies (*Dani* and *Slobodna Bosna*), plus the continuous campaign in the nationalist weekly *(Ljiljan)* against all of the independent-minded journalists and media outlets, and a variety of radio and television stations to boot. Bosniak leader Alija Izetbegovic prided his party on "allowing the greatest media freedom in the region." The fact is that it was not the party that "allowed" the freedom, but Bosnian journalists who won and preserved it in spite of their government. Izetbegovic himself, irritated by the criticism of his party in the independent media, attacked some of the Bosnian magazines as "media prostitutes," allegedly selling their services for a handful of dollars to the international donors. He was just replaying the same old song used by Milosevic and Tudjman in efforts to silence the opposition in Serbia and Croatia. He thought it was perfectly fine if the donor was, for example, his party but not the international organizations.

Izetbegovic—together with Muslim religious community leader

Mustafa Ceric—was instrumental in trying to impose further Islamization of public life in the territories under his control. In 1996, on the occasion of the first postwar New Year celebration, he openly criticized Bosnian TV for projecting images of public drinking, singing, and Santa Claus appearances "which are not our tradition." The fact is that Bosniaks not only traditionally celebrated the New Year but also shared in the religious holidays of their Catholic, Orthodox, and Jewish neighbors. Santa Claus bringing gifts to children was part of this celebration in schools, communities, and companies. Ceric also attacked Bosnian TV for using terms such as "the Holy Father" and "His Holiness" in reporting about Pope John Paul II's activities, accusing it of "Catholization" of Bosniaks. "That was just part of the systematic campaign against secularism, conducted through Dzemaludin Latic's *Ljiljan*," *Dani* editor Senad Pecanin said in an interview.[30] Latic was a close associate of Izetbegovic, who led *Ljiljan's* attack against mixed marriages, as well as a campaign against prominent Sarajevo poet Marko Vesovic and a number of secular Bosniak intellectuals.

Editors of the two best political weeklies in Bosnia, Pecanin of *Dani* and Senad Avdic of *Slobodna Bosna*, were a constant target of radical Bosnian Islamists' attacks. Pecanin said:

> There is an extremely high price attached to practicing independent journalism here. And very few people are ready to pay it. That includes threatening phone calls at 2 or 3 a.m. with the caller telling me where my car is parked or the exact route my child takes to a daycare center. Latic's *Ljiljan* once ran a doctored photo of me with Salman Rushdie depicting me as an "enemy of Islam." President Izetbegovic himself, after we ran a dossier on crimes committed against Serb and Croat civilians by renegade commanders of the Bosnian Army, accused us publicly of causing $200–300 million in damage for international assistance denied to Bosnia. Then Ceric repeats these accusations. And as a consequence, the printing company increases the price of printing us; some distributors refuse to sell us; and some advertisers cancel their contracts. Not to mention one of Sarajevo's notorious warlord's entry into my office pointing, fortunately, only a toy gun to my head, or a bomb exploding in front of *Dani's* office.[31]

Avdic was physically attacked and beaten in a downtown Sarajevo hotel on December 24, 1995. After that, he ran an open letter in *Slobodna Bosna* addressed to Izetbegovic, claiming that the police and military intelligence "enable the state to have information on every single politician, officer, or journalist," and concluding that the attack was an attempt "to settle accounts" with him. "I do not know how much of this you can control," Avdic wrote to Izetbegovic. "If you cannot, it is horrible, and one should flee this country. If you can but do not do it, it is no less dangerous and horrible."[32] Miljenko Jergovic, reporting on the Bosnian media in *Nedjeljna Dalmacija* concluded, "If you judge it by *Slobodna Bosna*, there are Western European standards of freedom of the press in Sarajevo."[33] But the price tag for Avdic's editorial independence included some fifteen court cases, two suspended sentences, and even an arrest at his office to take him to court. His case prompted High Representative Carlos Westendorp to intervene in Bosnia's judicial system by moving the alleged libel cases from the criminal to the civil courts, thus taking the threat to prosecute away from nationalist authorities (only individuals can bring charges in civil courts).

The state of the media was less satisfactory in Republika Srpska and even worse in the Croat-controlled territories of Bosnia. An international presence in the election process forced the ruling SDS to allow the existence of some alternative newspapers, including *Nezavisne novine (Independent Newspaper)* and *Novi prelom (A New Layout)* in Banjaluka, as well as *Alternativa* in Doboj and *Panorama* in Bijeljina, all of which constituted "opposition" more than "independent" publications. The International Crisis Group reported that "Of these, *Nezavisne novine* was by far the most influential, evolving from a fortnightly newspaper into a weekly in June and a daily in August [of 1996] with financial assistance from the UK's Overseas Development Agency, the U.S. Agency for International Development (USAID), and George Soros' Open Society Fund. Moreover, the daily boasted a circulation of 4,000 and the weekly a circulation of 9,000, which though objectively low was nevertheless far greater than any other publication in Republika Srpska."[34]

On August 25, 1999, *Nezavisne novine* ran an exclusive, entitled "Renegade group of Prijedor policemen massacred more than 200 Bosniaks; Republika Srpska Army saved survivors, murderers escaped prosecution." That report—on a crime that had happened seven years before, on August 22, 1992—was the first ever in the Republika Srpska media on war crimes perpetrated by Serbs. The paper published a thorough investigative report on how some 200 Bosniaks from the Prijedor area, former inmates of the notorious Omarska concentration camp, were bused to the Koricani cliffs on Vlasic mountain in Central Bosnia and summarily executed. Seven of them survived the massacre, and *Nezavisne novine* ran their testimony. The report prompted an avalanche of threats to the paper's staff, accusing them of "betraying the nation," but the paper continued to print new revelations of the crimes committed by the Serb paramilitary, known as "Mice," in the Teslic area.

The price of such reporting proved to be high. On October 22, 1999, Reuters reported that a Bosnian Serb editor had lost his legs in a blast. Zeljko Kopanja, 45, founder, publisher, and editor of *Nezavisne novine*, was on his way to his office at 7:15 a.m. when an explosive device planted under his car went off. The blast severed one of Kopanja's legs, and he was brought to Banjaluka Clinical Center in critical condition. Surgeons amputated what was left of both of his legs. His heart had stopped beating briefly, but he was resuscitated and temporarily put on a respirator. Two weeks later, fighting both physical and emotional pain, Kopanja asked his friends and family to put him in a wheelchair so he could "take a walk" down Banjaluka's main pedestrian street, he said in an interview. "Seeing people in the [Gospodska] street, some of them just shaking my hand, some sobbing, I knew I had done the right thing. And I knew I had to persevere [in exposing the war crimes] since I had sacrificed so much. I don't think that any nation is criminal. It's individuals and certain policies, not a whole nation," Kopanja said of his motives to continue publishing.[35] "After all, what would my life be like if I confined myself to a wheelchair and my home only!" He agreed that he was a victim not only of the Serb war criminals, who wanted to silence him, but also indirectly of the silence in other Serb media about the war crimes. "The silence of the others has left us too lonely, exposed to accusations and vulnerable to attack. No one else [in the Republika Srpska media] has joined us. But I don't think it was politically or ideologically motivated silence. It was fear," Kopanja said.

The Helsinki Committee of Bosnia Herzegovina reported that other media in Republika Srpska experienced other sorts of harassment. *Reporter* magazine, which published both Bosnian and Serbian editions, was seized at the border when it ran a story on corruption in government. An independent radio station in Zvornik had its offices demolished; PIM TV in Bijeljina had its electricity supply cut off when the manager of a neighboring power company disliked a report; and a correspondent for independent media from Doboj, Milan Srdic, was beaten up by the local mayor. Rajko Vasic, information minister in Republika Srpska's government, had his car torched after the acting president of the Serb Radical Party, Mirko Blagojevic, accused him of "committing a crime against the Serbian people" and announced that his case had gone before "a Chetnik court."

For four years after Dayton, the only information available in Croat-controlled territories came from Tudjman's HDZ-held media, with no independent or alternative voices. Independent publications from Croatia, such as the *Feral Tribune* and *Nacional,* did not have equal access to the market in those territories, while two journalists from the independent *Novi list* from Rijeka—Robert Frank and Ronald Brmalj—were taken by force from their rooms in Ero Hotel in Mostar and badly beaten, with the attackers smashing Frank's hand "so you can't write any more."[36]

Oslobodjenje cartoonist Bozo Stefanovic summed up the desperation for change in post-Dayton Bosnia in a cartoon for the New Year 1999. Number One, depicted as the Bosnian opposition, tells three happy Nines wearing the distinctive ethnic hats of the three Bosnian nationalist parties: "Go ahead, laugh! Next year you'll all be Zeroes." In response, Izetbegovic's close associate and successor in the Bosnian Presidency, Halid Genjac, attacked *Oslobodjenje*—"and your Bozo" (suggesting Stefanovic's Serb name)—for making all three parties, SDA–SDS–HDZ, equally bad "when it is well known who defended and who attacked Bosnia." The paper's editor-in-chief, Mehmed Halilovic, responded that the cartoon was not meant to be a lesson in history but a reflection of Bosnia's need for political instead of ethnic pluralism.

Serbian Media Support Milosevic's Fourth War

Media developments in Serbia in the post-Dayton period 1995–2000 were marked by the Milosevic government's continued control over all influential media outlets and its systematic suppression of surviving or newly established independent media. Ironically, in the tradition of Balkan leaders' not telling the public what's on their minds—particularly concerning decisions that affect people the most, such as war and peace—Milosevic's decision in summer 1995 to abandon the Bosnian and Croatian Serbs, the very people he had pushed into rebellion against their own states, was first noticeable in Serbian TV's weather forecasts. Beginning in early September, the map illustrating the weather conditions, which throughout the war had shown the whole of "Greater Serbia" including Serb-held territories in both Croatia and Bosnia, suddenly shrank to cover only what was left of Yugoslavia: Serbia and Montenegro. Tired of international sanctions and isolation, Milosevic decided to change his image from Balkan arsonist to Balkan firefighter, becoming more cooperative in the now American-led peace efforts. The man who rose to power projecting himself as the protector of all Serbs had nothing to say when Croatian forces reclaimed Serb-held territories in Croatia, prompting a mass exodus of Serbs. Milosevic's TV, once so passionate in supporting a self-styled "Serb Republic" in Croatia, chose to ignore tens of thousands of Serb refugees fleeing the Croatian Army's offensive. The same silence followed the Bosnian Serbs' losses in a combined offensive of Bosnian and Croat forces in the closing months of the war. The media focus was on Milosevic-the-peacemaker, not on the victims of his drive for "Greater Serbia." He was seen meeting and greeting U.S. broker Richard Holbrooke and his team, followed with message after message of peace rhetoric, including an endless litany of "telegrams of support" from miners and workers for their president's peace efforts. There was no mention of the long columns of Serb refugees streaming into Serbia from Croatia and parts of Bosnia.

This was also the time when some of Milosevic's earliest and most loyal supporters in the state media fell from grace. First it was the director of Serbian Radio and TV, Milorad Vucelic, too closely associated with years of war propaganda to be entrusted to lead the propaganda of peace. Then it was the head of Politika TV, Slobodan Ignjatovic, another veteran in the advocacy of Serb ultranationalism. By the time Milosevic went to Dayton for the final peace talks in November 1995, Zivorad Minovic, instigator of Serb nationalism in the late eighties to early nineties in the pages of *Politika*, was briefly arrested and then fired because his services were no longer needed. On March 27, 1996, at the bottom corner of page 16, the paper carried what amounted to his political obituary: "Former president of the Politika Company Zivorad

Minovic is no longer employed in *Politika* due to retirement. Minovic has met all conditions for retirement under the force of the law."

For Milosevic, it wasn't enough to change the guard in his party-orchestrated media. He needed to silence the independent media as well, to eliminate public reminders of who initiated the wars in the first place. The design, as illustrated by his government's takeover of *Borba*, was simple: Invalidate the laws on media independence, adopted during the reformist Yugoslav government of Ante Markovic in the late eighties, and declare the previous privatization of disloyal media illegal. Once the "social ownership" of the media was restored, the ruling party would take over. In *Borba's* case, it was the federal government; in the case of the Studio B TV station, it was the Belgrade city government. The same recipe was used in the takeover of a number of regional and local media outlets—usually radio stations—throughout Serbia.

Milosevic's wife, Mirjana Markovic, in her infamous diaries published in *Duga* magazine, laid the ground for the state harassment of both independent media and their international donors. Issuing an unveiled threat to both the opposition and the independent media, she wrote:

> Before long, it will be known who participated in the financing of some of the media in Eastern European countries. That will also point to who was financed, i.e., who was paid to act as a fifth column in their own country . . . . But in taking money to work against their own country and for another one, these people should think about their descendents. Those mercenaries and informers who organize "democratic parties" and "independent media" with foreign currency naively think that the truth about their activity will not see the light of the day. And they naively hope that if trouble finds them, their financiers will protect them.

With "enemies from within" silenced and defeated, Milosevic's propaganda machinery focused on "foreign enemies," those critical of his control over media and especially those who—like the Soros Foundation—tried to support the scattered, independent voices in Serbia. Now the state-controlled *Borba* led the charge, accusing Soros of offering "poison in the guise of humanitarianism" and undermining "Serbian identity." One media analyst wrote that "*Borba* headlines went so far as to proclaim that 'Soros is Turning Our Youth Into Jannissaries [forced conscripts under the Ottoman Empire]' and that it is time to 'Ban the Soros Foundation.'"[37] By the spring of 1996, Belgrade authorities did exactly that, by simply removing the Foundation from court-registered institutions.

The regime's witch-hunt against all "enemies" and "collaborators," foreign "mercenaries" and "traitors," might explain why the Serbian media showed no interest in investigating some of the internationally well-established facts on wartime abuses. There was near silence on war crimes, with outright denial at worst or attempts to spread the blame to "all sides of the conflict" at best. The early indictments and legal proceedings before the International Criminal Tribunal at The Hague were either ignored or dismissed as "politically motivated accusations aimed at blaming Serbs for everything." Even such a reputed publication as *Vreme* ran a story largely simplifying what is known as "the worst atrocity on European soil since the World War II": "The Serb forces entered Srebrenica last July after provocation by Muslim troops from inside the enclave, and they evicted the Muslims."[38] While the reporter noted with irony that Serbs who settled in the once predominantly Muslim area deny any knowledge of the crime ("I wasn't there!"), he wrote the article as if he "wasn't there" either. He chose not to offer the otherwise well-known facts on the mass slaughter and "disappearance" of more than 7,000 men from Srebrenica.

The silencing of the independent media was part of Milosevic's broader strategy to solidify his party's power in the elections scheduled for November 1996. His Socialists and their partner, the small JUL (United Yugoslav Left) party led by his wife, enjoyed a full support in the media leading up to the elections. When the opposition nevertheless won in fourteen of Serbia's nineteen largest cities, Milosevic's government decided to hold onto power by annulling their victory. Electoral fraud prompted protests in the streets of Belgrade, which grew day by day from the end of November 1996 to the beginning of March 1997 into a mass street rebellion against the regime led by *Zajedno* (Together), a coalition of opposition parties. Protesters especially targeted the state-controlled media, marching on Serbian Television and Politika buildings in downtown Belgrade, chanting slogans and throwing eggs and paint at Milosevic's propaganda headquarters. Coverage of the protests underlined the tragic state of media freedom in Serbia: Tens of thousands of protesters in Belgrade's squares and streets, even under their own windows, simply did not exist for the

Milosevic-controlled media. While citizens protested media manipulation, TV screens and *Politika* headlines insisted on foreign and domestic enemies, spies and traitors, vandalism and terrorism, followed by the well-rehearsed technique of endless "telegrams of support" for the "legitimate authorities" and "preservation of the constitutional order."

Biserka Matic, a longtime *Politika* reporter who, together with many of her colleagues opposed the nationalist propaganda during Milosevic's years and received a salary no higher than the company's janitors, wrote an open letter requesting the resignation of the paper's director general, Hadzi Dragan Antic. "I don't understand my colleagues [not joining her request]. I will retire soon, and they will continue to work in a paper that's stained and humiliated. *Politika* has never been stoned or pelted by eggs, and its journalists have never before been called egg-heads and thieves," she wrote, explaining her protest.[39] Two of *Politika's* foreign correspondents, Dusan Simic (London) and Verica Rupar (Budapest), also sent a letter stating that the paper's failure to take note of the protests in Serbia and the international reactions to them were in opposition to the role of the press in a democratic society and harmful to *Politika's* reputation. An independent Belgrade commentator observed, "Primitive day-in and day-out propaganda on 'vandalism' in the streets of Belgrade, fabricated polls on 'citizen dissatisfaction' with 'fascists throwing garbage on Belgrade streets, stopping traffic and destroying what we built over decades' was the most obvious sign that the central Socialists' (SPS)-JUL studio did not want to take chances."[40] In all the state media, newsroom personnel were instructed to rely on Tanjug, the official news agency, for their reports. Veteran Belgrade Radio journalist and media analyst Rade Veljanovski quoted editors issuing standardized orders to small-town correspondents telling them to send interviews with opponents of the Together coalition, making sure that the "polling in the street" included only those critical of the opposition.[41]

On December 3, 1996, during the second week of the protests, Radio B92, one of the lonely sources of pure reporting on the events in Belgrade, suddenly went off the air. "The program was cut at the moment the announcer read a statement by someone making an analogy between Hitler's rise to power and what had occurred in Serbia's election," B92's Slobodan Stupar told *Vreme*.[42] The rebellious radio resorted to new technology, using Real Audio software, which allows you to listen to the radio via the Internet, to continue reporting, making it possible for both the Serbian and international public to get first-hand reports on the Belgrade street protests. B92 also went back on the air through international broadcasters' frequencies, including the Voice of America, the BBC, and Radio Free Europe, all of which had local language services. Through their solidarity, the local radio station—which couldn't even cover all of Belgrade—suddenly reached audiences throughout Serbia. With international support, director Veran Matic was able to access a satellite linking thirty-two radio and sixteen television stations into an Association of Independent Electronic Media (ANEM), covering 70 percent of Yugoslavia.

But the months-long protests, labeled "Belgrade spring" in the Western media, failed on one crucial account: Focused exclusively on electoral fraud, the opposition never addressed Milosevic's responsibility for the wars of the 1990s. Once the government accepted the opposition's electoral victory in major Serbian cities, Milosevic moved to solidify his power.

Serbia's Information Minister Aleksandar Tijanic, who in June 1996 had surprised everyone who knew him by leaving a career as one of Serbia's most respected journalists to enter the government, resigned his ministerial post following the demonstrations in March 1997, saying, "The journalist in me has defeated the minister." He said he had joined the government only to try to improve the media environment. In the 1980s, he initially criticized Milosevic and was virtually blacklisted in Serbian newspapers, continuing to write almost exclusively in Croatia *(Danas* and *Nedjeljna Dalmacija)* and in Bosnia *(Oslobodjenje).* He returned to Serbian journalism as the editor of Politika TV and later as a founder of BK (Karic Brothers) TV before accepting the ministerial post. Many in Belgrade believed that his promotion to minister was due to his well-advertised friendship with Milosevic's influential wife. In an interview with *Vreme* following his resignation, Tijanic explained his many reasons for leaving the government:

> First, I wanted to stick to the law and put frequencies up for public auction every year, so anyone interested could set up a radio or TV station. Second, I wanted to enable licensing of all Serbian media that met basic professional criteria, from Radio B92 to local stations. Third, I was absolutely against the practice of other ministries (in party uniform or not) banning media across

Serbia while leaving the responsibility to the information ministry. Fourth, I was fiercely against limiting the entry of foreign journalists into the country and drawing up lists of unsuitable journalists. I think the Serbian government has no right to choose the press. Fifth, and most important, I think the Serbian media have the right to report on events in Serbia. Since I was prevented from reacting the way I wanted to, I resigned.[43]

Following the restoration of the opposition's electoral victory in major Serbian cities in spring 1997, a number of new media outlets—not necessarily independent, but in opposition to the government—were formed. There were new local or regional dailies, radio, and TV stations throughout Serbia.

Milosevic, meanwhile, resorted to a proven method to solidify his power once again: Create a new crisis and project himself as the protector of "the threatened nation." This time the target was Kosovo, where he had started his rise to power in 1987. Ever since their province had been stripped of autonomy in February 1989, Kosovo Albanians—more than 90 percent of the province's population[44]—had been practicing nonviolent resistance against the Milosevic government's repression. The government had imposed total segregation on the province, giving Serbs control over all the instruments of the state including the army, police, local governments, media, schools, and health care facilities. In response, Albanians developed their own parallel institutions. For Albanians, peaceful resistance had one unwanted consequence: Kosovo was completely forgotten in international efforts to stabilize the Balkans, giving rise to impatience, desperation, and radicalization. By early 1998, the first armed Albanian groups appeared, calling themselves the Kosovo Liberation Army (KLA) and challenging Serbian police control in some areas of the province. This of course provided a pretext for Milosevic to use force. He dispatched heavily armed special police that announced "a showdown with Albanian terrorists," stormed Kosovo villages, and killed whole families of alleged "terrorists." According to the U.S. Department of State's 1998 Country Report on Human Rights, in early March, Serbian police entered the compound of the Ahmeti family in Likosane, rounding up and executing twelve male members of the family. A few days later, they surrounded the family compound of Adem Jasari, destroying the compound and killing eighty persons, including women and children. In

the course of that year, police also executed at least five male members
of the Hamzaj family in Ljubenic and allegedly executed eighteen
members of an Albanian family in Gornje Obrinje. Albanian rebels
also committed crimes against Serb civilians, Albanian "collaborators,"
and some members of the Roma minority. Their attacks against Serb
police forces were regularly followed by Serb retaliation against
Albanian civilians, leading to an escalation of tensions and low-level
"ethnic cleansing," calculated to expel Albanians village-by-village and
not—like Bosnians in 1992—from whole regions in order not to provoke international intervention. The strategy was described as Milosevic's motto: "Take a village a day to keep NATO away."

The major Serbian opposition parties, which never challenged Milosevic's justification for his wars—some because they agreed with him,
others because they believed that being "patriotic" gave them a better
chance to win elections—either supported the government's actions in
Kosovo or kept silent. State television glorified the "heroic sacrifice" of
killed Serb policemen but never showed pictures of the dozens of mur-
dered Albanian civilians. Five independent newspapers were prosecuted
for, among other things, referring to the dead Albanians as "victims"
instead of "terrorists." The daily *Danas* was attacked for reporting that the
Serbian Assembly honored only the dead Serb policemen without
acknowledging the dead Albanians. State TV, Milosevic's ally of choice,
was the predominant source of news: According to a study done by the
Novi Sad polling agency, "As many as 53 percent of the population
obtains its information exclusively from television. . . . Only 12 percent,
or approximately 1.3 million people in Serbia read daily newspapers regularly or almost regularly. Less than 5 percent, or 500,000 people, read
weekly political magazines."[45]

Veran Matic of Radio B92 registered the escalation of anti-Albanian
rhetoric in the regime-controlled media in a 1998 article. He noted that
they began calling the Kosovo province "Metohija," the name they had
always used for the western areas of Kosovo, which are home to some of
the historic Orthodox monasteries; they also referred to Albanians as
"Shiptars." With the advance of repressive Serb operations, Milosevic's
media adopted their black and white technique, referring to Albanians as
"Shiptar terrorists," "Shiptar gangs," or "Shiptar secessionists" and to the
Serb special police backed by the army as "forces of order." Reporting on

another "Terrorist Hideout Destroyed," the state media, according to Matic, "pushed aside any data on civilian casualties, the scale of the operation, the impact on civilian facilities, or the strength of the forces involved."[46]

This one-sided reporting, well rehearsed during the war in Croatia and Bosnia, was in full force again. Citing the possibility of NATO intervention against Serbia, Milosevic's government strengthened its control over the media by issuing on October 8, 1998, a Decree on Special Measures Under the Threat of NATO Armed Assault Against Our Country. That same month a new information law was introduced, providing new instruments for strangulation of the independent media. The law—adopted under the emergency procedures—prohibited rebroadcasting of foreign news programs of a "political-propagandistic nature." Under the law, anyone could sue media outlets for "unpatriotic" articles or materials "against the territorial integrity, sovereignty, and independence of the country." A number of independent publications such as the dailies *Dnevni telegraf, Danas, Blic,* and *Glas javnosti,* as well as weeklies, such as *Evropljanin* and *Vreme,* were slapped with huge fines threatening their very survival.

With the beginning of the seventy-eight-day NATO air campaign against Yugoslavia on March 24, 1999, aimed at stopping ethnic cleansing in Kosovo and at helping expelled Albanians return to their homes, what was left of the independent media in Serbia faced a difficult choice: continue to publish under censorship or cease operations until better days. Challenging the government's propaganda line was hardly an option. One of those who openly criticized Milosevic, Slavko Curuvija, the founder and publisher of *Dnevni telegraf (Daily Telegraph)* and *Evropljanin (European)* weekly experienced all sorts of government harassment. His papers were banned in Serbia; in response, he registered them in Montenegro, printed them in Zagreb, and smuggled them into Serbia. In mid-October 1998, Curuvija published an open letter, co-signed by his colleague and friend Aleksandar Tijanic, to the Yugoslav president, entitled "What Is Next, Milosevic?" criticizing him for the decade of wars and suffering in the former Yugoslavia. Immediately following the publication of the letter, on October 24, *Evropljanin* was fined $150,000, a draconian sum by Serbian standards, and the assets of the company and its director Ivan Tadic were seized, including Tadic's personal belongings from his apartment.[47] Curuvija was sentenced to five months in jail for offending the "dignity and honor" of Serbia's deputy prime minister and he was still expecting a ruling on his appeal. Refusing to accept the censorship, he ultimately halted the publication of his papers. State television accused Curuvija of "supporting NATO's bombing of Serbia,"[48] which was not true. A day later when the NATO bombing began, the *Politika ekspres* headline read, "Curuvija Has Finally Got His Bombs." Five days later—on Sunday, April 11, 1999—two gunmen dressed in black killed him outside his apartment building in downtown Belgrade on his return with his wife, Branka Prpa, from their Orthodox Easter lunch.

Veran Matic, who issued public pleas against the bombing through Western media, including an Op-Ed piece in the *New York Times*,[49] was arrested during the police takeover of his station just before the first bombs fell on Belgrade. He said in an interview:

> Our program was critical of the government because Milosevic did not prepare the country for the bombing. Suddenly, late that night, March 24, 1999, the station went off the air. I called the office but no one picked up the phone, so I walked toward the station, knowing that I was followed. When I came to the radio station and called from downstairs, they told me, "Everything is finished; you don't have to come up." But my colleagues and friends were there, and I went in. Police asked for my ID and told me I had to go with them. In a car on our way to Belgrade's Central Jail, they told me, "Man, don't worry, everything will be taken care of." I wanted to call my wife, to tell her not to worry, but they would not allow me. They offered me a choice between "a single or a double room" and placed me with someone in a Giorgio Armani suit, who slept like a baby, while I was watching the sky expecting the planes and bombs. The guards were drunk, there were some loud Romanian black marketeers next door, and when my roommate woke up, he thought I was a police informer. He was accused of murder. The next day I was released, and B92 was soon occupied by a new, government-installed management.[50]

B92 staff refused to work for the regime's management and later resumed broadcast over the Internet.

People in Belgrade and elsewhere in Serbia, while exposed to the terror of the bombing, were served Milosevic-style versions of what was going on: "The Serb people" were punished for their legitimate defense of their ancient territories against "Shiptar terrorists" and "NATO fascists." While the unintended tragic deaths of Serb civilians in the NATO bombings were presented as a "Nazi-like crime" against the Serb nation, hundreds of thousands of Albanians who had been forced to flee their homes in a systematic "ethnic cleansing" campaign did not even get an honorable mention.

In the early hours of April 23, 1999, a NATO bomb hit the head-quarters of the Serbian TV in downtown Belgrade, killing sixteen employees, mostly technical staff, none of them a journalist or a senior employee. That night I received a call from a Serb colleague based in Europe, asking me to comment for her radio station on the "bombing of a media institution." I told her that my reaction was mixed: "My heart is bleeding for the innocent people on duty, who were there as hostages to their institution's propaganda war against NATO—why else would there be a make-up artist on duty at 3 a.m.?— but I honestly have trouble thinking of Belgrade TV as 'a media institution.' The mission of the media is to spread the news, while their mission was to deny the news; the media's role is to inform, their role was to misin-form; and, after all, force and even murder were used in imposing that TV station's propaganda on Bosnia in 1992." And it later became known that NATO had warned RTS of the pending attack and all employees could have been evacuated from the building.

Thinking of that institution, with deep sympathy for the innocent Serbian TV employees sacrificed by their own managers, who knew per-fectly well that their building was a potential strategic target, I couldn't remember Belgrade TV offering any professional solidarity during the Serb terror against Bosnian media in 1992–95. All the international TV networks—BBC, CNN, ABC, CBS, Austrian, French, and German—reported many times on the Serb shelling and destruction of *Oslobodjenje*, sending their crews to visit us in our atomic bomb shelter.[51] Serbian TV offered only a picture from the perspective of the Serb artillery besieging and bombing Sarajevo. While it was perfectly expected that international groups concerned with media freedom around the world would con-demn the attack on Belgrade TV, some of their moral recommendations, such as the one that propaganda should be confronted with the truth, not with bombs, sounded naïve in the Balkans realities of the 1990s. Because of Milosevic, there was no way to tell Serbs the truth. All the media were in his hands: censored or strangled.

Six months after the bombing of Serb TV, the parents and relatives of the sixteen staff members killed on duty unveiled a commemorative stone in front of the ruined building, dedicated to "The sixteen sacrificed, in eternal peace." A news report sums up the reactions to the incident: "Mirjana Stoimenovski, the mother of one of the victims, says that their loved ones died as 'victims of the cruel policy of the RTS, which put workers' lives, completely unnecessarily and consciously, on NATO's altar.' And the public is convinced that the families of those who died are right: 'the regime sacrificed RTS employees in order to raise anti-NATO feelings during the bombing.'"[52] According to that report, the families of the sixteen blamed RTS management for the deaths, saying that the NATO bombs were guided by the defiant words from their screens. Tatjana Lenard, a foreign news editor, said in an evening news broadcast, "Let [the NATO Supreme Commander Gen. Wesley] Clark shoot, we are waiting for him at number 10 Takovska Street." But she later claimed she had merely used a "figure of speech."[53] Rumors spread that some of the senior TV executives had left the building shortly before bombing.

At the time of the NATO bombing campaign, I remember meeting a friend in Washington, D.C., who was deeply involved in helping the Serbian independent media throughout a decade of Milosevic dictatorship: "Can you explain what is going on at *Vreme?*" he asked, shocked with the anti-Western rhetoric in a magazine known for its balanced and critical reporting on the wars in the Balkans. *Vreme*—like the rest of the Serbian media—could choose only to submit to censorship or not publish at all. "It was a difficult choice," Stojan Cerovic, the magazine's most respected writer, said in an interview. "My colleagues believed that once we stopped publishing, we'd never be able to come back."[54] Gordana Logar, at that time an editor with *Danas* daily, said *Danas* was motivated by the same consideration as *Vreme:* If they stopped publishing, it would most probably be forever. The government threatened to close any publication that ceased to operate during the NATO intervention. "*Danas,* like most of the rest, submitted to censorship," Logar said in an interview.[55] The editor took all stories to the information ministry, which had strict rules on what was allowed and what was not. Logar explained:

> It was easier to deal with the minister, Aleksandar Vucic, directly. He had some self-confidence that comes with the position, while his deputy was scared of everything. She had never been a journalist. Once she decided that we couldn't print the full six pages of *Danas.* When the editor asked her

what he was going to put in those six blank pages, she was surprised that the space had to be filled with something.[56]

Faced with this lose-lose situation, those in the independent media who decided to publish under censorship compromised their position with both the international donors and some prominent Serbian human rights activists. Natasa Kandic, director of Belgrade's Humanitarian Law Center, charged that there were "no significant editorial differences between the government, pro-government, and antigovernment media during the NATO intervention."[57] Others, however, such as media analyst Jovanka Matic of the Belgrade Institute of Social Sciences, did see a difference between state and private media. "State media sought to present this homogenization [against the bombing] as identical to support for the Milosevic regime, or indivisible from it; other media maintained a dividing line between the regime, the leader(s), and the national interest. Like it or not, national interest was widely perceived in wartime Yugoslavia as resistance to the bombing and defiance of the bombers."[58]

Others in Belgrade saw it as a question of credibility. One of the prominent antiwar activists, Svetlana Slapsak, wrote in *ProFemina:* "For someone who publicly protested when they, you-know-who, bombed Dubrovnik, Vukovar, Osijek, Zadar, Sarajevo, Mostar, there was no difficulty in opposing the [NATO] bombing of targets in Yugoslavia. For those who were silent then, it was more difficult." She noted that two groups, around *Republika* magazine and around Radio B92, became even more critical of the regime, pointing to the responsibility for the war and bombing, with serious analysis and human interest reporting on the Albanians and their tragedy.[59] Lepa Mladjenovic from the Autonomous Women's Center in Belgrade related her personal experience of being censored by an independent Belgrade publication. When she gave an interview to the independent daily *Glas*, she said that the women's center communicated daily with "our Albanian friends in Pristina" during the war. "The editor changed the word 'Albanian' to the derogatory 'Shiptar' and changed the word 'friends' to 'colleagues.' I ask myself, 'How does this fascist policy of eliminating the possibility of having friends among Kosovo Albanians and forbidding that we call them Albanians affect each of us?' Aren't we afraid of this [effect]?"[60]

Blaine Harden of the *New York Times* reported on Milosevic's propaganda following the defeat in Kosovo:

Kosovo episodes of this season's Big Lie, like previous "news" programming during the Bosnian war about how mendacious Muslims in Sarajevo were laying siege to themselves to get world sympathy, are part of the pattern of mass deception that has characterized a decade of Mr. Milosevic's nationalist wars. It is a strategy that sells defeat as victory, ignores the periodic floods of Serbian refugees flowing into Serbia from lost war zones and leaves millions of Serbs in ignorance or confused denial of human rights atrocities committed in their name by Mr. Milosevic's security forces.[61]

According to a survey conducted by the U.S. Information Agency in summer 1999, "six in ten Serbs watched Serbian state television 'frequently' or 'sometimes' and half listened to state radio at least sometimes during the NATO air strikes on the FRY [Federal Republic of Yugoslavia]. Nevertheless, other sources of information were widely used during the air strikes, including independent radio (46 percent), foreign television (31 percent), and foreign radio (28 percent). . . . Four in ten Serbs listened to RFE, VOA, BBC, RFI, or Deutsche Welle during the NATO air strikes."[62] Eric D. Gordy illustrates, in his book, the power of the Milosevic-controlled state television as "the authority of last instance." He quotes an older Belgrade woman, a strong supporter of the regime, who told him: "I understand why you think the way you do because you live in America and watch American television. But I live here and I watch Yugoslav television, so I think differently."[63]

Croatia: Tudjman's Media vs. "Enemies of the State"

In post-Dayton Croatia, two newspapers in coastal Adriatic cities, the weekly *Feral Tribune* in Split and the daily *Novi list* in Rijeka, bore the brunt of the Tudjman government's harassment. The *Feral Tribune*, a satirical weekly with a name alluding to the *Herald Tribune*, started as a weekly supplement first within *Nedjeljna Dalmacija* and then within *Slobodna Dalmacija*. Its first editor was Viktor Ivancic, who later brought in his friends Predrag Lucic and Boris Dezulovic. The three of them were also known under their common nickname Viva Ludez, meaning something like "Long live fun," which was based on the first letters of their names. When Tudjman's party occupied *Slobodna Dalmacija* in 1993 and its legendary editor Josko Kulusic was forced out of office, the *Feral* team left too. They were joined by respected TV reporter Heni Erceg, who later became the editor, and started to publish as an independent weekly. *Feral* became Tudjman's favorite "enemy of the state" for regularly poking fun at the Croatian president, with doctored cover pictures depicting him in a bathtub with Milosevic or as a successor to Ustasha leader Ante Pavelic; exposing his obsession with becoming a "new Tito," obvious from his taste for decorated imperial uniforms, presidential palaces, and ceremonial guard; contrasting the lavish lifestyles of the HDZ elite with the economic hardships facing the country and its people. Ivancic was not apologetic about the label. "I really am an enemy of such a state. Why shouldn't I be? Why should the whole Croat people serve the state? Why should I have to serve that state the way the government wants me to? For me, it is the state that has to serve the people, and especially to serve the individual. I want a state that will serve me."[64]

The government used many different methods in its efforts to silence *Feral*. HDZ-controlled *Slobodna Dalmacija's* printing press refused to print it; the HDZ-controlled distributor Tisak first refused to sell it and later refused to pay *Feral* the money for its sold newspapers; local kiosk owners and street vendors were intimidated and afraid to sell "that anti-Croat paper." The danger was real: HDZ extremists in Split burned piles of *Feral* at several locations throughout the city in June 1995. Tudjman's war against *Feral* included the imposition in 1994 of a 50 percent sales tax, normally reserved for pornographic literature—a tax the paper barely survived—and the adoption of a law by which the state could prosecute authors and editors offending the holders of high offices. The new law was, as expected, soon tested in *Feral's* case. Ivancic and another *Feral* journalist, Marinko Culic, were indicted on May 7, 1996, for ridiculing Tudjman's proposal to "reconcile in death" Ustasha fascists and their victims by burying their bones together. The paper compared the idea to that of the late Spanish dictator Franco about reconciling fascists and their victims in death by building a joint monument for "all victims of the war." *Feral* printed another photomontage of Tudjman receiving as a gift from Pavelic a replica of the Jasenovac concentration camp monument commemorating tens of thousands of victims of Ustasha crimes. The incriminating articles were published under the titles "Bones in a Blender" and "Jasenovac—the Biggest Croatian Underground Town." By comparing published quotes in the courtroom, Ivancic and Culic used the occasion to demonstrate the similarity between Tudjman's and

Franco's ideas. "This trial is aimed at criminalizing opinions different from those of Tudjman, but we will continue to think of his idea as sick. It is relativizing war crimes," Ivancic said.[65]

In September of the same year, the law protecting top state officials was tested against the Rijeka daily *Novi list* and the Zagreb weekly *Nacional,* both critical of Tudjman and his party. Two editors, Veljko Vicevic and Ivo Pukanic, were indicted for "spreading lies" and "muddying the leaders" of the ruling party and its members. After Tudjman and the HDZ took control of *Slobodna Dalmacija,* in addition to all statewide television and radio broadcasts, they controlled four out of five dailies in Croatia. Even though *Novi list* was not a national daily (it was published in Rijeka and wasn't available throughout Croatia), the paper had gained an international reputation for its open-minded approach to the controversial issues of democracy and to Croatia's role in the war in neighboring Bosnia. Summarizing the previous year in January 1996, *Novi list's* commentator Roman Latkovic observed that it would be remembered for "the final unmasking of Franjo Tudjman as a man who led the country to ruin." The comment was based on the fact that Tudjman had used his imperial presidential power to prevent the opposition-nominated Zagreb mayor from taking office despite the election results. "Croatia headed by Tudjman is being reduced to a dictatorship, a Mafia-type banana republic and everybody's worst nightmare," Latkovic's commentary said. Croatian state television (HTV) immediately fired back, stating on prime-time news that "certain forces personified by Roman Latkovic have taken off their masks" and should instantly be included among "Croatia's enemies."

HDZ attempted to "privatize" the Rijeka daily the same way it had privatized *Slobodna Dalmacija.* But the effort failed, mostly because Tudjman's party never won more than 20 percent of the votes in the traditionally cosmopolitan port city of Rijeka. However, soon after Latkovic's commentary, the government dispatched the financial police to *Novi list.* On March 28, 1996, they came up with a finding: The paper had to pay a 3.7 million DM ($1.8 million) customs duty for importing a printing press from Italy. The import had been previously exempted from duties because the press was brought to Rijeka as an Italian publisher's donation to the area's Italian minority and was used to print, free of charge, the Italian-language *La Voce del Popolo* in addition to *Novi list* and *Glas Istre (Voice of Istria)*.

The Tudjman government's intimidation did not silence *Novi list*. Vicevic and his staff, as well as some of the most respected Croatian columnists who contributed regularly to the paper, continued to report on even the most sensitive topics. These included reports on the crimes committed during the liberation of the Serb-held areas of Croatia and the Zagreb authorities' responsibility for the attempted assassination of Hans Koschnik, the European Union's administrator in the Bosnian city of Mostar, by Croatian extremists in February 1996. *Novi list* ran a commentary accusing state television of running Tudjman's election campaign while denying his opponents, Vlado Gotovac and Zdravko Tomac, any coverage. The commentary said that HRT had sponsored a celebration of the president's birthday and organized a musical cara-van throughout Croatia and even abroad celebrating Tudjman and his party ahead of national elections. "There is more. The HRT announced the military parade at Jarun in a special advertisement, with the inevitable picture of the president, and there was also a commercial for a Tudjman cassette issued by the HRT's Orfej Company," the com-mentary said.[66] Tudjman erupted in a speech to HDZ's youth wing in November 1997: "Various fools, crackpots, dilettantes, ignoramuses, and simply those who sold their souls, want to denigrate the magnifi-cent revival of Croatian freedom and independence, and the glorious and thunderous Croatian victories," he said, aiming his remarks at the independent media.[67]

Tudjman never got that angry at the continued embarrassing per-formance of the HDZ-controlled media. One of the worst examples included reporting by Zagreb Radio and *Vecernji list* on a visit to Cro-atia by the late U.S. Commerce Secretary Ron Brown. The American delegation was scheduled to land at Dubrovnik airport at about 3 p.m. on April 3, 1996, so the radio announced in its afternoon newscast that not only had they arrived but that the meeting between Brown and Croatia's Prime Minister Zlatko Matesa had already begun. In its first edition the next morning, *Vecernji list* "reported" that Matesa "had received the American delegation" at the airport at which Brown had stated: "This mission signals the next phase of American relations with Bosnia and Croatia."[68] Tragically, the plane had crashed near the

Dubrovnik airport minutes before its scheduled landing, killing Secretary Brown, the delegation of businessmen accompanying him, and
the crew.

With all of his instruments of intimidation, Tudjman never managed to silence the Croatian press completely. Individual Croatian journalists, intellectuals, and politicians as well as civic society activists, such
as a group around Croatia's Helsinki Committee led by Ivan Zvonimir
Cicak, constantly challenged Tudjman's authoritarian rule. Croatia's
Society of Journalists (HND) played a crucial role in providing its
members a forum to defend professional standards and values throughout a decade of HDZ. While the official Serbian Association of
Journalists followed the regime's line, challenged only by the disenfran-
chised independent union, and the Bosnian association disintegrated
along ethnic and territorial lines, HND remained active throughout the
1990s. Formed in 1910, the organization had a long tradition, and it
started its own Journalists' Workshop, which has offered three-month
courses to some 150 journalists, and an International Center for the
Education of Journalists in Opatija that has organized some fifty courses,
workshops, roundtables, and other media conferences. One of the most
serious challenges to the Tudjman government's total control of the
media came with the establishment in 1997 of Forum 21, bringing
together dissatisfied Croatian Radio and Television (HRT) journalists
who stood up against the ruling party's monopoly over state television.
Among the Forum 21 co-founders were Mirko Galic and Damir Matkovic, both of whom wanted to transform Croatian television into a
professional organization responsible to the public rather than to those
in power.

Galic had limited previous experience with television. He had been
in journalism for thirty-two years, almost half of that time as a correspondent in Paris, and he had also been the editor-in-chief of the leading Croatian newsmagazine, *Danas*, in its best years, 1985–88. Galic
came to the HRT only in 1997 as a managing board member with the
hope of helping to transform the organization that had become an
open advocate of Tudjman's party, the Croatian Democratic Union
(HDZ). "Five or six members of the television board were simultaneously members of the HDZ's Presidency," Galic said in an interview,
explaining his reasons for joining Matkovic and others in initiating the

HRT reform. Forum 21 was attacked as "an attempt to undermine the state," but—as Galic said—they wanted only to raise the issue of state television, to see what needed to be done for Croatia to have a public broadcasting company. He explained:

> Croatia was behind all the other countries in transition, and we argued for major changes. One was to establish an independent council, both to over-see the TV and to protect its editorial independence and institutional integrity. Next was to establish a private television, as a competitor to HRT; to separate the transmitter network into a new company serving all those who need access to the airwaves; and to adopt professional standards to separate journalism from politics, making it impartial and pluralistic. Forum 21 wanted to introduce professional standards that would protect both journalists and the public against manipulation, making it a rule that if the government says one thing, the opposition has the right to say something else. Arguing for public TV in Croatia, we aimed at changing the whole media landscape in the country.[69]

But after only a year and a half at HRT, Galic resigned in February 1999, "disappointed with both the business and editorial policies." In a public statement on his resignation, among his reasons for quitting Galic cited both governmental interference in his work and a lack of democracy. While Galic went to a new job as editor-in-chief of the weekly *Globus*, Matkovic, the founder and president of Forum 21, continued his struggle for the transformation of HRT. He was well equipped for this. A journalist since 1982, who had gone from a street reporter to a foreign correspondent visiting, among others, President Clinton and the Pope, Matkovic had been fascinated with television as a chaotic system in which there is some order after all: "No matter how chaotic it is throughout the day, there is always that prime-time news journal at 7:30 p.m." Matkovic said in an interview.[70]

Forum 21 ideas detonated into the public debate on the relationship between the state and television in a democracy. When U.S. Secretary of State Madeleine Albright visited Zagreb on August 30, 1998, assembled representatives of Croatia's independent media gave her a thorough overview not only of the pressures implemented against them but also of the battle Croatian journalists were waging to preserve the dignity of their profession. Members of Forum 21 told her they were fighting Tudjman's role as the de facto editor-in-chief of HRT. "We believe the HRT should be changed from an institution controlled by the president's office to a public institution," Dubravko Merlic said. Zrinka Vrabec-Mojzes, editor-in-chief of Zagreb Radio 101, which faced the government's ban through a denial of frequencies, told Albright how the demonstrations of some 120,000 Zagreb citizens prevented the planned shutdown of the station. She also said that, even though there were 120 radio and 15 television stations in Croatia, 90 percent of them were in the hands of ruling party members or loyalists, and that people in smaller towns didn't have the courage to demonstrate for media freedom as did people in Zagreb. Gordana Grbic and Zeljka Ogresta related their stories of being fired from state TV. And some in the audience spoke about the government's use of the privatization process, of government cronies' ownership of printing presses, and of distribution networks being used to break the independent press. Albright assured the group that, in her talks with Tudjman and other government officials, she would make freedom of the press "one of the benchmarks" Croatia would have to meet in order to be accepted into European institutions.[71]

The end of 1998 was marked by another embarrassing episode in Tudjman's relationship with the Croatian independent press. In mid-October, a new Zagreb daily, *Jutarnji list (Morning Newspaper)*, carried news that the president's wife, Ankica Tudjman, deposited some $137,200 in her confidential accounts at Zagrebacka banka (Zagreb Bank). That contradicted Tudjman's statement in a mandatory election disclosure form that his unemployed wife owned only a car. Damir Matkovic said in an interview that he was "professionally embarrassed" by the reaction of HRT: "On the evening after *Jutarnji list* broke the story, there was no word of it in the prime-time TV news. The next evening there was a debate on why the bank didn't protect the secrecy of deposits and why they allowed a breach of secrecy, but nothing about the obligation of public office holders to disclose their assets," Matkovic said.[72] Instead, state television offered Tudjman an opportunity to explain his wife's deposits in this way: "That's the result of fifty years of work and thirty published books."[73]

In 1999 there were more than 900 libel lawsuits against Croatian journalists and publishers. Seventy of them, twenty criminal cases and fifty private cases, were against *Feral Tribune* alone, with potential damages exceeding $2 million. Tisak, HDZ's crony-owned distribution network, continued to discriminate against independent publications, owing the weekly *Nacional* some $500,000 and the *Feral Tribune* $200,000 and bringing both weeklies to the verge of shutdown.

Nacional nevertheless deserves credit for exposing the most bizarre story of the Tudjman government's control of every walk of life. On June 2, 1999, the paper printed an article signed by Ivo Pukanic and Robert Bajrusi containing "state secrets." This well-documented article revealed that the state's mighty Service for the Protection of Constitutional Order was engaged in taping, following, and reporting on sports journalists, soccer officials, and referees in order to directly influence the outcome of the national soccer championship so that the president's favorite club, Croatia, would win.[74] Much later, it became known that Tudjman's government had spied on some 650 "enemies of the state," including 126 journalists, monitoring their private phone conversations; conducting apartment searches; and recording informants' reports on their private encounters, conversations, and love affairs.[75]

Tudjman died of cancer on December 10, 1999. Even the news of his death served as a reminder that dictators and the people around them have no respect for those who serve them unreservedly. Croatia's official news agency, Hina, was not even notified officially. They carried a report on Tudjman's death only after the international wire services had already reported it based on a Croatian TV announcement at 2 a.m. that Saturday. Hina's editor, Benjamin Tolic, protested to the government for being "betrayed," while director Ljubomir Antic resigned because "Hina's credibility had been damaged."

Tudjman's death immediately exposed the weakness of autocratic rule: Once the undisputed leader is gone, there are no democratic institutional mechanisms to provide continuity of his policies. A decade of Tudjman–HDZ rule in constant dispute with the rest of Europe over democracy and human rights and in continuing economic decline left Croatia desperate for changes. Tudjman's legacy was best described by the reaction of former U.S. Ambassador to Croatia Peter Galbraith, who said at the news of his death: "He was a man with two dreams. One was independent Croatia, and he achieved that, and the other was a European Croatia, which can be achieved only after he is gone."[76] The signs of imminent changes could have been detected even in Tudjman's obituaries written by some of his most enthusiastic propagandists. One of them,

Vecernji list editor Branko Tudjen, used his commentary on Tudjman's death to draw an until-then nonexistent line between the president and himself, stating "The president criticized me occasionally for being critical of the government." This was enough to provoke an ironic laugh among independent journalists. And anyone remembering Tudjen's servility to Tudjman now realized that the end of an era had definitely arrived.

The Year 2000:
The Beginning
of Change

FOR PEOPLE IN THE BALKAN COUNTRIES engulfed in the wars of the nineties—Bosnia, Croatia, Serbia—New Year's 2000 represented more than the much anticipated symbolic beginning of a new year, a new century, or even a new millennium. It was a moment of hope for a new beginning for the Balkans—a rebirth of sorts. It was a time to close a decade marked by the wholesale destruction of lives, families, homes, towns, and countries, a time to turn to the future. That symbolic year 2000 laid the ground for a long overdue change with the departure of Tudjman in Croatia, the rise of antinationalist pro-European parties in Bosniak majority areas of Bosnia, and the overthrow of Milosevic in Serbia. People of the former Yugoslavia, separated by newly established borders and identities, by their losses and bitter memories of wars and destruction, converged on a long journey toward a common European future. Only ten years earlier, decades ahead of other Eastern European countries in social development and standard of living, they now found themselves decades behind. Deeply divided in almost everything else, they were united in the shared goal to become part of an emerging

Europe, whole and free. These factors fueled the changes that began in the year 2000.

In Croatia, Tudjman's death in December 1999 opened the way for a dramatic turnaround. A coalition of pro-European democratic parties won the elections, removing the ultranationalist HDZ from power, and a new president Stipe Mesic, who opposed Tudjman's autocratic rule and his design for a partition of Bosnia, was elected. Mesic was the first leader in the region who denounced war crimes committed by his own country's armed forces, both against Croatian Serbs in Croatia and in the war in Bosnia, declaring that it was in Croatia's national interest to extradite all indicted war criminals. There had to be individual accountability "if we don't want the whole nation to bear collective responsibility for the crimes committed," he argued. "We can't be hostages of those individuals who committed crimes. I don't care what their names are or what positions they hold. Those indicted for war crimes have to face their responsibility."[1]

In Bosnia, which since Dayton had lived under a shadow of ultranationalist pressures from neighboring countries, with both Milosevic and Tudjman cronies still in power in Serb- and Croat-controlled areas, pro-European democratic forces began to take over, at least in Bosniak majority areas previously controlled by the nationalist Muslim SDA. The democratic forces won municipal and parliamentary elections in some of the largest Bosnian cities—Sarajevo, Tuzla, and Zenica. This raised hopes that the departure of Tudjman and Milosevic, and Croatia's and Serbia's subsequent announced respect for Bosnian sovereignty, might weaken the hold on power of the Serb and Croat nationalist parties in the rest of the country.

And in Serbia, on October 5, 2000, following another of Milosevic's attempts at electoral fraud, street protests finally brought change as the democratic opposition candidate Vojislav Kostunica, a constitutional lawyer, replaced Milosevic as Yugoslav president. Along with the defeat of Milosevic, the most noticeable change occurred in the state media, which had slavishly served him since 1987: With the same lightness that they had switched their loyalties from brotherhood and unity to nationalism and hatred, from Tito to Milosevic, they now screamed for joy over a "victory of democracy" in Serbia.

Croatia Opts for European Future

Visiting Croatia in January 2000, just weeks after the democratic opposition defeated the HDZ in parliamentary elections and days before the
final round of presidential elections, I saw signs of change everywhere.
Newspapers exhibited at the Zagreb Airport kiosks were all about
democracy and prosperity, not about "domestic and foreign enemies" as
they had been in Tudjman's decade. The taxi driver taking me to the
city was only too happy to discuss the end of the Tudjman era. Pointing
to the HDZ election posters that still clung to electricity poles along
the highway, he said, "It's good those thieves lost." The new government, with a coalition led by the Social Democrats winning the
Parliament and charismatic Stipe Mesic replacing autocratic Tudjman
as president, has pledged to free the media from a decade of strict party
control and has taken preliminary steps in that area. Journalists I met
over a drink at the cafe in the Croatian Radio and Television (HRT)
complex were looking forward to a change. "We've lost ten years, we
have to work hard to catch up with Europe," Damir Matkovic, Forum
21 president, said in an interview.[2] Having fought for "European TV"
in the years of the autocratic regime, Mirko Galic and Matkovic had
now been promoted to a position where they could implement the
changes they had advocated: Galic as director general and Matkovic as
his principal adviser. While Tudjman and his party were still in power,
Forum 21 had drafted a Charter on Public TV, inviting all political parties registered for the elections in January 2000 to sign it as a promise
to the public that if they came to power, they would support the HRT
transformation. Of the seventeen parliamentary parties, only seven
signed the promise, including—luckily for the Forum—all six opposition parties that won the elections, plus the Serbian People's Party. By
creating the Charter, "We set a precedent for a new way of dealing with
other major social issues. By accepting professionals' role in shaping
public television, the new government might also want to include edu-
cators in shaping the educational system or health professionals in
reforming the health care system," Matkovic said.[3]

Reformers' mission to transform Croatian Radio and Television
encountered immediate resistance from HDZ-appointed editors and
managers, who cried foul, describing the new managers as revenge-
seekers and portraying themselves in the Croatian media as "victims of

a witch-hunt." The last Tudjman-era editor-in-chief, Obrad Kosovac, asked publicly, "Why would I resign just because in HTV programs I supported Tudjman's option of a firm, upright, and stable state?"[4] Kosovac had earned the HDZ's trust by producing a series of documentaries on Tudjman's historic legacy of independent Croatia ("Dr. Tudjman—We Have Croatia," "From Wasteland to Croatia's Independence," "Creation of Croatian State"). But he was best known in public for his ability to adjust his own documentary work to changing political realities. During Communist rule, he made a documentary portraying World War II Croatian Cardinal Alojzije Stepinac as a Nazi collaborator, but—with HDZ rehabilitation of the pro-Nazi Croatian Ustasha movement—he changed the film to reflect Stepinac's promotion to sainthood. It took two sessions of the HRT council and Galic's public ultimatum—"If he stays, I go"—to remove Kosovac from the office. The fear of "revenge" among the leading propagandists of Tudjman's regime over the previous decade was founded in their own experience of coming to power. At that time the HDZ-appointed directors general, Hrvoje Hitrec and Anton Vrdoljak, had systematically purged the newsroom of all those considered "untrustworthy" by the new authorities.

As the new director general, Galic faced two major challenges in implementing the Forum 21 ideas he had helped develop: restoring the credibility of the newsroom, devastated by the loyal service to the ruling party throughout the 1990s, and making the HRT a viable public company. "Those who complain about possible 'revenge' are the same ones who made the HRT a one-party institution," Galic said in an interview. "They were brought into that position by the party, all key editors were party loyalists or activists, and now they accuse us of a 'showdown' if we want to replace an editor who was in the party leadership with one who was not, one who will guarantee a high professional standard. We have to replace party activists, depoliticize journalism, and liberate the profession from any party ties. It will take time and patience, but that's where we are going," he said.[5] His right-hand man in those efforts, Forum 21 president Matkovic, is equally eager to transform the HRT into a public company. He sees it as a "monster" reflecting the previous government's obsessions with the symbolism of big state institutions. Matkovic explained:

Running a three-channel state television 24 hours a day in a country with only 4.5 million people has been economic madness. We will ask for privatization of Channel 3, because two public channels are enough for a country with no more than a million subscribers. We also need to thoroughly revise our financial situation. In 1956, Zagreb was the first to have television in the former Yugoslavia, and since then it has always been in a "higher political interest" to pay its bills, no matter how much that cost.[6]

Matkovic wants HRT to support and encourage young talented writers by running public contests for the best screenplays, as well as sending its journalists to well-established European and American public television stations to learn in their newsroom environments how to make more professional, impartial, pluralistic TV programs. Forum 21 also argues for the regionalization of Croatian TV. One-third of Croatia's population is concentrated around Zagreb, while the rest of the country is losing population. "It's monstrous, like a huge head with no body," Matkovic said, adding that Croatia has distinct regions with their own traditions, culture, and literature that deserve expression in the media. "HDZ tried to erase those differences by centralizing everything in Croatia. We have ancient, 2,500-year-old cities in Dalmatia; we have regional centers such as Osijek, Split, Rijeka; but all you can do as a journalist in those cities is to serve the HRT evening newscast, following instructions from the center. You don't have a program of your own and no way to express your creativity. Our idea is to make Channel 2 a network of regional stations instead of serving the central authorities."[7]

Matkovic was asked in mid-April 2000 to comment on criticism in the independent press that changes were too slow, that many of those who served Tudjman's party were still anchoring the evening news. He readily admitted that the process has been slower than it should be. But while it's important to remove those who have lost the public trust, 'it's also important to ensure the continuity of the programs. "So the transition is an ongoing process," he said. "It's a question of who . . . is going to make sure we have our evening news every day." Some independent Croatian journalists criticized HRT reformers for being too soft in dealing with those who had lost their professional credibility serving Tudjman and HDZ. Galic countered that some of them deserve a second chance, and "we need to develop a system in which journalists will not lose their jobs whenever there is a change in government." In that, he was supported by at least one respected Croatian TV journalist, Tomislav Jakic, who himself had been a victim of HDZ purges. He was among the founders of the association called A Right to Profession, arguing that even though changes must be introduced in HTV, "it shouldn't be done the way HDZ did it."[8]

The change of government in January 2000 has been followed by major changes in Croatia's newspaper industry. The reexamination of the privatization process, in which Tudjman's loyalists acquired control over dozens of media outlets, has brought about changes in ownership and editorial staff in a number of regional newspapers and radio stations. The most spectacular event, however, was the arrest of the HDZ "media tycoon" Miroslav Kutle soon after the new government took office. Once a restaurant owner, by the mid-nineties—through his connections with Tudjman's party—he controlled more than 150 companies. In 1993, the HDZ used Kutle as a front to buy, with a party-sponsored loan of about $4 million, the respected Split daily *Slobodna Dalmacija*. That paper, once one of the finest in Yugoslavia, almost immediately became an HDZ frontline post, engaged in the nationalist crusade both in Croatia's war against neighboring Bosnia and against all opposition in Croatia. It took more than six years and the death of Tudjman for the Croatian Constitutional Court to declare the HDZ takeover of *Slobodna Dalmacija* unconstitutional. Ilija Marsic, president of the association of claimants of shares of *Slobodna Dalmacija*, commented, "After six years we have finally got satisfaction for the strike we organized because of the embezzlement [that was involved] in the takeover."[9]

Vecernji list, the highest-circulation daily in Croatia, also became the subject of controversy regarding its mysterious privatization. When Croatia's new president, Stipe Mesic, entered Tudjman's offices in February 2000, he found some 800 tapes and corresponding transcripts of the former president's conversations with his visitors. The tapes—many of which were made public with long transcripts running in newspapers like an ongoing crime story—contained evidence of the Croatian forces' involvement in some of the crimes committed in Bosnia, including the massacre of Bosniak civilians in Ahmici in 1993, as well as criminal activities and conspiracies regarding the privatization process. The scope of officially sanctioned looting of the country's resources was so great that Mesic was only half-joking when he said, "All countries have a mafia. But the Croatian mafia is the only one that has the entire country."

A transcript of Tudjman's conversation with his hard-line political adviser Ivic Pasalic on November 13, 1997, reveals how his party gained ownership of *Vecernji list*. Pasalic reported to Tudjman that he had developed a plan for a takeover. Two Croatian businessmen loyal to the HDZ would provide a cover with an investment fund registered in London, and even though they would formally own 55 percent of the company, the real majority owner would be the HDZ. "They will finance half of what we are supposed to pay, and everything is clean," Pasalic told Tudjman, convincing him that on paper it would look like a London-based investment fund coming to Croatia, registering according to Croatia's law, and bringing together investors interested in *Vecernji list*.[10] In the spring of 2000, *Vecernji list* was busy changing its editorial line from uncritical support for Tudjman and his party to newly expressed interest in their wrong-doings. When in mid-April the paper opened the "Gospic Dossier," a series of articles on crimes committed by Croatian forces against the Serbs in that area nine years earlier, *Feral Tribune* columnist Viktor Ivancic fired back in disgust: "The crimes in Gospic were possible because *Vecernji list* did not report on them." He asked whether the situation wouldn't be entirely different had the highest-circulation daily reported on the mass executions of Serb civilians, on firing squads killing at night and dawn, on gasoline poured over bodies to be burned, or bodies thrown into a nearby ravine and buried with the help of a few hand grenades. But that was not possible. Ivancic wrote:

> Such a turn of events was entirely impossible. It was important to secure, in advance, the silence of *Vecernji list* as an integral part of the killing logistics so the crimes could continue unobstructed, so the perpetrators didn't get discovered and tried, so the cycle of evil a few years later could reach its grandiose finale, with a pogrom of biblical proportions [the expulsion of Serbs from Croatia].[11]

According to media analysts, the new government was not quick enough in clearing up the mess Tudjman had left behind. By the end of 2000, of the three state-owned dailies, *Vjesnik* was barely surviving with no respectable circulation and no credibility; *Slobodna Dalmacija*, despite the illegal nature of its privatization, remained in the hands of

HDZ extremists who were running a campaign against the new democratic government; and *Vecernji list* was in transition between its
HDZ-approved owners and a prospective foreign investor. Prominent
Croatian media analysts Stjepan Malovic and Gordana Vilovic, sum-
ming up the first-year experience with a new democratic government,
said that it had not started with revenge against Tudjman loyalists in
the media, but it did not open the door for the most qualified either,
trying to appease members of the winning coalition parties. They
wrote:

> The political scene has changed drastically. From the once strong authority
> of president Tudjman and his weak opponents, there is suddenly a vacuum
> in which nothing is certain and no one has the final word. That's something
> unknown in these areas, so there is a cacophony of political views, some of
> which are unacceptable for some members of the same winning coalition.
> There are some attempts to form centers of power around the President of
> the Republic (Mesic), who is popular but with no powerful party behind
> him, or around the Prime Minister (Ivica Racan), who is president of the
> strongest party, Social Democratic Party (SDP), but not strong enough to
> govern by himself.[12]

Bosnia's Media Apartheid

The year 2000 found Bosnia in a state of "a more civilized apartheid."
Squeezed between Tudjman's Croatia and Milosevic's Serbia, both supporting extreme separatist parties in Bosnia and their hold on territories
"ethnically cleansed" during the war, Bosnians lived in three ghettos. In
Republika Srpska, the Serb half of the country, only a small number of
Bosniaks and Croats expelled during the war had returned. They were
met with mob violence, dynamiting and burning of rebuilt houses, and
"unexplained" murders of some of the returnees. The Bosniak-Croat
Federation, comprising the other half of the country, was far from being
a single entity as stipulated by the Dayton agreement. Croat HDZ-held
areas were as unfriendly toward any returns as was Republika Srpska, and
in Bosniak-majority areas the ruling Muslim SDA party was making "its
territory" increasingly unfriendly for Serbs and Croats. That ethnic
apartheid was best reflected in the country's divided media. Visiting
Bosnia in January 2000, I asked three prominent Bosnian independent
intellectuals—Zdravko Grebo, a professor at the Law School at Sarajevo

University; Zdravko Zlokapa, a professor at the Law School at Banjaluka University; and Slavo Kukic, a professor at the School of Economy in Mostar—for their comments as we watched tapes of the New Year's Eve 2000 TV newscasts shown in their respective cities. What were the mood, ideas, hopes, and fears that the local television offered for the new millennium to Bosnians divided into Bosniak-majority, Serb-majority, and Croat-majority territories? The decade that had begun on a high note, with the Fall of the Wall and with three nationalist parties—all with the word "democratic" in their names (SDA, SDS, HDZ)—promising to make Bosnia "a new Switzerland" was ending on a note of "sadness and uncertainty," Grebo said.

In contrast with separatist Serb TV in Pale or Croat TV in Siroki Brijeg—Bosnian Television in Sarajevo covered the New Year's festivities throughout the country, starting with a story on the celebration in Serb-held Banjaluka. There were also reports on the millennium celebration worldwide. Grebo noted that the traditional New Year's message, once reserved year after year for lifelong Yugoslav President Tito and later for the country's president, was delivered on the eve of the historic year 2000 by an American, the UN representative to Bosnia, Jacques Klein. "That reflects our country's total dependence on the international presence," Grebo said. Then, there was a segment presented as "good news for pensioners"—the post service had started to distribute August pensions at the end of December. Grebo reflected:

> Unfortunately, the pensioners have become a kind of paradigm for the shameful social status of most Bosnians. Those people, with their careers, lives, and current social status, are really a living testimony about the lost and betrayed hope for major change a decade ago. When the Berlin Wall was falling, with the promise of pluralism and democracy, there was hope for a better, more prosperous, happier life. That did not happen, and pensioners are a paradigm of that, living on the edge of misery. Instead of a European future, we in the Balkans had to experience wars, aggression, and genocide first. The people who took power here [in 1990] did not know how to lead a political or economic transition, and their kind of "democracy" did not help pensioners to avoid becoming a paradigm of lost hopes. It did not help my students either, who, almost without exception, desperately look for ways to flee this country. This should be the real issue for the New Year's Eve newscast.[13]

In Banjaluka, Zdravko Zlokapa commented on Republika Srpska's New Year's Eve TV newscast. Zlokapa, who had studied the role of

Yugoslav media in the 1990s, traces the roots of nationalist manipulation to the decades of Communist Party control.[14] It was during
Communist one-party rule in the former Yugoslavia that journalists
and all media outlets were shaped into instruments of political power.
Zlokapa argues that the Yugoslav public came to accept the idea that
the media serve those in power and that the government has the right
to use the media to serve its own interests. That explains the widespread
acceptance when control of the media was transferred from the old to
the new rulers after the fall of communism. "Journalists," Zlokapa said,
"continued to play the role they were used to playing, becoming the
most enthusiastic advocates of the new nationalist ideology: A huge
majority of them completely identified with this ideology, accepting
blindly, unreservedly, and uncritically the policies and political goals of
the ruling party."

Republika Srpska TV featured extensive New Year's messages from
four Serb politicians, with a heavy emphasis on their entity—and almost
no mention of Bosnia. It also featured High Representative Wolfgang
Petritsch's description of the year 2000 as "a decisive year for Bosnia's
future." Zlokapa noted that the programming had improved since the
Bosnian Serb television moved from Pale, the wartime capital of the Serb
entity, to Banjaluka, the new capital dominated by more moderate parties and politicians. Still, Bosnia was hardly mentioned in the newscast,
which carried New Year's messages from Yugoslav President Slobodan
Milosevic—internationally indicted for war crimes—and Montenegrin
President Milo Djukanovic. Zlokapa said that "the whole notion of
Bosnia as a single country has been pushed aside, like something that
should be forgotten. The impression being created is one of a deeply
divided society. There are no serious efforts to change that."[15]

On its New Year's Eve Journal of Herzeg-Bosnia, Erotel, the Bosnian Croat TV in Western Herzegovina, reinforced the impression of
a country deeply divided into three ethnic territories. While watching
the broadcast, Slavo Kukic recapitulated the meaning of the name
Herzeg-Bosnia:

> After Dayton, extreme elements of the Croatian Democratic Union
> (HDZ) in Bosnia Herzegovina had been forced to abandon their idea of a
> separatist Croatian Republic of Herzeg-Bosnia, as had their sponsors in the
> nationalist government of the late Franjo Tudjman in Croatia. Instead, they

established the Croatian Community of Herzeg-Bosnia, as a supposed citizens association or cultural community of Croats in Bosnia, but the organization is just a smokescreen for a separate Croat entity within Bosnia. They
just wanted to prolong the life of the Croat Republic of Herzeg-Bosnia in
this new incarnation.[16]

Erotel, which was in the hands of a radical group within the hard-
line HDZ in Western Herzegovina, broadcast a New Year's Eve
Journal focused on the January 3 elections in Croatia proper, openly
urging Bosnian Croats—who can vote in the elections in neighboring
Croatia—to vote for "those who will recognize and represent the interests of the Croatian people the best," essentially telling them that their
very future depended on a victory for the HDZ. (After the HDZ lost
and after a lengthy struggle against Bosnian-Croat hard-liners, the
Independent Media Commission (IMC) in Bosnia finally managed to
take Erotel off the air on February 17, 2000, in anticipation of the
launching of the Federal Television.)

Thus, in the spring of the year 2000, what we had in the Bosnian
radio–television environment was a media apartheid imposed by the
decade-long destruction of that country. Some appearance of civility
was brought about through a series of measures: (1) through force as in
the closing of Serb Pale TV in the fall of 1997 and Croat Erotel in
February 2000; (2) through patient persuasion as applied by media
monitoring and occasional sanctions by the international peace process
sponsors; and (3) through slow restructuring as in Republika Srpska
TV in Banjaluka and rebuilding as in plans to establish Federal TV
alongside Public Service TV in Sarajevo.

Two events in early 2000 made it clear that there is a long way to go
in achieving those goals. The sentencing to forty-five years in prison of
the Bosnian Croat wartime General Tihomir Blaskic by the
International Criminal Tribunal for the Former Yugoslavia in The
Hague and the arrest of the wartime speaker of the Bosnian Serb
Parliament, Momcilo Krajisnik, prompted protests both in Serb- and
Croat-controlled areas in Bosnia. Just covering different parties' condemnation of the Tribunal as both anti-Serb and anti-Croat, as the
"political instrument of the West" aimed at punishing "our guys only,"
as the "attack against our people" and "violation of the Dayton accords,"
was enough to polarize Bosnians again. Missing was a full report on

both Serb and Croat television on the accusations against the sentenced general and arrested politician. In Blaskic's case, charges included, among other crimes, the destruction of the village of Ahmici and the deaths of more than one hundred Bosniak civilians, including mothers and their children slaughtered in cold blood within his zone of responsibility. Krajisnik was charged with command responsibility for genocidal crimes against civilians, ranging from "ethnic cleansing" in the early stages of the war to the siege of Sarajevo throughout the conflict. Even four and a half years after the war, the public in the nationalist-controlled areas of Bosnia has not been told the full story concerning war atrocities.

There are calls by citizens' associations throughout Bosnia for the establishment of a Truth and Reconciliation Commission whose job would be to establish historic facts about the war; acknowledge its victims and suffering on all sides; and single out those responsible for war crimes, thus helping innocent people to move on with their lives without the burden of collective guilt of one or the other ethnic groups. The media has a critical role to play in that process. In the case of the ongoing International War Crimes Tribunal indictments and convictions, the "patriotic" cries by politicians and parties, who continue to exploit alleged victimization of "our own" in the hands of the "hostile international community," should be balanced in the media with thorough documentation of the crimes being prosecuted at The Hague. The ability to tell that story should be a major criterion in determining which media outlets are really independent and deserving of international support. Very few would qualify.

But it is not only domestic pressure that keeps the media from telling the public the full story of the war crimes. Even the international sponsors of the peace process, including the media-monitoring institutions, have contributed to a fear of reporting the wartime atrocities. By giving in to nationalists' claims that reporting on war crimes is "anti-Serb" or "anti-Croat," they not only deny the public a better understanding of what really happened in the Balkans in the nineties, but also strengthen nationalist hold on power and resistance to war crimes accountability. For example, when Bosnian TV broadcast the BBC-produced documentary drama *Warriors* on February 19 and 27, 2000, the IMC, charged with regulating Bosnian electronic media, received nine complaints by "Bosnian Croats" that the program "presents the Croats in a particularly bad light" at the beginning of the municipal election campaign. IMC Director General Krister Thelin agreed that there was a legitimate question of "timing" and an "absence of any comment or discussion" that would have provided some "additional information."[17] Thelin suggested a discussion in the studio immediately following the *Warriors* presentation or a special program providing a right of response within "a reasonable deadline." "In that sense, Bosnian TV did not violate the Code, but it did not meet the expectations of a responsible public radio and TV institution," Thelin wrote in a letter to the BHTV management on May 17, 2000.

The "media intervention" in Bosnia—despite all shortcomings—has achieved some initial results. The situation at the end of the year 2000 was much better than at the end of 1995. The warmongering nationalist Serb TV in Pale as well as nationalist Croat TV in Grude have been taken off the air; the IMC, established in June 1998, has played a major role in regulating the Bosnian electronic media jungle, adopting a Code on Radio and TV programming, establishing criteria, issuing licenses, and allocating frequencies to all qualified radio and TV stations. IMC also contributed to the creation of the Press Code and Press Council, which provide a more favorable framework for the development of both public and independent media in the country. In addition to nationalist Serb and Croat TV, the IMC took the nationalist Bosniak TV off the air as well. That action in October 2000 was based on a violation of the licensing rules: Bosniak TV registered as a private TV while its sources of funding, with a major investment from the Muslim political party (SDA) and unspecified other donors from Muslim countries, obviously made it something else. While the IMC justified its decision on strictly legal grounds as a case of "false representation," Bosniak nationalists—following the example of Serb and Croat nationalists in previous cases—were quick to denounce the decision as a case of ethnic discrimination, claiming it was against the interests of Bosniak people and against the freedom of the media.

A number of international media development institutions and donors, including the Soros Foundation and IREX ProMedia, have helped some of the existing newspapers and magazines survive and new ones to be launched, contributing to a gradual pluralization of the Bosnian media scene. In Sarajevo in the year 2000, there were three dailies: *Dnevni avaz*, which in that year broke from SDA political control and began to project an independent line; *Oslobodjenje*, tired and bruised, with declining editorial standards and without a clear long-term strategy, but still true to its reputation for tolerance; and *Vecernje novine (Evening Newspaper)*, transformed into *Jutarnje novine (Morning Newspaper)*, still in search of a new identity. *Dnevni Avaz's* break with the SDA prompted an angry public outburst by the Muslim party. Immediately following the April municipal election in which moderate, pro-European Social-Democrats defeated the SDA even in Sarajevo, their supposed base of power, SDA's federal Prime Minister Edhem Bicakcic told the party's Main Board they lost the election because of *Avaz's* betrayal. "We helped them financially at the beginning," Bicakcic said in an interview with *Dani*.[18] *Avaz's* founder, Fahrudin Radoncic, responded that his paper was actually never close to SDA, but only to SDA president Izetbegovic's "understanding of politics."[19] Nevertheless, the SDA acted like a cheated lover, attacking *Avaz* in public and—even worse—dispatching federal financial police to a predawn raid at the paper's building for a hand count of *Avaz's* circulation under the charge of tax evasion. They also froze the paper's bank accounts for several days, endangering the functioning of the company and prompting strong international condemnation. Radoncic said the frontal attack against *Avaz* was revenge for its persistent coverage of corruption in the privatization process, which enabled government officials and their cronies to purchase Bosnian hotels and other attractive businesses "under morally questionable" conditions.

In Republika Srpska the independent *Nezavisne novine (The Independent Newspaper)* became by far more popular than the once-privileged *Glas Srpski (Serbs' Voice)* among dailies, while *Nezavisne's* weekend edition printed 18,000 copies, according to June 2000 figures, becoming the first publication from Republika Srpska to reach the federation market.

One significant step toward greater media freedom was adoption, by the Office of the High Representative and the OSCE in Bosnia, of a Freedom of Information Act that provides public access to all information in possession of the government or public institutions. The law is aimed at fostering greater transparency and responsibility in the work of Bosnian institutions according to internationally accepted standards. But all these listed successes pale by comparison with the complete failure to develop—even five years after Dayton—a countrywide public radio and television system. Not that international supervisors of the peace process did not try. The problem was that they didn't know how to do it. Some of the people given a key role in developing the international community's media strategy in Bosnia did not have any noticeable expertise in journalism in their own countries. Most of the international institutions operating in Bosnia accepted, instead of challenging, the tripartite division of everything Bosnian—including the media. At one point, justifying yet another delay in restructuring Bosnian TV, international mediators said they were waiting for the Muslim SDA to delegate their new representative to a commission charged with restructuring. Thus the ruling parties had a built-in paralyzing influence on that process. There was no clear vision of what needs to be achieved—an open, pluralistic, high-quality, Europe-oriented, all-Bosnian TV. The process was held hostage to a bureaucratic obsession with rules, regulations, licenses, frequencies, all things of great importance but more like a frame without the picture. Representing all-powerful offices and enjoying the role of missionaries of free speech, most of the international participants in that effort failed to understand and appreciate that there was a Bosnian history of struggle for the ideals they came to represent. And that there were people who had fought for those ideals in prewar Bosnia. So they never realized the importance of bringing together, mobilizing, empowering, and supporting the best of Bosnian professionals as a key to any media development strategy. On the rare occasions when they looked for Bosnian professionals, they allowed the representatives of nationalist parties in media efforts to veto the possibility, as when they tried to recruit some of the journalists who had left the country, such as former Bosnian TV editor Ivica Puljic, who later worked with VOA in Washington, D.C. "Puljic can't be considered, he wasn't with us during the war," Izetbegovic's adviser Mirza Hajric objected in a local press report. Ironically, Hajric himself wasn't "with us" in the first years of the war, which found him in London, while Puljic spent months covering the Sarajevo siege. Illustrating what some critics of the process call the "colonial approach" to media development in postwar Bosnia, a Media Plan Institute report stated that international participants largely neglect local capacities and often without consideration, and sometimes in a belittling manner,

impose solutions not always the best suited to a situation. The report
said:

> One banal example tells with how little sensitivity the OBN project was run:
> the very name, OBN [Open Broadcast Network] doesn't mean anything to
> an average Bosnian viewer, since the very small number of people in this
> country understand English. Then, the obvious question is: how to expect the
> public to identify with something under a meaningless name? Unfortunately,
> the same mistake gets repeated: Independent Media Commission is called in
> Bosnia by its English abbreviation [IMC] and a public service is called PBS.
> As much as it might seem just a formality, it is exactly this symbolic dimen-
> sion of the media that is important if you want to have media, regulatory insti-
> tutions, and services fully integrated into not only the Bosnian media system,
> but in a whole society.[20]

Five years after Dayton, the international media intervention was
more successful in deconstructing than in reconstructing Bosnian
radio–television. By falling into the trap of automatic tripartite classifi-
cation, that everything has to be Bosniak or Croatian or Serbian, internationals decided early in the game that rebuilding the all-Bosnian TV
was not an option. They opted for a new TV, OBN, costing some $20
million over five years with all the limitations of such a project in
Bosnia's postwar landscape: limited area of coverage, expensive satellite
transmission, poor reporting from affiliated stations, the absence of a
functioning economy and advertising revenues, and a dose of suspicion
against internationally sponsored neutrality ("Bildt television"). While
OBN did provide a non-nationalist alternative at a time when Bosnian
air was poisoned by years of war propaganda and hatred, and it helped
break the inter-entity barriers, in the summer of 1999 the international
sponsors withdrew support for OBN and shifted focus to creating a
countrywide Public Broadcast System (PBS). But mired in all sorts of
obstacles, launching of PBS had been endlessly delayed, missing two
milestones in the peace process in 2000—local elections in April and
parliamentary elections in November—leaving democratic forces and
the Bosnian public without the benefit of television focused on the
country's European perspectives. OBN and the former Bosnian TV,
both abandoned and uncertain about their future, did their best under
the circumstances. But that wasn't enough to compensate for the
absence of nationwide radio and television free from nationalist governments' control.

The PBS project was held hostage to the internationals' limited understanding of Bosnia's complexities and to the agendas of the ruling parties in the Federation and Republika Srpska. Despite all the rhetoric in support of a multiethnic Bosnia, multiethnic institutions, and multiethnic spirit, international efforts to transform Bosnian television were in danger of actually helping preserve—if not enforce—the media apartheid created throughout a decade of violence. Like diplomats brokering the political settlement that even five years later left Bosnia fractured into two and three de facto entities, the international sponsors of Bosnian television restructuring for a long time gave in to nationalist claims that Bosniaks, Serbs, and Croats needed separate TV programs. In Republika Srpska, even the moderate government of Milorad Dodik in Banjaluka insisted that public information is strictly "the entities' business" and opposed any move to integrate the media space, seeing the prospect as the ghost of "unitary Bosnia."

In the federation, the appeasement of ethnic exclusivity reached a new high with a months-long debate on operating the federal television on two separate channels: one predominantly in Bosnian, the other in Croatian. The irony, which is costly in both money and resources, is that with all the nationalists' claims of historical, religious, cultural, linguistic, and all sorts of other differences, Bosniaks, Serbs, and Croats understand each of their, let's say three, languages, perfectly well. There is no single word, sentence, or public announcement in the Bosnian, Croatian, or Serbian language that can't be understood 100 percent by the people of all three ethnic groups. Yet just because a decade of nationalist madness taught the people to hate diversity of expression, instead of feeling enriched by it, Bosnians were supposed to have Serb-only, Bosniak-only, and Croat-only evening television news. Potentially, there are many problems with this. The major one is: How and why do you maintain an ethnic-news ghetto during an information explosion age? Is it really a good idea to invest in a my-entity-news-only television in a region that is supposed to integrate not only with the rest of the nominally single state of Bosnia but also with the wider region and the rest of Europe as called for by the Stability Pact, adopted by all post-Yugoslavia states? Also, does that separation along Bosnian-only, Serb-only, Croat-only lines mean that the public in those three viewing areas will be served reports only by their own journalists, interviews with their own politicians, and statements of their own artists, writers, and scientists? If so, this will reinforce institutional and cultural segregation, make dialogue and the exchange of ideas more difficult, and pose an obstacle to reintegration within the country and the region as a whole. If not, then the whole concept of separate channels in separate languages has no meaning because people will speak in Bosnian, or Croatian, or Serbian and be perfectly understood by everyone, preserving in this way both their individual and ethnic group values and Bosnia's diversity. Ivan Lovrenovic, a prominent Bosnian Croat writer, argued in his column in *Dani* that HDZ's insistence on a separate "Croat channel" was a way for that party to maintain its control over the Croat population. He said:

> HDZ has, exactly through media, and exactly in the sphere of mentality and culture, succeeded in making Bosnian Croats hate and neglect their own, authentic Bosnian identity, in favor of some abstract, non-existent, ideological all-Croat identity, which couldn't be accepted except by deleting and annulling everything in them that's Bosnian. Concretely, it means: learning in schools not Bosnian history but the history of Croatia, according to Croatia's official program. And learning Croatia's literature and cultural history. And learning a language ashamed of the way your elderly family members—your mother, father, grandfather, grandmother—spoke it, because the language they speak is not the Croatian they teach you in school, which is the only true, all-Croatian. To be ghettoized, as we always knew, means to disappear.[21]

"Bosnian identity," with which Lovrenovic and many like-minded Bosnians of all backgrounds grew up, was systematically destroyed and denied in the terror of the 1990s, in ethnic cleansing and the promotion of hatred, and it wasn't given a chance either in the Dayton talks or in the post-Dayton rebuilding of Bosnia. The absence of a vision in television "restructuring" was best reflected in a posting on the Bosnian TV bulletin board, inviting anyone "who wants to try out as a TV Journal or News anchor to come [to the newsroom] on Thursday, September 21, 2000 at 11 a.m."[22]

Serbia's Opposition Takes Power, State Media Change Allegiances

The year 2000 in Serbia was marked by dramatic events in the fall—the democratic opposition's victory in the September elections; the Milosevic regime's decision to annul election results; and the street revolution on October 5 overthrowing Milosevic and installing constitutional lawyer

Vojislav Kostunica as the new president—but it was also a year in which media oppression in Serbia had reached an all-time high. That final wave of government-led harassment against the media was announced by Serbian Deputy Prime Minister Vojislav Seselj. In a news conference in Belgrade on February 10, 2000, he accused the independent media of "complicity in the murder" of Yugoslavia's Defense Minister Pavle Bulatovic, who had been gunned down in a Belgrade restaurant on February 7. Seselj singled out *Danas* (the Belgrade daily); B-92 (radio); and *Glas javnosti, Vecernje novosti,* and *Blic* (dailies) as "American mercenaries, worse than any criminals" and "traitors, deliberately working for the murderers of Serbian children." He threatened them with "the worst imaginable consequences," issuing an unveiled threat: "You don't really think you will eventually survive our liquidation."[23] Just four days after Seselj threatened independent journalists, the state news agency Tanjug produced further ammunition for intimidation, implying in a commentary that a prominent Belgrade journalist, Aleksandar Tijanic, had something to do with the murder of the defense minister. A proof? Tijanic's January 16, 2000, article in the Banjaluka daily *Nezavisne novine,* in which he predicted a number of events for February, including the closing of a newspaper, the jailing of an editor, the leader of a major party facing charges in court, and the "relocation" of "one prominent individual . . . to the other world." The same charges against Tijanic were repeated by the state-controlled daily *Borba.*[24]

In Milosevic's Serbia, in which all the suffering of the nineties had been attributed to the "international anti-Serb conspiracy," Seselj–Tanjug style labeling of journalists as foreign mercenaries and traitors had already been proven to be life-threatening. In April 1999, a similar Tanjug commentary against *Dnevni telegraf* publisher Slavko Curuvija was followed in a matter of days by his assassination in cold blood in central Belgrade. On April 11, 2000, several hundred people gathered to mark the first anniversary of Curuvija's murder. A year later, no arrest had been made, and no official word on the investigation's progress was issued. Tijanic was quoted as saying that Curuvija "paid the full price for his words and his thoughts."[25] Even though some Belgrade journalists recall that Curuvija himself had previously enjoyed privileged access to government secrets, including his access to the police and to Milosevic's all-powerful wife, few doubt that the regime was responsible for his death. The suspicion was supported by the finding of a detailed police surveillance report on Curuvija's whereabouts on the day of his murder. "At 16:58 we stop any further surveillance as agreed with the head of the department," the report said. Some seventeen minutes later, Curuvija was shot in front of his apartment building. Curuvija's wife, Branka Prpa, who was with him on the last day of his life, strongly believed in the authenticity of the surveillance report. "There were some things in the report that only I knew, and which I had never said to anybody else either privately or publicly," she said.[26]

Milosevic's intolerance of any dissent in Serbia was demonstrated in the government's takeover of the highest-circulation Serbian tabloid, *Vecernje novosti,* on March 2, 2000. The paper was one of the bastions of Serb nationalism in the early years of Milosevic's rule, joining the state-controlled Serbian Radio Televison and *Politika* Publishing Company in providing the regime control of 90 percent of the Serbian media market. But in the first months of 2000, *Vecernje novosti* opened its pages to opinions critical of the regime. As a clear message to his supporters that there were limits to what they could say, Milosevic's government resorted to the tactics used in previous silencing of opponents, such as the daily *Borba* or weekly *Ekonomska politika:* They simply eliminated the Novosti Company from the court register, declaring its registration invalid. Once the regime's mouthpiece, the paper ran a commentary entitled "We Do Exist," stating that, "the Serbian legal system is showing its ugliest features today. . . . It doesn't allow us to defend ourselves, or to prove anything; not even the obvious thing: that we do exist."

Fines against independent dailies in Belgrade—such as *Danas, Blic,* and *Glas javnosti*—were too numerous to list. Using a draconian information law, adopted during the state campaign of terror against the Kosovo Albanian majority, Milosevic's government issued fines almost daily against media outlets, many of which—unable to pay—had their licenses revoked and equipment seized or had to close down. "What the regime likes most is total darkness. Thieves steal best in the dark. The only way to hide the horrible truth about the devastating effects of the regime's current policy is to turn off all those who provide information about it," Gordana Susa commented.[27]

Opposition Studio B, sponsored by Vuk Draskovic's Serbian Renewal Movement (SPO), avoided that fate for some time only after being forced to pay an astronomical fine by Yugoslav standards for alleged breach of law. But the station was nevertheless taken over in a 2 a.m. raid on May 17 when police wearing masks occupied its offices, which at that time also housed reborn Radio B2-92, Radio Index, and the mass-circulation daily *Blic*. Studio B Director Dragan Kojadinovic said that "the best illustration of the type of country we live in is the fact that a duly registered and legal TV station was closed down in a night raid on the station's offices by 100 masked policemen."[28] Even though the silencing of Studio B came at the time of rising resistance to Milosevic's rule in Serbia, and its political sponsor Draskovic, once known as the "king of the streets," called for mass protests against the takeover, the incident failed to generate a huge public response. The reason was, as one analyst put it, the public's recognition of the difference between regime and opposition media on the one hand and independent media on the other. Dragoljub Zarkovic, *Vreme's* editor-in-chief, said that "Studio B could not be defended because it never became the property of the citizens of Belgrade, so they did not feel it was their own TV, and because—in some stages—its editorial concept irritated viewers only a little less than the state TV irritated them."[29] He observed that the majority of citizens saw Studio B only as the reverse side of the state TV. Studio B promoted SPO leaders the same way the state TV promoted the regime; that party's announcements were more important than the news; there was wide-spread censorship of the activities of other political parties; and guests in the Studio B programs were selected according to their political views and affiliation.

Veran Matic, the editor-in-chief of Radio B92 and the founder of the Association of Independent Electronic Media (ANEM) network, described the media situation in Serbia in the year 2000 prior to Milosevic's defeat as tragic. "Serbia had a president whose only exit was to The Hague," Matic said in an interview. "Indicted for war crimes, Milosevic would do anything to remain in power. Facing October elections, it was only natural that he wanted to silence all independent media. He perceived them as his personal enemies, as a threat, and that's why he was closing them down."[30]

His strategy failed. That became clear to everyone on October 5, 2000. It wasn't just the sight of the Yugoslav Parliament building in flames, nor the triumphant victory celebration in Belgrade streets that

Thursday that made the people of Serbia realize that indeed "He's Done," as posters had claimed during months-long protests throughout Serbia. It was the appearance that evening of a new president, Vojislav Kostunica, on state television that made it crystal clear that Milosevic's thirteen-year-long rule was over. Literally overnight, media that had slavishly served him for more than a decade offered their unreserved loyalty to the representatives of the winning Democratic Opposition of Serbia (DOS). While Kostunica was introduced as the new president through a long and unchallenging conversation with a handpicked interviewer, other government-controlled television stations busily interviewed other opposition leaders. The same people who had been constantly portrayed as "traitors," "NATO mercenaries," "foreign spies," and "sold souls" were instantly promoted into the "liberators of Serbia." "People's Will Prevailed" exclaimed the once all-Milosevic daily *Vecernje novosti* the next day. And *Politika*—a daily that had helped lay the ground for hatred and war and promoted Milosevic into the leader of all Serbs—carried at the top of its front page Kostunica's speech and picture instead of reporting on the people's triumph in the Belgrade streets. Ivan Radovanovic, a writer who had left *Politika* in 1989 as it was falling under the control of Milosevic cronies, said of the paper's reporting: "I laughed when I saw *Politika*. A revolution had taken place outside its front door. There was tear gas, three people dead, the storming of parliament, and their entire front page was devoted to a speech by Kostunica."[31] Vojin Patronic, a thirty-year *Politika* veteran who assumed the position of acting editor-in-chief following the change in Belgrade, admitted the credibility problem his paper faced. "It will take a lot of detergent to clean the house. Maybe our readers will one day forget what the newspaper did," he said.[32]

Media critics were quick to recognize a familiar turnaround. The state media embraced the new rulers with the same ease they had first served Tito, then Milosevic. Only the top media bosses, those closest to the overthrown president, paid an immediate price for having served the once hallowed, now despised ruler. Protesters storming the Serbian TV building on October 5 nearly beat to death Dragoljub Milanovic, a man whose name had been used under the first articles announcing Milosevic's showdown with Serbian moderates in the late 1980s and who had subsequently been promoted as head of state Radio and Television. They knocked him down, kicked him, and beat him with a metal bar, sending him to the Emergency Center. His news editor, Milorad Komrakov, begged to be spared. They let him go, masked by a scarf over his face, but one demonstrator recognized him and hit him so he joined Milanovic at the hospital. Some of the other top editors escaped in disguise.

The state Radio and Television resumed broadcasting as The New Radio-Television of Serbia. The problem, of course, wasn't in the name. As Gordana Susa, a prominent Belgrade TV journalist who had left Belgrade TV in the late eighties to work for Yutel and then for an independent production, said, "There is a mental problem of people working for state TV who would equally serve Milosevic or the new authorities. They have forgotten the principles of professional journalism and become an agitprop [a Soviet-style propaganda arm] of ruling parties. The question is whether the new authorities want to accept that kind of slavish reporting. The sad picture of Milanovic's near-lynching should be a lesson to every single journalist."[33]

Biserka Matic, a new information minister who once wrote an open letter to *Politika* bosses appealing for professional dignity, told a Belgrade roundtable on the restructuring of the Serbian state Radio-Television (RTS) on December 7, 2000, "They [RTS journalists] are behaving as though they had spent a long time in prison and are now unable to cope with freedom." In an interview with Radio B92 she encouraged Serbian media to criticize the new government "as much as possible." As in the case of RTS, all other state-controlled media announced their "liberation." The state news agency Tanjug informed the public on the night of revolutionary change that they would be "with the people again" and "report according to professional rules." *Politika* used exactly the same language, greeting demonstrators entering its building on October 5 on ground-floor television screens with the promise "*Politika* is with its people again."

The sudden turnaround of all regime media was greeted with ironic approval among Serbian independent or, better, non-regime media, because not all of them were independent from sometimes extreme nationalist parties. The Association of Independent Journalists' Court of Honor had found in 1998 that regime media, and especially RTS, had been "instruments of ruling parties and circles following entirely the propaganda model—bending and not reporting important facts, manipulating information, which is often the same as lying, spreading ethnic and religious hatred and intolerance, as well as intolerance toward any different view and criticism of the authorities."[34]

Now the regime media have suddenly noticed the existence of independent news outlets. The Independent BETA news agency, set up in 1994 by nine journalists in Belgrade to provide objective and nonpartisan information, was one of the beneficiaries of the turnaround. The day after the revolution, *Politika* carried BETA's report instead of its own, and all other state media hurried to subscribe to the service. The agency, originally started by former Tanjug journalists dissatisfied with the agency's service to Milosevic's regime, had grown by the end of 2000 to employing 145 journalists, with an extensive network of correspondents and a reputation for professional reporting on domestic and international issues.

In the aftermath of the "liberation" of the state media, new editorial and management teams have been named, with some of the finest Serbian journalists, pushed aside in a decade of ultranationalism, assuming the leadership role in facing the challenges of democratization. The Serbian Association of Journalists, compromised by its support for the ruling elite, opened a series of hearings against prominent members who had violated professional principles. Their first ruling was the expulsion of the former news editor at state TV, Milorad Komrakov, for "several years of misinforming and deceiving the public, in contravention of journalists' ethics." The Court of Honor found Komrakov an "accomplice in disseminating hatred of all whom had different views."[35]

Few people know the price of the struggle for press freedom better than Miroslav Filipovic, a Kraljevo correspondent for the Belgrade daily *Danas*, Agence France Presse, and the London-based Institute for War and Peace Reporting (IWPR). On May 8, 2000, six officers of the Serbian secret service arrested him in front of his apartment building and searched his flat for about two hours. The key evidence they collected was a printout of some ninety pages of his stories, which included his reports on the regime's repression against the Muslims of the Sandzak region; Serbian military and police activities aimed at destabilizing Kosovo; and—the most critical one—atrocities committed by members of the Yugoslav Army in the province in 1999. Filipovic was imprisoned, interrogated, charged with "espionage and spreading false information," and on May 22, 2000, a military court in Nis sentenced him to seven years in prison (he served five months). After Milosevic was toppled, Filipovic wrote: "Now, I have been released and promoted to the role of hero, a symbol of the fight for freedom of speech in Serbia. I was there on the side of justice and freedom in the final clash with Slobodan Milosevic's regime. Now the hunter has become the hunted. The roles have reversed."[36]

With the fall of the Milosevic regime, the Serbian public was offered the first reports of the war crimes committed in his wars of the 1990s, from Croatia and Bosnia to Kosovo, and Matic himself launched a campaign to establish Serbia's version of a truth commission, which would provide a full accounting of responsibilities for that decade. Some of the darkest secrets of the repression surfaced with the opening of the once well-protected police files. One such item deals with the NATO bombing of the Serbian state TV at 2:06 a.m. on April 23, 1999, which left sixteen employees dead. Their families, who blame NATO for the bombing but also the TV management and Milosevic's regime for sacrificing their loved ones for propaganda purposes, had found the documents and credible international witnesses proving that both the Serbian government and TV's management knew that the station was to be bombed. An official memo signed by the TV's security chief states that he insisted that the production be moved to an alternative studio outside of the city, but the top executives, including director general Milanovic and chief editor Komrakov, refused to do it. A lawyer representing the families of the sixteen people killed announced he would file charges for premeditated murder against Milanovic and a group of his closest associates. Special UN envoy for human rights in the former Yugoslavia Jiri Dienstbier stated publicly that Milanovic and his deputy had been notified twenty-four hours in advance of the time of the attack.[37] The chief prosecutor at The Hague, Carla del Ponte, during her visit to Belgrade in January 2001, said that Milosevic knew beforehand that the TV was going to be bombed, prompting renewed calls in the international media community for a thorough investigation.

Mothers of the bombing victims insist on finding the truth. Mirjana Stoimenovski, mother of twenty-five-year-old TV technician Darko Stoimenovski, said in a Reuters interview, "We ask the top people at

RTS, why did you play Russian roulette with our dearest ones?"[38] In the same story, Borka Bankovic, the mother of seventeen-year-old Ksenija Bankovic, criticized Milanovic for saying the dead workers were heroes. "They are not heroes, they were doing their work, they were at their work place, and it was the officials' duty to protect them."

After thirteen years of oppression, it will take time, but—more important—hard work and a vision of a truly free media, to dismantle a legacy of serving the authoritarian regime. It will take transforming government-controlled radio and television stations into truly public ones and making many of the public media outlets, such as regional and local radio, television, and newspapers, into private ones. It will take not only renouncing the infamous information law of 1998 but finding ways to compensate media that had paid sixty-six fines totaling more than $30 million. It will take creating an environment in which people can freely debate the issues of both Serbia's past and its future. It will take transforming the experience and courage of those journalists who maintained independence under Milosevic into a media at the service of the Serbian public. These are the challenges of the new decade and the new century.

Policy
Recommendations

THE POWER OF TELEVISION in totalitarian societies to develop collective perceptions of what's right and what's wrong, to make people rally and even fight for causes shaped by TV images, has been illustrated in an ironic way by the reaction of residents of a small Serbian town to the Venezuelan soap opera *Cassandra*. According to one writer's account, "When the heroine Cassandra ended up in prison in one of the episodes, the furious people of Kucevo sent a petition (with around 200 signatures!) to the president of Venezuela demanding the immediate release of the innocent Cassandra. They went further still by writing to the Vatican to ask that Cassandra be proclaimed a saint, and then to The Hague tribunal, asking that it be made possible for Cassandra to get a fair trial in Serbia."[1] In this anecdote, the people who had nothing to say against their own army's real-time, real-life shelling of Vukovar, Dubrovnik, and Sarajevo—because the TV had made them believe that this constituted the "legitimate defense of threatened Serbs in Croatia and Bosnia"—suddenly felt a strong urge to stand for justice in faraway Venezuela.

More than a decade of systematic manipulation of the mass media in the Balkans, aimed at rallying nations—Serbs, Croats, Bosniaks—behind their respective nationalist leaders, has created many inaccurate and harmful collective perceptions. Some of the worst war crimes in post-World War II Europe, such as the siege of Sarajevo and the slaughter at Srebrenica, have been presented, at best, as "legitimate defense" and, at worst, as "Muslims bombing themselves." Mass murderers have been promoted as "national heroes" whose indictments, arrests, and convictions stir patriotic protests, condemnation of the international community, and the paranoid feeling that "everyone is against us." Once peaceful neighbors have become ancient enemies. The differences in religion, culture, and dialect—once a source of pride in diversity—have become invisible walls of suspicion and irrational fear. In Bosnia, for example, the drive for ethnic separation has resulted in separate Bosniak, Croat, and Serb networks for electric power, railway, and news distribution, and, worst of all, segregated schools in once multiethnic communities. In the five years after the Dayton Peace Agreement was signed (1995–2000), with all the investment in a variety of media development programs, not enough has been done to undo more than a decade of the systematic production of hatred.

Symbolically, nationalist manipulation of the Balkan media has come full circle in the tragic fate of a Serbian journalist who—better than anyone else—personifies a decade of "patriotic journalism." As described in Chapter 2, this story began in the fall of 1987 with Milosevic's propagandists using the name of Dragoljub Milanovic, a relatively unknown provincial journalist, to launch an assault against Serbia's moderate politicians. The story ended in the fall of 2000 with Milanovic—who had been rewarded for his "patriotism" with the most powerful position in the Serbian media as head of the state radio and television—being beaten in the street by pro-democracy demonstrators in Belgrade. Following the fall of Milosevic, Milanovic was arrested and charged with sacrificing the lives of his employees for propagandistic purposes during the NATO bombing of 1999. Ironically, when Milosevic himself was arrested on March 31, 2001, he was placed in a cell next to Milanovic's in the Belgrade Central Prison, symbolizing the end of an era of media manipulation and the abuse of power that had left a trail of death, destruction, and pain throughout the Balkans. It will take many years of hard work and—more than anything else—a clear vision of what needs to be done for the Balkan state-controlled media to end their propagandistic function and begin to play their rightful role in helping to promote and strengthen democracy.

The experience of the 1990s offers lessons for "media intervention" in the Balkans and in other countries and regions undergoing transitions to democracy. Most important among these, international peace agreements and international institutions that newly independent countries wish to join should lay out clear, explicit guidelines and criteria concerning the independence of the media. The Dayton agreement omitted this critical piece, leaving the media in all three states—Serbia, Croatia, and Bosnia—in the hands of those most responsible for the wars in the first place. No wonder the media continued to promote nationalist agendas and images, supporting their own leaders' and ruling parties' wartime goals, condemning neighbors, and resisting international efforts to bring about democratic reform and reconciliation.

What could or should have been done better? Following is a list of recommendations that might contribute to setting priorities and achieving better results in the next stages of "media intervention," not only in the Balkans but also in countries experiencing a less traumatic transition to democracy.

Ownership of the media. Ownership proved to be the single most decisive tool in the decade of nationalist media manipulation throughout the former Yugoslavia. In the decades of one-party Communist rule, media ownership was practically a non-issue. The ruling party enjoyed total control over all media in the country through various means, from the direct appointment of "most trusted" Party propagandists to key editorial positions to state-provided subsidies and benefits for publishers and journalists serving the cause. The tragedy of the Serbian, Croatian, and Bosnian media—and this is equally true for the whole public sector in those countries—was that their transition in the 1990s was not a real step from one-party monopoly to multiparty democracy. In all three cases, the Communist Party monopoly was replaced by a nationalist party monopoly, using the same totalitarian instruments of control. Milosevic in Serbia and Tudjman in Croatia—both products of hard-line communist ideology—established immediate and absolute

control over all state media. They took over state radio and television stations and the national dailies, *Politika* and *Vjesnik*, respectively, and they
expanded their parties' media empires by taking control of a number of
independent and regional media outlets. The method was the same: The
Milosevic and Tudjman governments took over almost all Serbian and
Croatian newspapers, declaring that their privatization during the late
1980s under Yugoslav reformist Prime Minister Ante Markovic was illegal, and making them a part of their propaganda machinery. This was the
fate of *Borba, Vecernje novosti,* and *Ekonomska politika* in Serbia, of *Slobodna Dalmacija* and *Danas* in Croatia, among others.

The winning coalition of nationalist parties in Bosnia after the first
multiparty elections in 1990 tried to use the Milosevic–Tudjman recipe
to subjugate the media in the republic, but Bosnian journalists challenged the law adopted in the nationalist-controlled parliament in
spring 1991. They rejected the nationalist claim of "the right of the
democratically elected parliament to appoint media editors and managers." By the end of that year, journalists had won a Constitutional
Court case, arguing that even if the Bosnian media, as elsewhere in the
former Yugoslavia, enjoyed some state support, the money belonged to
the Bosnian public and not to the ruling parties. At *Oslobodjenje*, we
went so far as to reject publicly any further state subsidy if it would be
used as blackmail over our editorial policy. The Bosnian media victory
was soon overshadowed, however, by the media war drums over the rivers
separating Bosnia from Serbia and Croatia. Milosevic's radio and
television signals were imposed over all the Serb-occupied territories of
Bosnia, and Tudjman's over the Croat-controlled territories. The Bosnian
voices of tolerance were replaced by voices of hate. Their dominance in
all three states continued long after the Dayton Peace Agreement was
initialed on November 21, 1995. Until the year 2000, the media remained
in the hands of warmongers, creating obstacles to reconciliation.

Lesson learned: Make the independence of the media an important
part of future peace agreements and one of the must-do requirements
for international acceptance of states in transition. These requirements
must include the overhaul of laws regulating the media and the acceptance of international standards of freedom of expression. In Serbia,
Croatia, and Bosnia, the still-prevailing concept of state media needs to
be replaced with the concept of a truly public media.

Representative managing and advisory boards. While state and regional government support of public media may still have a role until there is a functioning economy, it is necessary to develop a legal framework to protect independent media from political, party, and parliamentary control. One way to do this in postwar and transitional societies is through the internationally supervised establishment of representative managing and advisory boards comprising a broad civil society spectrum. These boards might include representatives of independent associations of journalists and their labor unions; scholars and writers; artists and athletes; human rights and other NGO activists; prominent public figures and religious community leaders; international organizations concerned with press freedom; and other international institutions engaged in democracy building. Their role should be to oversee and assist in the development of internationally acceptable standards and practices, providing protection for, rather than control of, the newly independent media. For a full five years after Dayton, this process has been stalled because the ruling nationalist parties were partners in "democratizing" the media they had manipulated in the first place. In Croatia following the fall of the Tudjman regime, political parties represented in the parliament remained a dominant factor in supervising the state radio and television. Not enough power was delegated to the broader civil society, to journalists and their associations. In Serbia following the fall of Milosevic, a radical move toward civil society participation in the management of radio and television took place—with an understandable absence of criteria on how to achieve broad representation, competence, and credibility.

Professional associations of journalists. Throughout the region, professional associations of journalists have an important role to play in efforts to restore the credibility and raise the standards of journalism. Except for the Croatian Society of Journalists (HND), which remained active in its efforts to protect and educate its members throughout a decade of oppressive HDZ rule, most other regional associations have disintegrated along ideological or ethnic lines. In Serbia, there was a deep divide between the officially sanctioned pro-Milosevic association and the Association of Independent Journalists. In Bosnia, there was not only a divide between associations of professional and not-so-professional journalists, but also between associations based on ethnic exclusivity. In the highly politicized, nationalistic environment of the 1990s, supposedly professional associations of journalists rallied behind "patriotic causes." They neglected their primary responsibilities: to establish, uphold, and develop standards and ethics of journalism; to organize and represent journalists in their search for decent pay, job security, benefits, and better work conditions; to protect their member-ship—regardless of ethnic backgrounds—against political and eco-nomic pressures from governments and political parties. If they were to shift their focus away from the nationalist policies of the past toward real-life issues and challenges, Balkan journalists would soon find that their common interests and concerns are more numerous and more vital than their differences.

Watchdog journalism. A crucial missing link in rebuilding media credi-bility in the postwar Balkans is the absence of a tradition of watchdog journalism. In post-communist societies, the media had no experience in critically examining and reporting on the work of state and party institu-tions, and no institutions were responsive to public interests. The nation-alist parties of the 1990s—like the Communists in the post-World War II period—did not have to answer questions about what they were doing or why. It took almost five years after Dayton for the first major break-through in this area, when the international High Representative in Bosnia, Wolfgang Petritsch, introduced the Freedom of Information Act providing citizens access to most information possessed by the govern-ment and other public institutions. While the Act creates a legal frame-work for greater media access to the secretive world of power, there is a need to develop a wide public information network: public affairs offices within major governmental and public institutions; a communications culture in which individuals and institutions are more responsive and available for legitimate public concerns, interviews, and press conferences; and access to records and databases of government and other public insti-tutions. To help create that culture of transparency and public accounta-bility, much more needs to be done to oblige public institutions to have their own public relations officers, to train communications specialists for these positions, and, more than anything else, to train journalists to ask questions of the greatest public relevance.

Education for journalism. Postwar Balkan journalism has a desperate need for creative educational initiatives. While there are some positive experiences—including the BBC School of Journalism within the Soros Media Center and the High College of Journalism within the Media Plan Institute in Sarajevo, as well as educational programs run by the HND in Croatia—the region needs a thorough overhaul of its formal schools of journalism. For the most part, these schools are based in former socialist schools of political science that have no tradition of educating modern media professionals. These schools, insisting exclusively on faculty with formal academic credentials—often earned in a vastly different political environment—could substantially improve their teaching of the practical aspects of journalism by bringing in accomplished and respected professionals. Journalists with "equivalent experience" teach in Western schools of journalism, providing students with valuable practical guidance and serving as role models.

During the decade of war and propagandist manipulation, the newsrooms in Serbia, Croatia, and Bosnia were devastated. Some of the best professionals have left or been forced to leave; they have been replaced with young, often uneducated and inexperienced reporters and editors who have practiced more party propaganda than real journalism ever since. To meet both the short-term demand for qualified journalists and long-term development needs, the postwar Balkan media must pursue innovative educational approaches. These could include on-the-job training within the newsrooms of major media outlets such as national radio, TV, and dailies, conducted by experienced regional and international "editors-in-residence." Working with journalists on their major daily assignments, leading them through story development—from the initial idea, to finding proper sources and documents, to shaping the story and providing adequate photos and graphs—would help establish some basic standards in regional journalism. Even some simple rules, such as consulting multiple sources for each story and always looking for "the other side" of an argument, would greatly improve the quality and credibility of the media. On-the-job training should also work on the more demanding elements of good journalism, such as a daily focus on the most relevant issues and developments; the introduction of investigative journalism techniques and teamwork on major stories; and improvement of story composition, from a captivating lead to the proper use of the most interesting quotes and headlines. Practical educational efforts within the newsrooms of major media could be expanded by including selected journalists and editors from smaller regional media outlets and by providing student internships.

Another innovative approach might include cooperative efforts in developing and executing coverage of major ongoing issues and events, such as election campaigns, truth and reconciliation processes, economic reforms, and international integration processes. A local–regional –international team of editors and journalists working together to shape major media coverage of critical issues would provide valuable learning experiences for working journalists and help set standards for future coverage of these issues. For example, media development institutions operating in the Balkans could sponsor election campaign coverage by selected media outlets—statewide radio and TV and leading dailies and weeklies in Serbia, Croatia, or Bosnia—including hands-on participation by competent regional and international advisers. Since Balkan media are more preoccupied with day-to-day survival than with long-term educational or development concerns, international donors could help by offering comprehensive educational projects, soliciting applications, and offering professional and material support to those who qualify. Working on such projects, with the full participation of regional and international advisers, would provide local editors and journalists with the skills for future coverage of political campaigns in their countries.

International exchange. Expanded international exchange should be an integral part of journalism education. There should be a more systematic effort to provide talented Balkan journalists who work for relevant national media with an opportunity to spend some time—three months, a semester, or an academic year—in an international newsroom environment interacting and working with scholars and practitioners. The combination of research, newsroom exposure, and internships at major international media organizations would offer a valuable learning experience for work in the region.

Recent history offers a powerful example of how stimulating and inspiring international exposure can be: It was the former foreign correspondents of the major Yugoslav media, those who had spent years reporting from the West, who in many cases became the most articulate critics and opponents of nationalist media manipulation throughout the region in the 1990s.

Education of media managers. Of equal importance for a long-term media development strategy is education for media management. Training managers to develop a sound business strategy—with the proper balance of news and advertising; the optimum balance between full-time staff and freelancers; and the best methods for increasing circulation, classified advertisement, subscriptions, and other income-generating initiatives—is key to the gradual move from media dependency on donors to self-sustainability. The direct involvement of international media business experts, such as Americans Herman J. Obermayer and Betty Nan Obermayer who worked in Slovenia and Macedonia, could provide regional media managers with valuable on-the-job training. The Obermayers have produced extensive analyses of leading national newspaper publishing companies—Delo in Ljubljana and Nova Makedonija in Skopje—identifying specific weak points, developing proposals to improve general business strategy, and offering concrete savings and income-generating measures.

Refocusing donor strategies. International media donors still have a valuable role to play in the development of independent Balkan media, but they, too, need to refocus their strategies. Instead of sometimes indiscriminate spending on projects of dubious quality or relevance, they might identify—on the basis of their performance in the 1990s and their creative and business potential—media outlets deserving support in their search for higher professional standards and profitability. These outlets should be offered a comprehensive aid package including financial support, investment, and lines of credit to achieve their goals. However, the aid should start with an expert overview of their business practices and prospects and—based on that overview—help in developing a sound long-term business strategy. This approach requires that international donor institutions improve their ability to analyze and identify regional media with the most credibility and potential; to engage competent international journalists and media business practitioners; and to include the full participation of proven regional professionals. Such measures could improve standards of journalism, develop respectable national-level media outlets, and help ensure their long-term economic stability.

Developing the media market. A competitive media market is needed to reduce media dependence on public funds. In the Balkan experience of the 1990s, even internationally supervised privatization left nationalist governments in charge of the instruments of economic harassment against independent media. The governments could silence the media at will by controlling—through networks of their cronies—printing presses, distribution networks, newsprint supply, discriminative taxes, allocation of radio frequencies, and manipulation of advertising. Prospects for the development of independent media would be substantially improved through lower taxes, equal access to basic supplies and frequencies, nondiscriminatory sales networks and advertising, and the development of smaller, less expensive, and more competitive printing facilities. Equal access, with no discriminatory sales taxes, to kiosks and subscribers throughout the region is one of the prerequisites for the creation of a competitive newspaper market. The goal would be for publications from Belgrade, Sarajevo, or Zagreb, for example, to circulate freely in all three states. These steps, together with an increased exchange of TV programming, would help overcome the media apartheid created by a decade of warmongering. Once a competitive media market exists in conjunction with long-term support for the most relevant media outlets, the market will decide, for example, which of the approximately 80 television and 200 radio stations currently operating in Bosnia Herzegovina should continue as economically viable businesses.

Truth and reconciliation. Just as the Balkan media participated in the ultranationalist crusades of the 1990s, preparing the ground for war and justifying the worst atrocities in Europe since the end of World War II, they now have a crucial role to play in truth and reconciliation efforts. Five years after Dayton, the public in Serbia and Croatia still has not been told the truth about the Bosnian war of 1992–95. As long as this is so, not only the history but also the future of the region will be vulnerable to nationalist distortions and the accumulation of hatreds for new tensions and conflicts. It was just such a manipulation of history that helped to generate the hatred that spurred the atrocities of the 1990s—blaming present-day Bosnian Muslims for the Turkish occupation 600 years ago, blaming all Croats for Ustasha crimes during World War II, and manipulating the number of those killed in Ustasha concentration camps such as Jasenovac, with the Serb nationalist historians exaggerating the number and Croat nationalist historians minimizing it. Experience tells us that acknowledging and honoring the victims on all sides, examining the record of atrocities, and neither denying crimes nor blaming everyone equally provide the best bases for reconciliation and coexistence in the Balkans. Documenting and making public the atrocities and sufferings on all sides would help the people of the region understand the complexities of the conflict and the pain of the innocent: presenting to the Serbs the full extent of the siege and killings of Vukovar and Sarajevo, the concentration camps in the Prijedor area, and the Srebrenica massacre; educating the Croats about atrocities committed in their name against Bosniaks in Herzegovina and Central Bosnia and against Serbs in Operation Storm in Croatia; and telling Bosniaks about the crimes committed against the Serbs during the siege of Sarajevo and against the Croats in the Konjic and Bugojno areas.

Once confronted with documents and pictures of these crimes, presented to them during the previous decade as part of a heroic and even sacred fight for survival, people will be better able to understand and support bringing war criminals to trial. Such efforts to uncover the truth and mete out justice are a precondition for the children of this tragic region, in which every generation of the twentieth century has experienced war—my grandparents' generation in 1914, my parents' in 1941, my children's and mine in the 1990s—to finally join a peaceful and prosperous Europe. This book is written with that hope in mind.

Appendix A
Historical
Timeline

May 4, 1980—Yugoslavia's President Josip Broz Tito dies at the age of 88, leaving a vacuum of power with the eight-member Presidency—one representative from each of six republics and two provinces—rotating on annual basis as the president.

February 1981—Riots break out at Pristina University in Kosovo with Albanian students chanting, "Kosovo-Republic." They demand that the Autonomous Province of Kosovo (with a population 90 percent Albanian) be given the status of a republic within Yugoslavia instead of being one of the provinces within the republic of Serbia (the other province is Vojvodina). The protests are labeled "counter-revolution" by the Yugoslav authorities and are followed by a brutal police crackdown against mostly young people, students, and teachers who participated. Hundreds are sentenced to long-term imprisonment for such "counter-revolutionary activities" as chanting slogans, carrying banners, or participating in rallies calling for "Kosovo-Republic," mostly under the incrimination of "association for hostile activities."

1981–1986—Two parallel processes develop: On the one hand, state repression against the Albanians; on the other, increasing claims in

Serbian nationalist media that the ones really oppressed are the Serbian-Montenegrin minority in Kosovo; this leads to organized political pressure to protect "threatened" Serbs and Montenegrins as justification for constitutional changes that would abolish provinces' autonomy and give Serbia full control of its "whole territory."

Fall 1986—Serbian Academy of Sciences and Arts produces a document called Memorandum, supporting Serb nationalists' claims that Serbia was a victim of the Yugoslav federal arrangement: that the Serbs as the largest ethnic group were left without their national state (with Serbia weakened by the existence of two provinces and Serbs living in three republics—Serbia, Croatia and Bosnia); that it was Tito, half Croat, half Slovene, who favored Yugoslavia's more advanced republics of Croatia and Slovenia; that the Serbs were even subjected to a "genocide" in Kosovo. The document—the existence of which is initially denied—provides the intellectual ground for intensified nationalist propaganda, including the calls for constitutional changes that would lead not only to Serbia's full control over the two provinces but also to "unification of Serb lands," i.e., annexation of Serb-inhabited areas of neighboring Bosnia and Croatia in order for "all Serbs [to live] in a single state." That is the initial element in what will become the drive for a "Greater Serbia."

April 1987—Slobodan Milosevic, then the president of the Central Committee of the League of Communists of Serbia, takes the banner of Serb nationalism a step further. He goes to a rally of Serbs and Montenegrins in Kosovo Polje and, following their preplanned clashes with the police, promises them, "No one is allowed to beat you anymore!" Milosevic becomes an instant hero of the Serb nationalist cause heading toward the confrontation with more moderate Serbian politicians, who still prefer constitutional changes within slow-emerging consensus with others in Yugoslavia.

Fall 1987—Milosevic condemns moderates for not being resolute enough on Kosovo and calls for the infamous Eighth Session of the Central Committee of the League of Communists of Serbia at which he manages to get a majority in condemnation of moderates, prompting the downfall of the president of Serbia, Ivan Stambolic, and the president of the Belgrade City Committee of the League of Communists of Yugoslavia, Dragisa Pavlovic. Becoming an undisputed leader of Serbia and "protector of all

Serbs" throughout Yugoslavia, Milosevic purges all major media in Serbia, giving his loyal propagandists a free hand in a nationalistic campaign against an ever-increasing list of enemies within Yugoslavia: Albanian "separatists" and "terrorists"; "anti-Serbian Catholic alliance" (of Croats and Slovenes); "Vojvodina autonomists" (those who oppose suspension of autonomy); and, later, "Muslim fundamentalists" in Bosnia.

Summer 1988—Milosevic takes his crusade for constitutional changes to the streets, organizing "Meetings of Truth" in support of "threatened Serbs and Montenegrins" from Kosovo, with hundreds of thousands of people supporting his drive against everyone else in Yugoslavia; street protests, with direct threat against the security of his political opponents; and forced resignation of the moderate leadership in Vojvodina and Montenegro, bringing Milosevic's loyalists to power and giving Serbia increasing control over Yugoslav federal institutions.

February 1989—Milosevic unilaterally changes Yugoslav federal arrangement by imposing constitutional changes giving Serbia direct control over Kosovo and Vojvodina and—through his proxies—over Montenegro. Protests in Kosovo lead to the police–army crackdown with Albanians reduced to second-class citizens.

June 28, 1989—Now firmly in control of Serbia, Milosevic goes to Kosovo Polje again to address a "million-Serb" rally celebrating the 600th anniversary of a historic battle with the Turks; he issues an unveiled threat to anyone opposing his drive for Serb domination in Yugoslavia: "Our battles are not armed battles yet, but such battles can't be excluded."

1989–1990—Milosevic's drive for domination prompts a drive for independence in the other republics, especially in Croatia and Slovenia. Pro-independence parties win elections in both republics in 1990. Croatian president Franjo Tudjman and Slovenian president Milan Kucan coordinate their countries' plans for independence. Tudjman's party takes over most relevant Croatian media running a nationalist campaign of its own. In Bosnia, a coalition of three nationalistic parties—Muslim (SDA), Serb (SDS), and Croat (HDZ)—wins elections in November 1990. This threatens the survival of the republic because SDS represents Milosevic's ideology of "Greater Serbia" and HDZ Tudjman's ideology of "Greater Croatia." But the SDA—as an exclusively Muslim party—fails to attract not only moderate Bosnian Serbs and Croats but also moderate Bosnian

Muslims (this means that those still in favor of the Bosnian tradition and culture of ethnic tolerance—including Bosnian media—do not have a representation in the decisions leading to the dismemberment of their country).

May–December 1991—Slovenia and Croatia declare independence. Yugoslav Army tries "to secure external borders" provoking a brief war with a hastily organized Slovenian territorial defense. With no Serbs to "defend" in Slovenia, Serb-dominated Yugoslavia lets Slovenia "go" but, under pretext of protecting Serbs in Croatia (12 percent of Croatia's population), the Yugoslav Army supports local Serb territorial forces and paramilitaries coming from Serbia in a takeover of "Serb lands" in Croatia; this results in a total devastation of the town of Vukovar, bombing of the Adriatic city of Dubrovnik, and numerous crimes against civilians throughout Croatia. The Serbian–Croatian war, which lasts for six months, is fueled and followed by an unrestrained "media war" with each country's media competing in glorifying their own and satanizing the "other."

April 1992—The international community (UN, EU, U.S.) recognizes the independence of Bosnia, Croatia, and Slovenia. Recognition of Bosnia's independence prompts Serb nationalists' violent response: Local paramilitary forces—armed and organized by the SDS and with artillery support from the Yugoslav Army and full participation of paramilitary groups from Serbia—proclaim "Serb autonomous regions" throughout Bosnia, taking control of up to 70 percent of Bosnia's territory that strategically connects Serbia proper with Serb-held territories in Croatia and creating what is supposed to be "Greater Serbia." In the process of the takeover, hundreds of thousands of Bosnian Muslims and Croats are expelled from their homes and towns: 200,000 are killed, many more are imprisoned in concentration camps, thousands of women are raped in systematic terror, and a million and a half Bosnians become refugees. Milosevic-controlled media from Belgrade and newly established "Serb media" in Bosnia take over radio and television transmitters throughout Bosnia, making it almost impossible for voices of tolerance from Sarajevo-based Bosnian media to be heard outside of their besieged and terrorized Bosnian capital. Propaganda of war and hatred, coming from Serbia and later from Croatia, dominates Bosnia's airwaves.

May–November 1993—With Serb "ethnic cleansing" of large areas of

Bosnia completed, Croat nationalists—encouraged by international mediators who continue to produce new sets of maps for ethnic partition of Bosnia—begin "ethnic cleansing" of their own in areas they consider "historically Croatian," along the lines agreed upon by Tudjman and Milosevic in the series of their talks on the partition of Bosnia. Anti-Bosnian campaign in Croatian media reaches proportions of previous anti-Serb campaign.

March 1994—The U.S. brokers an end of the Croatian war against Bosnia creating a Bosniak–Croat federation in territories controlled by Bosnian and Croat forces.

Summer 1995—Two events prompt greater international involvement in the efforts to end the war. On July 11, Serbian forces take over supposedly UN-protected "safe zone" of Srebrenica and, in less than a week of systematic terror in what was known as "the worst massacre on European soil since World War II," kill more than 7,000 men and boys trying to leave the enclave. In Croatia, in a surprising offensive the Croatian army takes over areas occupied by Serb forces in 1991. Joint Bosnian–Croat offensive leads to a withdrawal of Serb forces from some areas in Bosnia, which puts additional pressure on Serb nationalistic leadership to end the war. Limited NATO airstrikes against Serb positions in Bosnia, following a massacre of civilians in Sarajevo marketplace, and the possibility of further territorial losses force Bosnian Serbs' leadership to accept American-brokered framework for peace and to authorize Yugoslav President Milosevic to negotiate on their behalf.

November 1995—Three-week-long negotiations in Dayton, Ohio, chaired by the U.S. diplomat Richard Holbrooke, lead to a peace agreement under which Bosnia remains a single state with two multiethnic entities, the Bosniak–Croat Federation in 51 percent of the territory and the Republika Srpska (Serb Republic) in 49. The agreement is signed by the presidents of Bosnia (Alija Izetbegovic), Serbia (Slobodan Milosevic), and Croatia (Franjo Tudjman).

December 1995—NATO sends a 60,000-strong peacekeeping force to Bosnia, one third of them American. Efforts to rebuild Bosnia include a large-scale "media intervention" with considerable investment in local media. But following the Dayton compromise with "guys with guns," international mediators accept as partners in that process the individuals and institutions mostly responsible for the war and the propaganda of hatred (e.g., Momcilo Krajisnik, later arrested under war crimes charges, was left as a president of the Advisory Board of Bosnian Serb TV in post-Dayton Bosnia). Operating under the Dayton constraints of the partitioned country, international media efforts fail to identify and support potential strategic multiethnic media enterprises.

December 1996—Serbian coalition of democratic parties Zajedno (Together) wins municipal elections throughout Serbia, but Milosevic refuses to accept the results. Months-long street protests follow, forcing Milosevic to concede defeat in some of the largest Serbian cities, including the capital, Belgrade. Opposition takeover of the cities leads to an explosion of new media, some of them truly independent, some controlled by opposition parties and politicians. Milosevic's regime responds by adopting an Information Act that provides the regime with instruments to harass, fine, and eventually close media challenging his power.

March 1999—Renewed Serbian terror in Kosovo, and Milosevic's refusal to accept the internationally brokered peace deal that would include restoration of Kosovo's autonomy within Serbia, leads to the NATO air strikes against Serbian military targets. Milosevic uses the "NATO aggression" to censor, ban, and silence all of the independent or opposition media. A number of newspapers and radio and TV stations are forced to close down; some agree to operate under censorship or self-censorship.

December 1999—Croatian president Tudjman, who controlled Croatian state media with the same methods used by Milosevic in Serbia, dies. In elections following his death, a coalition of democratic parties defeats Tudjman's nationalistic HDZ, and liberal democrat Stipe Mesic becomes the new president. The slow process of rebuilding Croatian independent media begins.

April 2000—Moderate Social-Democratic Party wins municipal elections in some of the largest Bosniak-majority Bosnian cities, including Sarajevo, leading to a gradual removal of nationalist Muslim SDA from power. International media intervention still fails to restructure Bosnian state radio and television into a statewide Public Broadcast System.

October 5, 2000—Serbia's Democratic Opposition wins elections, but Milosevic refuses to accept the results, leading to street protests throughout Serbia and the opposition's takeover of Serbia's institutions. The process of rebuilding Serbia's independent media begins.

Appendix B
Overview of the Media Landscape: Serbia, Croatia, and Bosnia Herzegovina

Radio-Television

In all three Balkan countries engulfed in the wars of the 1990s—Serbia, Croatia, and Bosnia Herzegovina—the most influential media outlets were their state Radio-Television stations.

Before the war, the stations were named after the capitals of the republics: RTV Belgrade, RTV Zagreb, and RTV Sarajevo. With the dissolution of Yugoslavia and international recognition of the new states in 1992, the stations were renamed as RTV Serbia (RTS), RTV Croatia (HRT), and RTV Bosnia Herzegovina (RTVBiH).

Within those state-controlled radio-television companies, in all three cases the ruling nationalist parties exerted tighter control over television, while radio stations managed to maintain varying degrees of profession- alism through different periods of time; however, ultimately all radio sta- tions ended in the hands of their respective governments.

Following the Dayton Peace Agreement, which ended the war in Bosnia in November 1995, Bosnian TV shared the fate of the Bosnian state: It had to be practically dismantled in order for a new, decentralized structure, to be put in place. In 2002, the new Bosnian Public Broadcast System gradually took shape within the country's three separate entities:

☐ TV of Bosnia-Herzegovina, producing the evening News Journal at 7 p.m. for the whole country, and coordinating joint coverage of major international sports events;

☐ Federal TV, producing the prime time News Journal and other programs for the Federation; and

☐ Republika Srpska TV, doing the same for the Serb entity.

In all three countries—Serbia, Croatia, and Bosnia Herzegovina—the restructuring of the former state Radio and TV stations into public broadcast services has been frustratingly slow, with the ruling political parties and parliaments having too much control over the process in Serbia and Croatia, and international supervisors of the peace process having too little experience or regional expertise to handle this task in Bosnia.

In addition to the state-public electronic media, numerous new—some independent, some opposition, some regional—radio and TV stations have been established in all three countries.

In Serbia, Radio and TV B92, BK (Karic brothers) TV, Studio B, TV Politika, and TV Pink have been among the most influential, as well as Radio Index in Belgrade and radio stations in Pancevo, Sokobanja, and Nis, and the provincial RTV station for Vojvodina in Novi Sad.

In Croatia, Radio 101 and Youth TV in Zagreb, as well as regional RTV centers such as those in Split and Rijeka and others, have the widest audience.

In Bosnia, with a long delay in restructuring the state RTV, the new Open Broadcast Network (OBN) TV and the new FERN Radio played an important role in providing unbiased information throughout the country in 1996–2000. Following the establishment of the public broadcast structure, international sponsors abandoned OBN, and FERN was integrated into the new BH Radio 1. TV Hayat, Studio 99 TV, and Radio Zid in Sarajevo, as well as independent TV stations in Tuzla and Zenica, provided a valuable alternative to the nationalist-controlled electronic media outlets throughout the country.

Newspapers

In post-WWII Yugoslavia, each republic had its own, socially owned and Party-controlled publishing house. In Serbia, that was *Politika (Politics);* in Croatia, *Vjesnik (The Herald);* and in Bosnia Herzegovina, *Oslobodjenje (Liberation).* Besides leading dailies of the same name, those companies gradually developed other editions, including tabloid newspapers and political weeklies, as well as magazines for women, children, and families, and sports newspapers and radio and TV guides. Politically influential publications within each republic's publishing company included: the daily tabloid *Politika ekspres* (sometimes called *Ekspres*) and the weekly *NIN* in Belgrade; the daily *Vecernji list (Evening Newspaper)* and weekly *Danas (Today)* in Zagreb; and the daily *Vecernje novine (Evening Newspaper)* and weeklies *Svijet (The World)* and *Nedjelja (The Week)* in Sarajevo.

In addition, the federal daily, *Borba (The Struggle),* in Belgrade had its own tabloid, *Vecernje novosti (Evening News),* which prided itself as the largest-circulation daily in Yugoslavia.

In all three republics, there also were a number of regional newspapers. The most respected was the daily *Slobodna Dalmacija (Free Dalmatia)* in Split, Croatia, and then other dailies such as *Novi list/Glas Istre (New Newspaper/Voice of Istria)* or *Glas Slavonije (Voice of Slavonia)* in other parts of Croatia; *Dnevnik (Daily)* in Novi Sad, Serbia; and *Glas (Voice)* in Banjaluka, Bosnia Herzegovina.

In the late 1980s, the reformist Yugoslav government of Ante Markovic introduced liberal legislation allowing for privatization of previously Party-controlled newspapers. Some papers used the opportunity to project a new, independent editorial line and ownership structure, including *Borba, Slobodna Dalmacija, Oslobodjenje,* and a number of other publications.

When nationalists took power in Serbia and Croatia, they abandoned Markovic's laws, annulled privatization of the media, and in Serbia and Croatia, the Milosevic and Tudjman governments, respectively, established complete control of all influential media outlets. The Bosnian media successfully resisted the nationalist government attempts to control them, but then suffered irreparable damage during the three and a half years of war in April 1992–November 1995.

Following the fall of Milosevic in October 2000 in Serbia, *Politika* and

Politika ekspres as well as *Vecernje novosti* are struggling to regain respect and readership after more than a decade of loyalty to the regime; the federal government of ever-shrinking Yugoslavia declared that it didn't need a daily and offered *Borba* for sale; and a number of new dailies emerged to fight for their share of the market, with the Belgrade daily *Danas (Today)* gaining public respect for open-mindedness and free debate on Serbia's recent past. The most influential weeklies include *NIN* and *Vreme*. The monthly publication *Republika (The Republic)*, edited by Nebojsa Popov, has been the most consistent anti-nationalist voice in Serbia during and after the war years.

In post-Tudjman Croatia, the 1993 nationalist takeover of *Slobodna Dalmacija* was declared illegal, but the paper has not regained its prewar readership or liberal editorial line. *Vjesnik* remained government-supported with a poor circulation, while *Vecernji list* regained its status as the largest-circulation daily in Croatia, supported by fresh foreign investment. The Rijeka daily *Novi list* established itself as a widely respected publication and the new Zagreb tabloid, *Jutarnji list (Morning Newspaper)*, successfully competed for its share of readership. The *Feral Tribune* maintained its independent standards, remaining a constant critic of both the nationalist legacy and the slow pace of democratic change in Croatia. Two other weeklies, *Globus* and *Nacional*, have a considerable readership.

In post-war Bosnia, *Dnevni avaz (Daily Voice)*, sometimes called *Avaz*, became the largest-circulation newspaper, changing loyalties but remaining the most accepted paper among Bosniaks. The paper was initially loyal to the Muslim nationalist SDA, which had established it with generous support, then loyal to the pro-European Social-Democratic Party, which briefly supported it, and then promoted the political agenda of the Party for Bosnia Herzegovina. *Oslobodjenje* lost most of its best journalists and most of its readership. The former *Vecernje novine (Evening Newspaper)*—now *Jutarnje novine (Morning Newspaper)*—has been a distant third in the Sarajevo newspaper market. The Banjaluka daily *Nezavisne novine (Independent Newspaper)*, with considerable international support, has been trying to project the image of the "paper for all Bosnia" with limited success in Sarajevo.

The leading weeklies *Dani (Days)* and *Slobodna Bosna (Free Bosnia)* have been joined by a new publication, the bi-weekly *Start* magazine, which distinguished itself for provocative in-depth interviews and a less confrontational yet critical examination of the post-war country. In Republika Srpska, the weekly *Reporter* maintains a largely independent editorial line.

Agencies

In pre-war Yugoslavia, the federal news agency Tanjug (Telegraph Agency of New Yugoslavia) enjoyed a monopoly and had a huge network of correspondents throughout the country and dozens of foreign correspondents on all continents. With its propagandistic role in the decades of socialist Yugoslavia, the agency produced not only news, but supplied Yugoslav media with must-read commentaries, spreading the ruling Party's line throughout the country—on all radio and TV frequencies and the front pages of all newspapers. The same method was widely used during the Milosevic years with Tanjug becoming the mouthpiece of the Serbian strongman's regime. The post-Milosevic government has been struggling to consolidate Tanjug's huge debts and expensive bureaucracy.

Tanjug's traditional monopoly has been successfully challenged in Serbia by the new independent BETA news agency, started by disgruntled former Tanjug journalists. In Croatia, Tudjman's regime established the national wire service (HINA), with the only competition coming from the Split-based independent agency (STINA). In Bosnia, different wartime authorities ran their own wire services, which settled in the post-war period into the two entities' agencies: FENA for the federation and SRNA for Republika Srpska. The Sarajevo-based ONASA, founded by *Oslobodjenje*, provides an independent professional alternative to both.

Notes

Introduction

1. Elie Wiesel, "Perils of Indifference," The White House Millennium Lecture Series, April 12, 1999.

2. Gordana Logar, taped interview by author, McLean, Va., January 15, 2000.

3. Manjo Vukotic, telephone interview by author, Belgrade, April 25, 2000.

4. "In Memoriam, Posljednji Joskov dispet" ("Josko's Last Act of Defiance"), *Novinar,* March 1998.

5. "Pocast sjor Josku" ("In Honor of Mr. Josko"), *Slobodna Dalmacija,* February 22, 2000.

6. Nebojsa Popov, "Media Shock and Comprehending It," in *Media & War,* ed. Nena Skopljanac Brunner, Stjepan Gredelj, Alija Hodzic, and Branimir Kristofic (Zagreb: Centre for Transition and Civil Society Research; and Belgrade: Agency Argument, 2000), 10.

1. The Yugoslav Media in Tito's Time

1. A condensed version of events following the occupation of Yugoslavia can be found in Noel Malcolm's *Bosnia: A Short History,* first published in 1994 by Macmillan London Limited and simultaneously in paperback by Papermac.

2. Bozo Novak, telephone interview by author, Zagreb, April 18, 2000.

3. Ibid.

4. Figures on the number of people killed in World War II in Yugoslavia vary in different sources, but most historians agree that it was no fewer than 1 million. While official Communist history emphasizes the number of those killed "in liberation struggle," more critical examination points to the fact that the majority of those killed died at the hands of their compatriots serving different causes: Ustasha fascists, Chetnik royalists, and members of the partisan liberation movement.

5. Gertrude Joch Robinson, *Tito's Maverick Media: The Politics of Mass Communications in Yugoslavia* (Urbana, Chicago, London: University of Illinois Press, 1977) 18.

6. Ibid., 19.

7. Ibid.

8. As with anything else in the Yugoslav history books, the figures vary to the extremes depending on whether they come from "winners" or from "losers," from Titoists or anti-Titoists, from ideologically motivated official history or revenge-seeking opponents of the regime. In an article titled "Yugoslavia: A House Much Divided," published in *National Geographic,* August 1990, Kenneth C. Dannfort reported, "Tito silenced dissent by sending at least 7,000 critics to living hell on Goli Otok, a barren island in the Adriatic." (No page number; read on the Internet.)

9. Nevertheless in January 1955, Djilas was put on trial for "hostile propaganda." Serge Schmemann, "Milovan Djilas, Yugoslav Critic of Communism, Dies at 83," *New York Times,* April 21, 1995.

10. Milovan Djilas, *The New Class: An Analysis of the Communist System* (New York: Praeger, 1997).

11. I met Djilas in the spring of 1991 when he came to Sarajevo to participate in an open TV debate and visited me at *Oslobodjenje.* The man who spent years in Tito's jails even had some kind words for his long-time captor compared to the nationalists who replaced him. He felt that "socialism with a human face" could have succeeded had it accommodated the right to factionalism, the clash of ideas for which he argued so unselfishly. Djilas believed that communism actually helped nationalism triumph because it prevented the development of institutions that could have confronted nationalism, such as a democratic system, a market economy, and a prosperous middle class. "Communism buried itself," Djilas told me. He died in 1995 at the age of 83.

12. Aleksandar "Sasa" Nenadovic, telephone interview by author, Belgrade, April 21, 2000.

13. Novak interview.

14. Robinson, *Tito's Maverick Media,* 33.

15. Novak interview.

16. Ibid.

17. Ibid.

18. Nenadovic interview.

19. Rizo Mehinagic, telephone interview by author, Sarajevo, April 26, 2000.

20. Ibid.

21. Bozo Stefanovic, telephone interview by author, Sarajevo, April 26, 2000. At the time of this interview, Stefanovic was still a regular, best-regarded, cartoonist with *Oslobodjenje*, often causing trouble for the paper with Bosnian nationalists in power.

22. Novak interview.

23. Nenadovic interview.

2. Serbia: Manufacturing Enemies

1. Goran Milic, interview by author, Zagreb, January 19, 2000.

2. Branka Magas, *The Destruction of Yugoslavia: Tracking the Break-Up 1980–92* (London and New York: Verso, 1993).

3. Ibid., 7–8

4. A tendency among Serb nationalist propagandists to exaggerate murder and rape statistics is discussed by Magas, 62.

5. This was the predominant line in the Serbian media during the escalation of the Kosovo crises in 1981–89, with anyone in Serbia or elsewhere in Yugoslavia questioning that line being labeled "Serb traitor" or "Serb hater." The propagandistic effect was a gradual silencing of voices of moderation, primarily in Serbia.

6. Magas, quoting the Belgrade weekly *NIN*, says that "some 15,000 Serbs left Kosovo between 1968 and 1971, and another 30,000 (estimated) left over the next decade. Since the unrest, a further 9,000 have either left or applied to leave, which represents an acceleration of the outflow—up to 1981 the numbers had not gone beyond the regional pattern of inter-regional migration," 47.

7. Magas, *Destruction of Yugoslavia*, 49.

8. The SANU Presidency published a full text of the document in a book titled *Memorandum of the Serbian Academy of Sciences and Arts: Answers to Criticism*, written by Kosta Mihailovic and Vasilije Krestic (Belgrade: SANU 1995). The authors claim that critics of the Academy's unfinished document "resorted to slander and insults against the highest learned institution of the Sebian nation, its members, and the entire Serbian people." They say that work on the Memorandum was launched by the Academy's Assembly on May 23, 1985, because SANU "found it hard to bear the subjugated status of Serbia in Yugoslavia." On June 13, the SANU Presidency appointed a "committee to prepare a memorandum on current social issues," which included the following members: Pavle Ivic, Antonije Isakovic, Dusan Kanazir, Mihailo Markovic, Milos Macura, Dejan Medakovic, Miroslav Pantic, Ljubisa Rakic, Radovan Samardzic, Miomir Vukobratovic, Vasilije Krestic, Ivan Maksimovic, Kosta Mihailovic, Stojan Celic, and Nikola Cobeljic. The Working Group—chaired by Isakovic—was still editing the draft document when the story appeared in *Vecernje novosti* on September 24, 1986. Following the public uproar, the work on the Memorandum was suspended and the Presidency of SANU "assumed responsibility for the further fate of this document."

9. According to Mihailovic and Krestic *(Memorandum),* Cosic took part in the work on the Memorandum, which was coordinated by Antonije Isakovic. "Academicians Dobrica Cosic, Jovan Djordjevic, and Ljubomir Tadic were also invited to sit in on some of those meetings" of the Working Group, 15. Cosic himself elaborated his " winners in wars—losers in peace" thesis the following way: "Which kind of people are we, which kind of men, who in a time of war die for freedom so much only to lose it in their victories? How is it possible that someone among us, someone in the house, grabs from us what a much stronger enemy couldn't take away on a battlefield? How is it possible that people so dignified, so proud, so brave in war, accept humiliation and obedience in peace? . . . It is tragic to be a descendant of those who are forced to have more strength for war than for peace, and who after the biggest victory in Serbian history did not have the strength to confirm it in peace." (Dobrica Cosic, *Stvarno i moguce: Clanci i ogledi* [*Real and Possible: Articles and Essays*] [Rijeka: Otokar Kersovani, 1982], 171–172.

10. Mihailovic and Krestic, *Memorandum,* 10.

11. Laura Silber and Allen Little, *Yugoslavia: The Death of a Nation* (TV Books, Inc., 1996), 39. Distributed by Penguin, USA. The book is based on the television series of the same name, produced by Brian Lapping Associates Ltd., Great Britain.

12. Djukic's biography of Serbia's most powerful couple of the 1990s was also published in English: Slavoljub Djukic, *Milosevic and Markovic: A Lust for Power* (Montreal/Kingston: McGill-Queen's University Press, 2001).

13. Slavoljub Djukic, *Izmedju slave i anateme (Between the Glory and Anathema)* (Beograd: Filip Visnjic, 1994), 60.

14. B. Jovanovic, "Zasto ministar kulture brani antititovsku liniju?" (Why Is the Minister of Culture Defending an Anti-Titoist Line?"), *Politika,* May 26, 1987.

15. Djukic, *Izmedju slave,* 66.

16. Slavoljub Djukic, *On, Ona i mi* (Beograd: Radio B92, 1997), 66.

17. Ibid., 65

18. Djukic, *Izmedju,* 69.

19. Ibid., 71.

20. Silber and Little, *Yugoslavia,* 43.

21. Djukic, *Izmedju,* 78.

22. In the Yugoslav context of the time, that would constitute a serious breach of Party rules and a misuse of Stambolic's high office to protect his friend Pavlovic against the Party action: The Communist hierarchy was based on the so-called "democratic centralism" principle, with no room for a lower ranked organ (City Committee) to disobey a higher one (Central Committee).

23. Silber and Little, *Yugoslavia,* 44.

24. Djukic, *Izmedju,* 88.

25. Snjezana Milivojevic, *"Nacionalizacija svakidasnjice"* (*"Nationalization of Everyday Life"*), in *Srpska strana rata: Trauma i katarza u istorijskom pamcenju (Serbian Side of the War: Trauma and Catharsis in Historic Memory),* ed. Nebojsa Popov (Beograd: BIGZ, 1996), 673.

26. Zekerijah Smajic, e-mail to the author, May 6, 2000.

27. Aleksandar Nenadovic, *"Politika* u nacionalistickoj oluji" (*"Politika* in a Nationalistic Storm"), in *Srpska strana rata: Trauma i katarza u istorijskom pamcenju,* ed. Nebojsa Popov (Beograd: BIGZ, 1996) 586.

28. Zvonko Logar, "Smole, kao Slovenac crvenim zbog tvog politikantstva," *Politika,* September 23, 1988.

29. Milivojevic, *Nacionalizacija,* 674.

30. Nenadovic, *Politika,* 607.

31. Ibid., 596.

32. Borisav Jovic, *Poslednji dani Yugoslavije (The Last Days of Yugoslavia),* (Beograd: Politika, 1995), as quoted in Petar Lukovic's article, "Yugoslavia to Karlovac and Virovitica," *Vreme,* November 20, 1995.

33. Dobrica Cosic, "Writer's Notes," *Vecernje novosti,* April 15, 2002.

34. Milivojevic, *Nacionalizacija,* 674.

35. Milic interview.

36. Ibid.

37. Ibid.

38. Silber and Little, *Yugoslavia,* 66.

39. Milan Milosevic, "The Media Wars: 1987–1997," in *Burn This House: The Making and Unmaking of Yugoslavia,* ed. Jasminka Udovicki and James Ridgeway (Durham and London: Duke University Press, 1997), 109.

40. Zoran M. Markovic, *Nacija—zrtva i osveta (Nation—a Victim and Vengeance)* in *Srpska strana rata,* 650.

41. Rade Veljanovski, "Zaokret elektronskih medija" ("The Electronic Media Turnaround"), in *Srpska strana rata,* 610–36.

42. "Novi Sad TV Editors Suspended Over Editorial," Tanjug, April 12, 1990.

43. Zeljko Kliment, "Istina jednog psihijatra" ("One Psychiatrist's Truth"), *Vjesnik,* November 17, 1990, 16.

44. Milivojevic, *Nacionalizacija*, 682.

45. Raskovic's interview with Yutel was quoted by *Vreme* on January 27, 1992.

46. Stojan Cerovic, taped interview by author in Washington, D.C., July 15, 2000.

47. Ibid.

48. Veran Matic, taped interview by author in Boston, Mass., May 3, 2000.

49. Slobodan Antonic, "Hostages of the TV Journal," *Vreme*, May 25, 1992.

50. Milic interview.

51. Ibid.

52. Ibid.

53. Ibid.

54. Ibid.

55. Cerovic interview.

56. Dusan Simic, e-mail to author, December 27, 1999.

3. Serbo-Croatian War: Lying for the Homeland

1. Mirko Galic, taped interview by author, Zagreb, January 20, 2000.

2. Zivko Gruden, taped interview by author, Zagreb, January 20, 2000.

3. Hido Biscevic, "A Year with a New Identity," *Vjesnik*, January 5, 1991.

4. Nena Skopljanac Brunner, "Media Strategies of Constructing the Image of 'Other' as 'Enemy,'" in *Media & War*, ed. Nena Skopljanac Brunner, Stjepan Gredelj, Alija Hodzic, and Branimir Kristofic (Zagreb: Centre for Transition and Civil Society Research, and Belgrade: Agency Argument, 2000), 141.

5. Galic interview.

6. Ivica Djikic, "From Bordello to Public Television," *Feral Tribune*, No. 748, 2000.

7. Ibid.

8. Danko Plevnik, *Hrvatski obrat (Croatia's Turnover)* (Zagreb: Durieux, 1993), 97.

9. Miljenko Jergovic, taped interview by author, Zagreb, January 21, 2000.

10. Dubravka Ugresic, *The Culture of Lies: Antipolitical Essays* (University Park, Pa.: Pennsylvania State University, 1998), 72.

11. Blaine Harden, "Serbia's State Media Help to Inflame Yugoslavia's Rising Ethnic Passions," *Washington Post*, December 27, 1999.

12. Manjo Vukotic, telephone interview by author, Belgrade, April 25, 2000.

13. Goran Milic, taped interview by author, Zagreb, January 19, 2000.

14. Noel Malcolm, *Bosnia: A Short History* (London: Papermac, 1994), 179. The book was first published by Macmillan in London in 1994.

15. Yutel Newshour, June 30, 1991.

16. Emir Kusturica, "I Didn't Know, Now I Do," *Politika*, October 22, 1991.

17. Milan Milosevic, "The Media Wars," in *Yugoslavia's Ethnic Nightmare: The Inside Story of Europe's Unfolding Ordeal*, ed. Jasminka Udovicki and James Ridgeway (New York: Lawrence Hill Books, 1995), 117.

18. Nebojsa Popov, "Media Shock and Comprehending It," in *Media & War*, ed. Nena Skopljanac Brunner, Stjepan Gredelj, Alija Hodzic, and Branimir Kristofic (Zagreb: Centre for Transition and Civil Society Research, and Belgrade: Agency Argument, 2000), 10.

19. Ejub Stitkovac, "Croatia: The First War," in *Yugoslavia's Ethnic Nightmare*, 152–53.

20. Heni Erceg, *Ispodvijesti o ratu u Hrvatskoj (Undernews on War in Croatia)* (Split: *Feral Tribune*, 1995), 61.

21. Heni Erceg, e-mail to author, September 25, 2000.

22. Ibid.

23. Sandra Basic-Hrvatin, "Television and National/Public Memory," in *Bosnia by Television*, ed. James Gow, Richard Paterson, and Alison Preston (London: British Press Institute, 1996), 68.

24. Mark Thompson, *Forging War: The Media in Serbia, Croatia and Bosnia Herzegovina* (London: Article 19, International Centre against Censorship 1994), 161.

25. Damir Matkovic, taped interview by author, Zagreb, January 21, 2000.

26. Ibid.

27. Milic interview.

28. Nena Skopljanac Brunner, "An Analysis of Media Presentation of Reality by RTV Serbia," in *Media & War*, ed. Nena Skopljanac Brunner, Stjepan Gredelj, Alija Hodzic, and Branimir Kristofic (Zagreb: Centre for Transition and Civil Society Research, and Belgrade: Agency Argument, 2000), 250

29. "An Action Against the Terror of Croatian Forces," *Politika*, October 3, 1991.

30. "Crimes Before the Eyes of the World," *Politika*, November 22, 1991.

31. Momcilo Petrovic, Junaci naseg doba/Heroes of Our Time: Veselin Sljivancanin, Vitez za jednokratnu upotrebu/A Disposable Knight, *SAM—Srpska anarhisticka mreza* [website]/Serbian Anarchist Network, December 16, 1995.

32. Stojan Cerovic, "In the Trap of Patriotism," *Vreme News Digest,* December 2, 1992.

33. Jagoda Martincevic, "Decisions a Natural," *Vjesnik,* November 9, 1991.

34. Darko Hudelist, *Novinari pod sljemom (Journalists Under Helmets)* (Zagreb: Globus, 1992), 38–47.

35. Drago Hedl, "Javna rijec u Hrvatskoj, *Glas Slavonije"* ("Public Word in Croatia, *Voice of Slavonia"*), *Erasmus Magazine,* July 1996.

36. *Vecernji list,* end of 1992. Author lost the actual article in a computer crash and was unable to find it again.

37. Erceg e-mail.

38. Jelena Lovric, "Javna rijec u Hrvatskoj, *Danas"* ("Public Word in Croatia, *Today"*), *Erasmus Magazine,* July 1996.

39. Milos Obrenovic ruled Serbia as an autonomous province still under the Turkish Ottoman Empire from 1815 to 1839 and again 1858 to 1860.

40. Dusan Simic, e-mail to author, December 27, 1999.

41. Ibid.

42. *Vreme,* February 17, 1992.

4. Bosnia: Ground Zero

1. Population census 1999, Statisticki bilten 219 (Statistics Bulletin 219), Republic's Bureau for Statistics, Sarajevo, May 1991.

2. Senad Pecanin, taped interview by author, Sarajevo, February 2, 2000.

3. Kemal Kurspahic, *As Long As Sarajevo Exists* (Stony Creek, CT: The Pamphleteer's Press, 1997), 21–60.

4. Zlatko Dizdarevic, taped interview by author, McLean, Va., February 5, 2001.

5. Ibid.

6. Tudjman and Milosevic met at one of Tito's favorite hunting villas, in Karadjordjevo near Belgrade on March 25, 1991, and later in a series of meetings of the presidents of all six Yugoslav republics. There are numerous indications that the main point of agreement between the two was their design for the partition of Bosnia in order to create both "Greater Serbia" and "Greater Croatia."

7. Branka Magas, "The Destruction of Bosnia and Herzegovina," in *Why Bosnia? Writings on the Balkan War,* ed. Rabia Ali and Lawrence Lifschultz (Stony Creek, CT: The Pamphleteer's Press, 1993), 253.

8. Gordana Knezevic, e-mail to author, July 28, 2000.

9. Zoran Udovicic, "Media Plan Research: 'Hate Speech' Losing Its Colors," *AIM,* February 13, 1996.

10. Miljenko Jergovic, taped interview by author, Zagreb, January 21, 2000.

11. Gojko Beric, taped interview by author, Sarajevo, January 29, 2000.

12. Miljenko Jergovic, "Risto Djogo Died of Laughing," *Nedjeljna Dalmacija,* September 23, 1994.

13. I watched this report myself, but didn't make a note of the date at that time.

14. Pale TV, Evening Journal, April 11, 1995.

15. Roger Cohen, "Sarajevo Girl Killed, Yet Serbs Suffer," *New York Times,* April 26, 1995.

16. Mladen Vuksanovic, *Pale: Dnevnik (Diary), 5.4.–15. 7. 1992* (Zagreb: Durieux, 1996).

17. Ibid., 10.

18. Ibid., 17.

19. Ibid., 21.

20. Ibid., 42.

21. Ibid., 79.

22. In mid-April 1992, Nedim Smajlovic, son of Kjasif Smajlovic, called the author to tell him about the circumstances surrounding his father's death.

23. Mehmed Husic, interview by author, Sarajevo, February 2, 2000.

24. Beric interview.

25. Knezevic e-mail.

26. Mark Thompson, *Forging War: The Media in Serbia, Croatia and Bosnia-Hercegovina* (London: Article 19, International Centre Against Censorship), 249.

27. "A Million People Watching Television in the Cellar," *Slobodna Dalmacija,* March 15, 1993.

28. Senad Hadzifejzovic, taped interview by author, Sarajevo, January 28, 2000.

29. Goran Milic, taped interview by author, Zagreb, January 19, 2000.

30. Ibid.

31. Zeljko Garmaz, "Where Are the Politicians Heading," *Globus,* April 1, 1994.

32. Zilhad Kljucanin, "Partizana ne smije biti" ("There Shouldn't Be Any Partisans"), *Zmaj od Bosne,* June 17, 1993.

33. Dubravko Horvatic, "Muhammedan Genocide Against Croats," *Vjesnik,* June 24, 1993.

34. Emir Imamovic, "Instructions for Genocide," *Dani,* June 26, 2000.

35. Ibid.

36. Adnan Jahic, "A Vital Muslim State," *Zmaj od Bosne,* September 17, 1993.

37. Following Cosovic's attack, one of *Oslobodjenje's* editors was forced to send his family from Serbia to exile in Sweden; one of the Serb reporters asked for an assignment as a copy editor so his name wouldn't appear in a paper for some time; while others continued to work concerned for the fate of their loved ones within the reach of the Serb authorities.

38. Kurspahic, *As Long As Sarajevo Exists,* 213–14.

39. Knezevic e-mail.

40. Jergovic interview.

41. Petar the First Karadjordjevic was the King of Serbia, 1903–1918, and the King of the Kingdom of Serbs, Croats, and Slovenes, 1918–1921.

42. Warren Zimmerman, "The Captive Mind," *New York Review of Books,* February 2, 1995.

43. The UN Security Council adopted Resolution 757 on May 30, 1992, imposing economic sanctions against rump Yugoslavia, i.e., Serbia and Montenegro, for failing to meet the Resolution 752 of May 15, 1992 demand for withdrawal of their troops from Bosnia Herzegovina.

44. Thompson, *Forging War,* 103.

45. Milica Pesic later moved to London and became the director of the Media Diversity Institute.

46. Media Report, Radio National, Australian Broadcasting Corporation, May 21, 1999.

47. BBC Summary of World Broadcasts, November 6, 1993.

48. Stanko Cerovic, "The Truth About Violence," *Vreme,* April 25, 1994.

49. Nenad L. Stefanovic, "The 115-Year Old Orphan," *Vreme,* November 28, 1994.

50. Dusan Simic, e-mail to author, December 27, 1999.

51. Ibid.

52. Gordana Logar, taped interview by author, McLean, Va., January 15, 2000.

53. Patrick McCarthy, *Srebrenica Survivors in St. Louis: After the Fall* (St. Louis. Mo.: Missouri Historical Society Press, 2000), 47.

54. David Rohde, *Endgame: The Betrayal and Fall of Srebrenica—Europe's Worst Massacre Since World War II* (New York: Farrar Straus and Giroux, 1997).

55. "Srebrenica—A Defensive Action," *Politika,* July 15, 1995.

56. Press release issued by the International Criminal Tribunal for the Former Yugoslavia (CC/PIO026-E), November 16, 1995, The Hague.

57. Report of the Secretary-General (of the United Nations) Pursuant to General Assembly Resolution 53/35 (1998): Srebrenica Report, New York, November 16, 2000.

58. Ivan Radovanovic, "Derby in *Politika,*" *Vreme,* November 13, 1995.

59. Nenad Ivankovic, "The World Accepts Partition of BH," *Vjesnik,* June 8, 1993; "Milosevic Satisfied: The Plan Buried, Bosnia in Three Parts," *Vjesnik,* June 18, 1993; and "Kozirev Doesn't Exclude Even the Change of the Borders," *Vjesnik,* June 28, 1993.

60. Mugdim Karabeg, *Fasade* (Mostar: Rondo, 2001).

61. *Vjesnik's* one-sided headlines included "War and Crimes, a Muslim Name for Cease-fire," May 8, 1993; "Jihad and Holocaust Hand in Hand," June 11, 1993; "Unheard of Crimes by Muslim Forces," June 15, 1993; "Muhammadanian Genocide Against Croats," June 24, 1993; "Muslims' Bloody Trail," August 1, 1993.

62. "British Intelligence Officers Caused the War Between Croats and Muslims," *Vjesnik,* September 19, 1993 (reprinted from *Danas*).

63. Mario Marusic, "35 Croats Hanged in Zenica!" *Vjesnik,* August 9, 1993.

64. Miljenko Jergovic, "Goals Journalists Scored on Themselves," *Danas,* June 25, 1993.

65. Heni Erceg, e-mail to author, September 25, 2000.

66. Jergovic interview.

67. "A Knife Soaked in Croat Blood," *Vjesnik,* June 14, 1993.

68. Chuck Sudetic, "Mostar's Old Bridge Battered to Death," *New York Times,* November 9, 1993.

69. Jure Ilic, "Weeping Over a Bridge or Over Mostar," *Vjesnik,* November 10, 1993.

70. Jergovic interview.

71. John F. Burns, "U.N.'s Grim Documentation at a Massacre Site in Bosnia," *New York Times,* October 28, 1993.

72. Aleksandar Milosevic, "No Excuses," *Vjesnik,* October 29, 1993.

73. Thompson, *Forging War,* 197.

74. Dubravko Merlic, *Slikom na sliku (Frame on Frame)* (Zagreb: Dual, 1994), 6.

75. Damir Matkovic, taped interview by author, Zagreb, January 21, 2000.

76. HTV Evening News, 19:30 p.m., February 1, 1993.

77. Milic interview.

78. Ibid.

5. Balkan Media Post-Dayton: Missed Opportunities

1. Richard Holbrooke, *To End a War* (New York: Random House, 1998).

2. Dayton Peace Agreement, Annex 3, the Agreement on Elections.

3. International Crisis Group Report, *Media in Bosnia and Herzegovina—How*

International Support Can Be More Effective, March 17, 1997, 5.

4. Carl Bildt, e-mail to author, March 16, 2002.

5. Ibid.

6. Zoran Udovicic, taped interview by author, Sarajevo, February 2, 2000.

7. Mark Wheeler, *Monitoring Media: The Bosnian Elections 1996* (Sarajevo: The Institute for War and Peace Reporting with Media Plan, Sarajevo, 1997), 33.

8. Ibid., 44.

9. Chris Hedges, "TV Station in Bosnia Feeds Serbs Propaganda," *New York Times,* June 9, 1996.

10. "Bijela knjiga: Mediji i demokratizacija u Bosni i Hercegovini" (White Book: Media and Democratization in Bosnia Herzegovina), Independent Media Commission, Sarajevo, December 6, 2000.

11. Author's analysis of HTV Journal rebroadcast on Channel 56 in Fairfax County, Va., in February 1997.

12. *Monitoring Report,* Volume 3, Issue 2, July 26, 1997 (Sarajevo: Media Plan and Institute for War and Peace Reporting).

13. Ibid., Issue 1, July 12, 1997.

14. Ibid., Issue 4, August 23, 1997.

15. *New York Times,* "Bosnia's Polluted Airwaves," September 6, 1997.

16. Associated Press report from Sarajevo, October 30, 1997.

17. Wheeler, *Monitoring Media,* 2.

18. *Monitoring Report,* Volume 3, Issue 1, July 12, 1997.

19. Ibid., Issue 6, September 12, 1997.

20. Goran Milic, taped interview by author, Zagreb, January 19, 2000.

21. Jadranko Katana, taped interview by author, Sarajevo, January 28, 2000.

22. International Crisis Group Report, "Media in Bosnia and Herzegovina: How International Support Can be More Effective," Sarajevo, March 18, 1997.

23. Ibid.

24. Zoran Udovicic, "Media in BiH—Conquering of Democracy" (Sarajevo: Media Plan Institute, 2000).

25. ICG, "Media in Bosnia and Herzegovina," 6.

26. Fahrudin Djapo, "Soon, *Dnevni avaz,* as the Pro-Regime *Oslobodjenje* in the Past, Will Only Be Used for Window Cleaning," *Ljiljan,* July 2, 1997.

27. Senad Pecanin, "Instead of Fighting Saja, They Fight Avaz," *Dani,* July 15, 2000.

28. Zlatko Dizdarevic, taped interview by author, McLean, Va., February 5, 2001.

29. David DeVoss, "Independent Journalists Fill Political Vacuum—And Pay a High Price for It," *Los Angeles Times,* November 14, 1999.

30. Senad Pecanin, taped interview by author, Sarajevo, February 2, 2000.

31. Ibid.

32. Sanja Despot and Snjezana Pavic, "Wait Until the State Starts Thinking," *Novi list,* January 7, 1996.

33. Miljenko Jergovic, "*Ljiljan* Carries the SDA Banner," *Nedjeljna Dalmacija,* June 14, 1996.

34. ICG, "Media in Bosnia and Herzegovina," 6.

35. Zeljko Kopanja, interview by author, Washington, D.C., November 16, 2000.

36. *State of the Media in Bosnia Herzegovina in the Context of Human Rights* (Sarajevo: Helsinki Committee for Human Rights in BiH), Issue 31, December 1999, 3.

37. Stan Markotic, "A Potent Weapon in Milosevic's Arsenal," *Transition,* April 28, 1995.

38. Dragan Todorovic, "On the Spot: Srebrenica and Bratunac, I Wasn't There!" *Vreme,* May 7, 1996.

39. Marijana Milosavljevic, "A Letter on Silence," *NIN,* December 13, 1996.

40. Ivan Torov, "The Truth Swallowed by the Dark," *Nasa Borba,* December 17, 1996.

41. Rade Veljanovski, "Once Upon a Time, There Was a Radio," *Vreme,* December 21, 1996.

42. Filip Svarm, "What Would They Say If They Could," *Vreme,* December 7, 1996.

43. Uros Komlenovic, "Minister vs. Citizen," *Vreme,* March 15, 1997.

44. This figure of Albanians representing more than 90 percent of the population in Kosovo has been the most cited estimate internationally; the exact figure is not available because ethnic Albanians boycotted the official census in 1991.

45. Miklos Biro, Novi Sad, "Is Anybody Out There?" *War Report,* February –March 1996 .

46. Veran Matic, "Terms of Estrangement," *Index of Censorship,* July/August 1998.

47. Investigative Team Report, "Medijska slika Srbije—Zivot u represiji" ("Media Picture of Serbia—A Life Under Repression") (Beograd: Media Center, December 4, 2000), 22.

48. Radio–Television of Serbia, Evening TV Journal, Monday, April 5, 1999.

49. Veran Matic, "These Bombs Don't Help," *New York Times,* April 1, 1999.

50. Veran Matic, taped interview by author, Boston, May 3, 2000.

51. *Oslobodjenje* published daily throughout the three-and-a-half-year siege of Sarajevo from an underground atomic bomb shelter beneath its obliterated building. Two books have been published in the United States on *Oslobodjenje's* wartime struggle: Tom Gjelten, *Sarajevo Daily: A City and Its Newspaper Under Siege* (New York: HarperCollins, 1994) and Kemal Kurspahic, *As Long As Sarajevo Exists* (Stony Creek, CT: The Pamphleteer's Press, 1997).

52. Vlado Mares, "Sacrificed for Serbia?" *International War and Peace Reporting,* October 30, 1999.

53. Tatjana Lenard, "No Official Announcement of RTS Bombing," ANEM (Association of Independent Electronic Media) Weekly Report, Belgrade, February 3, 2001.

54. Stojan Cerovic, taped interview by author, Washington, D.C., July 15, 2000.

55. Gordana Logar, taped interview by author, McLean, Va., December 18, 1999.

56. Ibid.

57. Ljiljana Smajlovic, "Don't Shoot the Messenger," *Transitions,* October 7, 1999.

58. Ibid.

59. Svetlana Slapsak, *ProFemina,* Spring–Winter 1999.

60. Lepa Mladjenovic, "The Women in Conflict Zones," Conference Paper, A comparative study of the issues faced by women as a result of armed conflict, Budapest, October 1999.

61. Blaine Harden, "Live, in Belgrade, the Milosevic News," *New York Times,* June 27, 1999.

62. Opinion Analysis, USIA, September 16, 1999.

63. Eric D. Gordy, *The Culture of Power in Serbia: Nationalism and the Destruction of Alternatives* (University Park, Pa.: Pennsylvania State University Press, 1996), 99.

64. Zeljko Rogosic, "In Croatia, a Phantom Curse 'Enemy of the State' Has Been Created, and I Really Am an Enemy of Such a State," *Nacional,* December 11, 1996.

65. Vesna Peric-Zimonjic, "Press Freedom for Whom?" Inter Press Service, July 17, 1996.

66. Gordana Grbic, "The Huge Risk for Gotovac and Tomac," *Novi list,* May 27, 1997.

67. "The Tudjman Tirade," *New York Times,* Editorial, November 27, 1997.

68. "Conversation with a Ghost," *Feral Tribune,* April 8, 1996.

69. Mirko Galic, taped interview by author, Zagreb, January 20, 2000.

70. Damir Matkovic, taped interview by author, Zagreb, January 21, 2000.

71. Federal Information Services, Federal News Service, Washington, D.C., August 30, 1998.

72. Matkovic interview.

73. "Croatia's Tudjman Hits at Rumors of His Wealth," Reuters, December 31, 1998.

74. Mladen Plese, "Police Started the Searches of Newsrooms and Journalists' Apartments," *Nacional*, June 6, 1999.

75. Jozo Petricevic, "Records Against Freedom and Morality," *Novinar*, 10-11-12/2001.

76. Peter Galbraith, interview by CNN on the occasion of Tudjman's death, December 19, 1999.

6. The Year 2000: The Beginning of Change

1. Stipe Mesic, interview, "Necu biti fikus!" by Heni Erceg and Marinko Culic, *Feral Tribune*, 759, 2000.

2. Damir Matkovic, taped interview by author, Zagreb, January 21, 2000.

3. Ibid.

4. Ivana Erceg, Media After Elections, Alternativna informativna mreza (AIM), January 16, 2000.

5. Mirko Galic, taped interview by author, Zagreb, January 20, 2000.

6. Matkovic interview.

7. Ibid.

8. Erceg, Media After Elections.

9. Ibid.

10. Ivica Djikic, "Pasalic: We Have Vecernjak!" *Feral Tribune*, May 20, 2000.

11. Viktor Ivancic, "Vecerbljak," *Feral Tribune*, April 14, 2000.

12. Stjepan Malovic and Gordana Vilovic, "Media Picture of Croatia: Structure and Economy of a Media System," *Media Online*, November 28, 2000.

13. Zdravko Grebo, taped interview by author, Sarajevo, January 27, 2000.

14. Zdravko Zlokapa, "The Media in Republika Srpska: A Painful Transition," *The Yearbook of the Banjaluka Law School*, no. XXIII, 1999.

15. Zlokapa, taped interview by author, Banjaluka, January 29, 2000.

16. Slavo Kukic, taped interview by author, Sarajevo, February 2, 2000.

17. *Media and Democratization in Bosnia Herzegovina*, White Book of the Independent Media Commission, June 12, 2000.

18. Senad Pecanin, Interview, "Logicno je da sam ja Izetbegovicev nasljednik," *Dani*, July 14, 2001.

19. Senad Pecanin, "Umjesto da ruse Saju, ruse Avaz," *Dani,* July 14, 2001.

20. Zoran Udovicic, Tarik Jusic, Mehmed Halilovic, Radenko Udovicic, and Media Plan Institute Research Team, "Media at Turning Point: Media Picture of Bosnia Herzegovina," Sarajevo, January 2001.

21. Ivan Lovrenovic, "Bosnian Croats and Television," *Dani,* January 21, 1999.

22. Emir Suljgaic, "Out of Control," *Dani,* June 10, 2000.

23. "Seselj Threats Provoke Media Boycott," Institute for War and Peace Reporting, Balkan Crisis Report no. 117, February 18, 2000.

24. "Media Situation in Serbia: Threats Against Journalists," BETA News Agency, February 16, 2000.

25. Steven Erlanger, "Belgrade Stepping Up Intimidation of Journalists," *New York Times,* April 12, 2000.

26. Zeljko Cvijanovic, "Curuvija Murder Mystery," Institute for War and Peace Reporting, November 3, 2000.

27. "The New Energy of Resistance," East-West Institute, March 31, 2000.

28. Ivana Jankovic, "The End in 10 Days," *NIN,* May 18, 2000.

29. Dragoljub Zarkovic; "Say A, and Then B," *Vreme,* May 27, 2000.

30. Veran Matic, taped interview by author, Boston, May 3, 2000.

31. Michael Dobbs, "Yugoslav Allegiance Blows with the Wind," *Washington Post,* November 2, 2000.

32. Katarina Kratovac, "Tough Times for Yugoslavia's Media," Associated Press, October 27, 2000.

33. Aleksandar Djuricic, "A Picture of Lynching as a Warning," *Reporter,* October 16, 2000.

34. "A Media Portrait of Serbia—Life in Repression," Media Center Research Team, Belgrade, October 22, 2000.

35. Jasminka Kocijan *(Danas),* "Court of Honor Expels Komrakov," as quoted by Media on Media, Media Center Belgrade, December 6, 2000.

36. Miroslav Filipovic, "The Price of Truth," *IPI Global Journalist,* Fourth Quarter 2000.

37. "Milanovic and Associate Charged with Premeditated Murder," *ANEM Weekly Report,* November 4–10, 2000.

38. Beti Bilandzic, "Relatives blame NATO, Officials for Serb TV deaths," Reuters, April 23, 2000.

7. Policy Recommendations

1. Dubravka Ugresic, *The Culture of Lies, Antipolitical Essays* (University Park, Pa.: Pennsylvania State University Press, 1998), 263.

Index

Bijedic, Dzemal, 14
Bildt, Carl, 143–144, 152
Biscevic, Hido, 63–65
Blagojevic, Mirko, 161
Blaskic, Tihomir, 193–194
Blic, 201
Boban, Mate, 131
Bobic-Mojsilovic, Mirjana, 93–94
Borba, 15, 18, 69, 124–125, 163,
    xiii–xvii
Bosnia
    conflict with Croatia during 1993,
        128–131
    creation of Serb Democratic
        Parties, 52
    destruction of Mostar bridge,
        131–132
    independence of, 119
    media changes in the mid-1980s,
        87, 88–100
    nationalists' control of postwar
        media, 140–161
    New Year's 2000 broadcasts,
        191–193
    psychiatrists' mobilization of
        Serbs, 52–53
    Srebrenica massacre, 126–127,
        225
    Stupni Do massacre, 132–133
    takeover by antinationalist pro-
        European parties, 183–184,
        190–200
Bosnia Herzegovina
    newspapers, 231–233
    Radio-Television stations,
        229–230
Bosniak, 116
Bosniak-Croat Federation, 135,
    139–140, 190, 225
Bosniaks, 114–119, 128
Bosnian Radio and TV, 146
"Bosnian spring," 88–100
Bosnian TV, 113, 151, 158, 194–195

Bozanic, Dragan, 101, 102, 144
Bozic, Marinko, 136
Brcin, Dragutin, 124–125
Breadline massacre, 103, 104,
    120–121, 225
Brmalj, Ronald, 161
Brown, Ron, 177–178
Bulatovic, Pavle, 201
Bulatovic, Vukoje, 24

Causevic, Enver, 117
Central Committee, Eighth Session,
    39–40, 222
Ceric, Besim, 100
Ceric, Mustafa, 158
Cerkez, Veseljko, 147
Cerovic, Stanko, 123
Cerovic, Stojan, 54–55, 79–80
Charter on Public TV, 185
Cicak, Ivan Zvonimir, 178
Civic Alliance, 59
Cominform, 7–8
Committee to Protect Journalists,
    148
Communist Information Bureau,
    7–8
Contemporary Journalism, 11
Cosic, Dobrica, 47, 237n
Cosovic, Dragisa, 117
Crncevic, Brana, 47
Croatia
    cease-fire agreement, 85
    changes following Tudjman's
        death, 183–184, 185–190
    conflict with Bosnia during 1993,
        128–131
    creation of Serb Democratic
        Parties, 52
    declaration of independence,
        71–72, 224
    "ethnic cleansing" crimes, 75
    media coverage of war during
        1991, 96–97

About the Author

Kemal Kurspahic was editor-in-chief of the Sarajevo daily *Oslobodjenje* in 1988–94. He has received numerous awards including the World Press Review's International Editor of the Year in 1993 and the International Press Institute's World Press Freedom Hero in 2000. Kurspahic is the author of three previous books: *As Long as Sarajevo Exists, Letters from the War,* and *The White House.* He is currently a spokesperson for the UN Office on Drugs and Crime in Vienna.

This book is a fine example of the work produced by senior fellows in the Jennings Randolph fellowship program of the United States Institute of Peace. As part of the statute establishing the Institute, Congress envisioned a program that would appoint "scholars and leaders of peace from the United States and abroad to pursue scholarly inquiry and other appropriate forms of communication on international peace and conflict resolution." The program was named after Senator Jennings Randolph of West Virginia, whose efforts over four decades helped to establish the Institute.

Since 1987, the Jennings Randolph Program has played a key role in the Institute's effort to build a national center of research, dialogue, and education on critical problems of conflict and peace. Nearly two hundred senior fellows from some thirty nations have carried out projects on the sources and nature of violent international conflict and the ways such conflict can be peacefully managed or resolved. Fellows come from a wide variety of academic and other professional backgrounds. They conduct research at the Institute and participate in the Institute's outreach activities to policymakers, the academic community, and the American public.

Each year approximately fifteen senior fellows are in residence at the Institute. Fellowship recipients are selected by the Institute's board of directors in a competitive process. For further information on the program, or to receive an application form, please contact the program staff at (202) 457-1700 or visit the Institute's website, www.usip.org.

Joseph Klaits
Director

8349   56